EROTIC MENTORING

WRITING LIVES

Ethnographic Narratives

Series Editors:
Arthur P. Bochner and Carolyn Ellis
University of South Florida

Writing Lives: Ethnographic Narratives publishes narrative representations of qualitative research projects. The series editors seek manuscripts that blur the boundaries between humanities and social sciences. We encourage novel and evocative forms of expressing concrete lived experience, including autoethnographic, literary, poetic, artistic, visual, performative, critical, multi-voiced, conversational, and co-constructed representations. We are interested in ethnographic narratives that depict local stories; employ literary modes of scene setting, dialogue, character development, and unfolding action; and include the author's critical reflections on the research and writing process, such as research ethics, alternative modes of inquiry and representation, reflexivity, and evocative storytelling.

Volumes in this series:

Erotic Mentoring:
Women's Transformations in the University
Janice Hocker Rushing

EROTIC MENTORING

Women's Transformations in the University

JANICE HOCKER RUSHING

Walnut Creek,
California

LEFT COAST PRESS, INC.
1630 North Main Street, #400
Walnut Creek, CA 94596
http://www.LCoastPress.com

ISBN 1-59874-026-1 hardcover
ISBN 1-59874-027-X paperback

Library of Congress Control Number: 200593270

Printed in the United States of America

This title is printed on Perfection Antique Recycled paper containing a minimum 30% recycled waste. The balance contains virgin fiber. The paper is acid free and meets the minimum requirements of ANSI/NISCO Z39.48-1992 (R 1997) (Permanence of Paper).

Cover photo: *Psyche Revived by Amor's Kiss.* Marble statue by Antonio Canova (1757–1822) in the Louvre, Paris. MR 1777. Photo by C. Jean. Reprinted by permission of Réunion des Musées Nationaux/Art Resource, New York.

Grateful acknowledgment is made for permission to reprint excepts from the following: Page 14: Excerpt from *Dream Work,* by Mary Oliver. "Wild Geese." Reprinted by permission of The Atlantic Monthly Press. Copyright © 1986 Mary Oliver. Pages 79, 237, and 241: Excerpts from "The Way I Should" by Iris DeMent. Copyright © 1997 Songs of Iris. Used by permission. All rights reserved. Page 82: "In Blackwater Woods." Excerpt from *American Primitive,* by Mary Oliver. Copyright © 1978, 1979, 1980, 1981, 1982, 1983, by Mary Oliver. By permission of Little, Brown and Co., Inc.

06 07 08 09 10 5 4 3 2 1

CONTENTS

FOR TOM

FOREWORD

Janice Hocker Rushing died on February 19, 2004, just a few short months after completing this book. So it is left to us, her husband Tom Frentz, and her sister Joyce Hocker, to take up a task we so wish Janice were here to finish. Where to begin? Not everyone knew that Janice was a deeply spiritual person, not in any specific, denominational sense, but through her unshakeable belief that all of life is interconnected in important, but seldom recognized, ways. "Our time is marked by a yearning for wholeness," she once wrote to open an article on the film *E. T.* She was right when she penned those lines twenty years ago, and she's even more right today. Her belief that we are connected, and that we yearn to examine that connection, made her radical, for writing about spiritual wholeness is about as unwelcome to the everyday life of the university today as being into sexual promiscuity would have been twenty years ago. Janice lived her life to challenge and reconcile oppositions—within her self, within the academy, and within her scholarly work. For Janice, personal growth was indistinguishable from professional growth, self was intimately connected to other, and living a responsible life meant becoming more consciously aware of our unconscious moral potential. Janice was loved and respected by her students precisely because she asked them to examine their own lives in the same way she examined hers. Through their relationship with Janice, many students realized their hidden potential and felt enabled to be themselves.

Janice studied texts, but it was *the way* she studied them that made her unique. She interpreted texts in light of myths, those long-enduring stories that define the moral ground upon which cultures walk. She took to Jung more than Freud, Campbell more than Barthe. Where it is fashionable to see myths as simplistic, archaic tools of ideological power, Janice always looked beyond such reductionist visions and saw the cultural complexity in their humanizing values. And she liked movies—not obscure avant-garde films that no one can understand, but rather big-budget, immensely popular Hollywood blockbusters, the ones we all grouse about, but shamefully sneak off to see. She believed that when a film inspires our imagination it is never solely because of its star power, clever marketing, or "whiz-bang" special visual effects, but rather because the film taps into some unconscious mythic reservoir that we need to recognize consciously and then act upon.

Janice was an ultra-feminine feminist, and while that phrase might be an oxymoron in some feminist circles, it surely wasn't for Janice, who always preferred both/and to either/or. As her picture clearly shows, she was a beautiful woman (granting that "beautiful woman" is little more than some socially constructed masculine ideal!). As you'll learn from her book, she was an adept backpacker and camper, but she also loved shopping and being, as she used to put it, a "girlie girl." In her fifties, she giggled openly at teenagers while shopping in the Juniors section for petite size-2 low-rise jeans.

Even her feminism was unusual. Rather than rehashing the ways in which women continue to be oppressed in contemporary society, Janice looked for the historical origins of that oppression. Long before Dan Brown made it the controversial centerpiece of *The Da Vinci Code,* Janice found that well-known and beloved myths were, in fact, patriarchal makeovers of older, decidedly female stories. As a feminist, Janice sought to discover, and then recover, those older narratives that taught women how to live and be—for themselves, as opposed to how to live and be for men.

Janice was first and foremost a writer, a remarkably gifted writer. Early in her academic career, she confided to Tom that she always thought she got published more for how she said things than for what she said. For years she labored, as many creative academics do, under the crushing conventions of academic prose, that often arid style of intellectual pretension that nobody would ever read unless it were assigned in class. But then, in the last decade of her career, she encountered Art Bochner, Carolyn Ellis, "Bud" Goodall, and that small cadre of autoethnographers in the field of communication who believe that good scholarly writing should both advance knowledge *and* impact the lives of scholarly readers. Under Art's encouragement and guidance, Janice's gradually "came out" to be what she was born to be—a creative writer who preferred to write nonfiction.

This book was ten years in the making. It is about some pivotal experiences in the lives of important women in Janice's life, but it is also about Janice's own life. She tells of complicated, relationally intricate, sometimes erotic (not always sexual) mentoring between these women and older, more established male professors, using the explanatory precision of ancient myths to frame and make sense of these relationships for the women who lived through them, and for herself. For those who read closely, a subtle change occurs as the book unfolds; Janice turns more inward, to her own dreams and to the dreams of the women, trying to recover an ever-deeper sense of what these relationships meant then and what they mean today.

Janice asked Joyce to read her last chapter aloud to her very shortly before she could no longer understand. "Isn't that wonderful?" she exclaimed of the final dream in the book. When Janice's agent, Sally von Haitsma, finished reading the last chapter, she e-mailed Tom and asked "Do you think Janice knew she was dying when she wrote the last chapter?" Tom didn't know, of course, but it does seem clear to both of us that Janice intuited something dangerous and transcendent happening to her and that it weaves unconsciously in and out of the last part of her book.

Janice was grateful for the many special people in her life who made her book possible. First and foremost she thanks the women who shared their mentoring experiences with her. Many spent hours reliving the moments—sometimes in pain, sometimes with pleasure—that came to define so much of their lives in, around, and beyond academia. Tom remembers how some would call, at all hours of the day or night, with fragments of thoughts or feelings just recently recalled, or things they said previously that they wanted to amend *right now*. He remembers their reading and editing Janice's accounts of their experiences, always trying to capture a more nuanced fidelity.

Without their passion, compassion, and generosity, this book could never have been written.

Janice would also thank Tom and Joyce. Tom was her soul-mate of nearly twenty-five years. She often expressed how comforting his presence was during her bouts of insomnia. She gratefully received his unconditional love, his support through all of her projects, even his reckless and off-beat humor. Tom made many attempts, not always successful, to be the boundary between Janice and others that she was not always able to erect for herself. She would thank her sister Joyce, who was there when she came into this world, who mothered, sistered, loved, and mentored her, who shared a closeness with her of unsurpassed depth and meaning, and who, with Tom, helped to usher her out of this world. Joyce and Janice both went to Texas Christian University, studied with some of the same professors, and developed an early passion for reading mythology. Later, in long conversations, they made sense of complexes, personal histories, family relationships, and dreams. Janice once thought of becoming a clinical psychologist, which Joyce later did. Instead, Janice became an analyst of film, culture, and relationships.

Janice would thank her family. Her mother Jean loved her dearly and always encouraged her as a writer. Jean would often stay up with Janice, editing, making suggestions, asking questions. Janice thought of Jean as her first writing teacher. Joyce and Janice often spoke about daughter(s) living the unlived life of the mother. Janice honored and appreciated her father Lamar, a liberal minister who loved justice and carried a passion for unfashionable social views. In this way he helped his children understand that to be accepted by others was not the most important thing; that to follow one's call was a challenge and a privilege. He introduced Janice to C. G. Jung and to the significance of dream work in life. Janice adored her younger brother Ed, who is peacemaker, environmentalist, and spiritual traveler. Janice was awed by Ed's devotion to the love of his life, Dianne Rice Hocker, whom he married in the hospital just one month before she died of cancer in 2002. Ironically, Janice's last convention paper told about this event.

Janice felt deeply grateful for the longstanding love, insight, encouragement, and assistance of her perceptive Jungian analyst, Anne deVore. Anne helped open Janice to the magical world of dreams in her adult life.

There are three more people without whom this book would not exist. Janice would thank Sally von Haitsma, for allowing Janice's work to touch her heart as well as her head, for agreeing to be her agent, for having unflagging confidence in the book, and for working tirelessly to get it published. Art Bochner believed in Janice and in this project. He patiently and perceptively mentored Janice with the utmost equality, respect, and collegiality, in a way that helped her find her deeply personal voice. At one point in a personal communication to Art, Janice wrote of her new voice, "I like it; it takes the . . . style that you helped coax out of me down about five more notches in accessibility, I hope. . . . I'm trying to write in a style people would actually want to read . . . I can't thank you enough for insisting that I loosen up." Art introduced Janice's book to Mitch Allen of Left Coast Press, Inc.. Thank you, Mitch, not only for agreeing to publish Janice's work but also for trusting that a work of this high quality will find an audience.

Finally, Janice would want to thank her extended family and friends, who never left her side during the final weeks, days, and hours of her life. Her parents, Jean and Lamar Hocker were there, as always, "for the long run" (although both died within a year of Janice's passing). Jean wrote memos to Janice about her memories of her as a child, as we all fought the monster of forgetting. Her brother, Ed, left his home and job in Colorado Springs and stayed until the end. Her very special friend of thirty years, Gale Young, flew in from California and never left. Joel Doelger and Jean Kebis, close friends in Arkansas, were there every day with food, organization, wine, and support. Paula Maxwell, nurse extraordinaire and close friend, tended to Janice gently and helped us understand what was occurring. Joyce's husband, Gary Hawk, was not just there, but was the spiritual center holding us all together, as he played songs on his flute, built a rock wall with Ed in Janice's honor, prayed and sat with us all. And, of course, we were there as well. Janice would thank the medical support people and hospice for knowing what we didn't always know, and for doing what we were not always able to do. There were countless others who brought food, taxied people around, made calls, received calls, and were "there" when we needed somebody to be. In Janice's study hangs the title of a poem by Robert Frost, "Happiness Makes Up in Height for What It Lacks in Length." We all feel that way about Janice's life.

Janice would surely want to thank her beloved cat, Mollie, for being the joyful daughter she never had, for never leaving her side even to chase lizards, and for trying (except for our intervention) to "knead Janice back to life" when she sensed her spirit leaving on that windy February night.

~

On her marker in the Tincup, Colorado, cemetery, is inscribed "Born of love, bearer of the light of kindness." Those words capture much that was wondrous about Janice, but they hide something too. It was hard for Janice, very hard, to refuse anything that anyone might have wanted from her or asked of her. And, given her considerable gifts, many asked for and wanted much. We'd like to close this Foreword with a poem (Janice loved poetry) written by Janice's brother-in-law expressly for Janice in her final hours.

Tom Frentz and Joyce Hocker
June, 2005

The Fate of Beautiful Women

For Janice

On this side of your dying
in the room where you felt most alive,
writing your way to clarity
about your own life and generations
of women who wanted more
than to be used for the purposes of men,
I see how they made you
into something they needed for themselves.
They looked on your bright mind
and chased you in the hope
of catching you for their muse.
They looked on your fine, delicate body
and, in their desire to possess and enfold,
made you their maiden and lover.
They looked on the light of kindness
that seemed to shine from your fair hair,
your smooth skin and smiling eyes,
and they made you sister, or more often,
the human form of some imagined angel.
What weight to carry to your dying
where your body labored through the night
to consume in the fire of your breathing
the imposed fictions of their need.
If only you could have been less permeable,
less like a blue lake taking all
that falls to the surface into your depths
and more like a diamond
reflecting the light off interior walls,
multiplying it for your own delight.

Gary W. Hawk
February, 2004

PART ONE

THE MAN-MADE MAIDEN

Women often form personal relationships in academia with men who attempt to mold them to fit their own masculine ideals. Such relationships quickly became a dominant *leit-motif* in my conversations with women. Partly because the higher ranks in academia are still overwhelmingly populated by men, many romantic pairings still occur between an older man, such as a professor, and a younger woman, such as a student or assistant professor. The pivotal myth that helps enlighten such relationships is "Pygmalion and Galatea," the story of a beautiful woman sculpted by the hands of an exacting master who falls in love with her. What I have called the "Maiden Lover" springs from the romantic love between Pygmalion and his Galatea.

Galatea also blends her voices with those of other mythological characters in the women's stories. The "Muse" aestheticizes romance, inspiring the man to re-create himself, often giving her own poetic powers over to him. Pygmalion owns the "Mistress" as an object of his physical pleasure, and she tends to lose her creative self to his attempts to dominate her. Pygmalion, or more centrally, Zeus, gives birth to an Athenian "Brainchild" as a perfect mirror image of his masculine intellect—one unstained by the messiness that is the feminine flow of life. These four voices—Maiden Lover, Muse, Mistress, and

Brainchild—take their names from the man's projections onto the woman—that is, they are more the reflections of his search for his own soul than they are the woman as she is herself. She may identify with a role and try to live it out, project her own complementary image onto him, or reject his demands and struggle to define herself. Together, these roles narrate a progression from incipient radiance to loss of self, although not everyone I interviewed went through all the phases, or in this order.

CHAPTER 1

ALMA MATER

Al'ma Ma'ter [L. alma mater, bounteous mother.] A title given by the Romans to several goddesses, especially to Ceres and Cybele, and transferred in Eng. to Universities and schools regarded as "fostering mothers" to their alumni.

Oxford English Dictionary

When I was four, I had a ritual I performed exactly the same way each time, never missing a step, as if my life depended on it. I would remove the drawers from the small painted chest holding my clothes in the bedroom my older sister and I shared. Placing a pillow and a blanket in the bottom and lining the back and sides with *Little Golden Books*, I climbed inside and spent blissful hours reading, away from whatever cares might have troubled a pre-kindergartner. In the words of my father's favorite song, I "let the rest of the world go by."

My family did me the great honor of taking this observance seriously. My sister Joyce, herself an astonishing reader who carried home her quarry from the public library in an orange crate each week, never ridiculed me, even though this bureau held her clothes too. When asked why I wasn't at the dinner table, she would say "Janice can't come, she's in the chest." They simply resumed the meal without me, perhaps understanding that this particular hiding place was my temple, a sacred space, an *alma mater* where my love of learning could be felt body, mind, and soul. Virginia Woolf could have a room of her own; I wanted a chest of drawers, and this one fostered me like any good mother would. It was my first school.

While writing my PhD dissertation a couple of decades later, I became a "freeway professor," driving to the furthest reaches of greater Los Angeles to teach classes at three different colleges. This was not the life of the mind, but the grind of the road; not the Ivory Tower, but a fast-imploding Edsel. My first husband traded his piano to an Indian for this car while driving down a back road in New Mexico. He kept a screwdriver under the floor mat for when the gear shift lever came off in my hand between first and second, which was often enough. My favorite songwriter Guy Clark's "If I could just get off of this L.A. freeway/ Without getting killed or caught" became my eight-track refrain. At least as a graduate student at the University of Southern California, I had been able to wait out the freeway hours with my peers and professors at the 901 Club, a foul-smelling bar held together with duct tape and chewing gum. The pitchers were lite, the conversations heavy, and the drunk pissing just outside the screen door lent an odor of solidarity with the oppressed that complemented our awakened leftist sensibilities. Now, here on the 405, I yearned for the ivy-covered walls that were my birthright.

Miraculously, I landed a full-time job at UCLA the next year. I was only a lecturer with no prospect of tenure, and my first assignment was teaching the introductory course in Communication Studies to five hundred students. "Comm 10," as it was called, had become a monster draw because its first teacher, the wife of a famous Hollywood producer, had the performance skills and timing of Richard Pryor. Facing a disappointed ocean of faces from an elevated stage and trying not to trip over the microphone cord, I heard my opening joke fall flatter than the Texas Panhandle. It was going to be a long quarter. But I soon learned from my more-experienced TAs that "teaching is the lowest form of showbiz," and I slowly improved. Unaware that Proposition 13 would soon cost me my job, I had begun to realize my dream. Walking one perfect day from Royce Hall to the student union across expansive lawns connecting the archetypally collegiate buildings, I felt I was in one of those Hudson River Valley paintings where the beneficence of God shines down through the clouds, surrounding the tiny human figure with an otherworldly column of light. "This is it," I thought. "I've arrived."

I have to admit that not all my academic episodes have been so mystical—even those expressly designed to evoke such a feeling. At the commencement ceremony for my PhD, I sat on the front row of the soon-to-be-hooded elite and threw up, right after "Pomp and Circumstance." The best slant I can put on this is that it was outdoors. The faces on the people sitting next to me struggled between compassion and repulsion, the latter gaining an edge as I helplessly wretched on the green grass of USC. Since I was not sick before or after the exercises, this ill-timed eruption has long been something of a mystery. By all accounts, I had a fulfilling stint in graduate school, despite the inevitable stresses of concentrating on papers rather than life for five years. So, ruling out medical explanations, I have to entertain the possibility of regurgitation as metaphor. Maybe I was not as completely nourished as I had thought—perhaps not everything I took in agreed with me—and my stomach was suggesting what my mind could not yet entertain.

I have remained in school, on one side of the desk or the other, all my life. Whenever the stacks of papers filling my weekends get thicker than my patience, I consider other callings—practice dummy for a massage therapy school might be nice. But reasoning from sign, perhaps academia is the best place for me. I don't understand the inner essence of Power Point or the profit motive, and nine-to-five would drive me to misdemeanors. I do still love a classroom buzzing with nascent epiphanies, as well as "the life of the mind," even though I often have to trick myself into believing that's more than a platitude.

Even so, higher education has not always been an *alma mater*, as with each successive grade and professorial rank I learned to separate academic performance from the warmth and safety of my early self-made cave. A critic of popular culture by trade, I am sufficiently versed in the Oedipal complex to know that everyone, even a girl, must inevitably climb out of the womb, separate from a sticky dependence on Mother, and attain a thick enough skin to enter the properly phallic world of the Fathers. Nowhere is this more true than in academia, where to succeed we must engage in single-combat warriorship—grasping for renown by driving a sword into the scholarly contributions of another and producing prominent protégés who will carry on our legacies for at least a few years before doing the same thing to us.

I have managed these initiation-into-manhood tasks reasonably well. But now that I am a full professor they are not sustaining me in this second half of life. It is painful to realize that academia envisions the mother image, not as a secure foundation, but as a hazardous trap that should be buried by the Ivory Tower, altogether and for good. We may sing the *alma mater* tearfully at football games, but it is not the main event. Somewhat rankled herself about the status of the maternal, Simone de Beauvoir once wrote, "Man is in revolt against his carnal state, he sees himself as a fallen god: his curse is to be fallen from a bright and ordered heaven into the chaotic shadows of his mother's womb."[1]

At the university this fear of things feminine remains, despite the considerable advances of feminism. After all, as Jean Markale points out, Plato's Allegory of the Cave, a pillar of the academy's philosophy, "portrays men as prisoners chained up in a cave, their backs turned towards the entrance so that they cannot see the reality of the outside world except as shadows on the opposite wall." Water castles and caves are, in fact, some of the most common symbols for the womb in mythology.[2] They are the perpetual dwelling places of dangerous and alluring figures, those who once were princesses and queens, but later got demoted into witches and sirens. I was as impressed with Plato's parable as anybody else when Professor Gus Ferré, a brilliantly wild-eyed Swede, told it to us in freshman philosophy with a tone both reverential and ecstatic. We knew the code: if he gestured hazardously with his glasses and his yellow hair rose impossibly from his six-inch forehead, it was going to be on the test. Surely, this *is* a great meditation on the veils of Maya that separate us from the truth of existence. But could it also be significant that Plato represents illusion in terms of the mythic feminine—as the snare of the enlightened *man*?

This book is about my experiences as a woman in academe—mostly as a professor, but reaching back for perspective into grade school and forward through college and graduate school. It is also about other women's experiences, some of which I have observed on my own and many that they have told me. I have found that our stories must be buried in order for us to be "successful." Certainly they should be hidden from those who evaluate us and whose esteem we seek, but also from ourselves. It is too hard to succeed, especially on a tenure track, when we allow our USDA non-approved "feminine" lives to intrude on this tightly constrained path. Like bulges of unsightly fat, they must be exercised away or squeezed into Body by Victoria.

But traces of what we've kept in the dark come to light in our night dreams, our longings, our bodily eruptions, and our emotional rebellions. Sometimes we surreptitiously air our misgivings to each other in the hallways—like last week when three of us profs spontaneously lamented our chronic insomnia and the next day exchanged remedies tightly wrapped in foil. Or we type our dis-ease on e-mail, where we can pepper it with expletives and feel a semblance of insurrection. For the most part, however, we stay under control, couching even our feminism in ready-for-prime-time terms, acceptable to refereed journals and university presses.

Some have published eloquent first-person accounts of their navigations through academia and relationships to people within it; a few who I have found inspiring are bell hooks' *Teaching to Transgress: Education as the Practice of Freedom*; Carolyn Ellis' *Final Negotiations: A Story of Love, Loss, and Chronic Illness*; Jane Tompkins' *A Life in School: What the Teacher Learned*; and Arthur Bochner's "It's About Time: Narrative and the Divided Self."[3]

At first I thought I'd better read *everything* relevant, and as friends discovered what I'm writing about they helpfully suggested more titles. Assuming I could actually accomplish this, though, I'd probably never get around to writing myself. I also didn't want, as my husband Tom puts it in his Research Methods seminars, to "sew a new teat on the udder of knowledge" because, in academic conventions, this means you need to savage someone else (see above on the "single-combat warrior"). One of Tom's graduate students actually did this—sewed on a new teat, that is. She presented him with a perfectly stitched pillow, a satin cow's udder with four attached teats in light pink and one in bright fuchsia; across the surface she had printed in large block letters, UDDER OF KNOWLEDGE. It is his favorite visual aid. Whenever I pass by Tom's classroom and see him earnestly explaining this to his red-faced students, I still think about her subtle feminization of the ritual by which one cements one's study atop the road-kill of somebody else's. Or, in the words of Abby, a professor who was thinking of quitting her job as director of a large research center, "Writing a research article is so *penetrative*: you have to find a hole and fuck it!"

"All the good stories are out there waiting to be told in a fresh, wild way," Anne Lamott says about writing. "Life is like a recycling center, where all the concerns and dramas of humankind get recycled back and forth across the universe. But what you have to offer is your own sensibility, maybe your own sense of humor or insider pathos or meaning. All of us can sing the same song, and there will still be four billion different renditions."[4]

Maybe I'm not absolutely free of guilt over not providing a complete literature review; as a student I never failed to turn in my homework—not even once. Or perhaps by the time I get to the end of these pages, I will mercifully give it a rest. You can decide which is appropriate. Meanwhile, I'll proceed with my "archaeological" project—an attempt to dig up shards of what lies beneath the surface, piece them together into whole figurines, and make inferences about a culture that still remains mostly in the dark.

I am concerned here with what are often considered "feminine" ways of valuing and knowing that are absent from the collective vision of academe. The book is about women, but I hope to also touch what men call, usually with self-reassuring mockery, their "feminine sides"—what they, too, have to suppress in order to make it in this manly arena. And it is more generally about an absence of feminine soul in the academy as an institution. I believe academia is ailing from its one-sided insistence on rationality and intellect, like the Fisher King whose groin wound festers while his kingdom dries up into a Wasteland. The Ivory Tower is all "up" and no "down." The "scholarly" and the "collegiate" depend upon the suppression of what lies beneath, which is, ironically, the very thing that could coax it to life. But mostly, I'd just like to help real women I know and some I don't to have an easier time of it at the university.

FLOATING

This is the place in the introduction where, as a good academic, I should tell you how I went about my work. I will do that, but in a bit of a roundabout way, since that is how this book came about. When I hit mid-life at the same time as I published a book and made full professor, I crashed hard, finally realizing what a product of the academic patriarchy I was, working almost all the time to prove my worth. My beleaguered body cried "Foul!" at my nonstop pace, as if finally fulfilling the yucky prophecy of my graduation *ritual ad nauseum*. I looked back upon the "body of work" that constituted my *curriculum vita* with a mixture of pride and aridity, as if the bucket in my creative well had come up dry. I contemplated the costs of learning to talk the parched talk of academic prose and walk the soulless walk of what my friend Art Bochner calls "institutional depression."[5] I wanted to play, to grow flowers, to just sit. I published no refereed articles for two years, instead writing a science-fiction screenplay with a friend, hoping Hollywood might rescue me from school on the strength of just one script and without returning to L.A.

This was unexpected.

I knew all about mid-life crises, having (typically) read books about them and observed many of my peers do things like leave their mates for less seasoned game and trade in their SUVs for Harley's—the kids could walk to their own damn soccer games. Of course, these were mostly men, who tend towards flashier blowouts; women's are just as keenly felt but less entertaining to watch. I never thought I would lose the inestimable thrill of seeing my name on page proofs. Although I didn't think of myself in these terms, since in my opinion I could never accomplish enough, friends called me "prolific" when they wanted to be nice, "driven" when they didn't. From preschool on I had been a model pupil, winning more good citizenship awards than I could remember and counting an A– as categorical defeat, allowing myself a modicum of absolution only if it was gotten in science. So what was I doing here on the couch, reading *Better Homes & Gardens*, skipping over the hard parts?

But what was absolutely shocking was my realization that all this time I had valued men more than women, unwittingly considering "feminine" ways of being and doing less legitimate than "masculine" ones, even when arguing the opposite in my teaching and writing. One of the worst things, I now had to admit, was to be considered "soft" or "girlish" by the princelings of the theoretical court—always double jeopardy for me, since my subject was mythology, or what Tom playfully calls "that squirrel and the unicorn stuff," and I knew how to sneak "pretty words" into prestigious forums. But now I wanted to be around women, to enjoy their company. Suddenly women became very important to me, not only for how they could illuminate my own story but also for their friendship.

Several years ago I began intensive interviews with women I knew who were willing to talk. This would allow me to meet two needs at once, or, as my Ukrainian friend used to put it, to "kill one bird with two stones." If I spoke to women about their lives in the university, maybe I could get to know them. Meanwhile, I could fulfill the requirements of a quasi–social scientific study, what I learned in graduate school to call "qualitative research" or "intensive interviewing." I asked women at home and at conferences if they would tell me their personal stories of life in academia. Then with the help of a modest grant from my university, I flew around the country to interview women from a wide variety of fields, ages, geographical regions, countries, and ethnicities. In positions, they ranged from undergraduate to graduate students, from assistant to full professors, and from deans to a university president. Most of the women I interviewed either were or had been committed to academia at some point, whether for a graduate degree or for their careers. Most of the undergraduate experiences recounted here, then, were the reflections of women who had gone beyond that status.

Almost everyone was so enthusiastic that I sensed there were nerves out there relatively untouched. Many suggested other women to contact. Their friends called me. I got unsolicited e-mails. Men asked to be included. We met in offices, living rooms, hotel rooms, coffee shops, restaurants, bars, campus hallways, and parks. Several women whispered their stories to me at lunch or during social occasions while others nearby carried on separate conversations. As I write this, I am still a beneficiary, in that when I attempt to answer the question "What is your book about?" many people spontaneously share their own stories. This ongoing stream convinces me that the narratives included here, although always personal, are rarely singular.

The more I talked and the more I wrote, however, the less committed I became to standards of "external validity," even the comparatively mushy ones of qualitative methods, and the more enamored I became of the interdisciplinary movement in research known as "new ethnography," "autoethnography," or "personal narrative."[6]

Harold Lloyd Goodall, Jr. defines this new ethnography as "creative narratives shaped out of a writer's personal experiences within a culture and addressed to academic and public audiences."[7] This kind of writing "is constructed out of a writer's ability to hold an interesting *conversation* with readers."[8] That means that the standards of creative writing—shaping what one sees and hears into a story that is engaging to the reader—are at least as important as the standards of accurately representing that "reality." Autoethnographic mantras include "Show instead of tell." One should "bring life to research. Bring research to life."[9] This tradition strives to avoid the very dryness of academic prose—not to mention *life*—against which I was rebelling, and to elicit actively the emotions of readers rather than to regard those as a dark blot on the white slate of scholarly objectivity.

In fact, new ethnographers have taken seriously the realization that "reality" can never be "represented accurately," because all representations are constructed by the presenter. That also means there is no one-to-one correspondence between the language used to represent reality and reality itself. Rather, what counts as reality depends upon who is looking at it, how they interpret it, and what they want to do with it. What we have often considered to be "logical" or "scientific" has much to do with who asserts it—and that has been mostly Western, white, and male speakers—than with any kind of universal truth that is independent of scientists and logicians. As Goodall puts it, "'Who has the right to speak for a culture?' is very much a question about *who is entitled* to represent it."[10]

One of the ways that new ethnographers try to address this "crisis of representation" is to acknowledge their biases in interpreting cultures and the people within them, while inserting themselves into the stories they tell. This means that, as an autoethnographer, I do not hold myself up as some omnipotent observer, but examine myself while I tell the stories of others. As Carolyn Ellis says, "Understand self to understand others."[11] As a matter of fact, I continued to learn about myself throughout the writing of this book; aspects of my experience that I thought were artfully wrapped up in neat packages continually came unbound as I listened to others, wrote their stories, and was forced to re-evaluate my own. In addition, as a reader, if you are to come to your own conclusions about what I say here, you need to know something about me—where I stand when I converse with other women, how I react to their tales, and how we play off one another. Thus, like several other women whom I came to know well, I am a recurring character within this book.

When an "interview"—which I gradually began to refer to as a "conversation"—was intentional, I generally secured permission to tape-record it. I often started with something about myself. If the women were young, I recounted how burdened, yet excited, I felt as a graduate student or assistant professor. If they were older, I told them about my mid-life burnout. Or if the woman had indicated why she was interested in talking with me, I questioned her about that. I followed whatever thread she picked up, whether or not her story related to mine. I was amazed at the extent to which women's narratives intertwined with mine over time, such that I thought about them when I was doing other things, they caused me to go about my daily work differently, and they even appeared as characters within my dreams.

What you will read here are "real" tales—mine and those of others I met—as well as some gleaned from movies, literature, autobiographies, biographies, music, and dreams. I have shaped some of what women told me into the voices of "composite characters," which means that I condense two or more persons' stories into one, like a character in a play. When this is the case, the context is "real" for at least one of the persons, but not necessarily for others. This is one way that I can protect the identities of women who did not wish to be recognized; it also reduces somewhat the number of people I am asking that you get to know. Many of the names, locations, and disciplines are also changed. Other than these changes, most of the time I give their stories to you pretty much as they were told to me or as I observed them unfolding.

It would have been fascinating to also interview the men to whom the women referred, or who entered into relationships with them. Because of the sensitive nature of what many women said, however, as well as the impossibility of finding many of these men or securing their cooperation, I decided that I could not tell these men's stories here. Obviously, their perspectives are just as important, just as "real," as those of the women. But it is also the case that men's perspectives within academia are often the "norm," the standard against which those of women are measured or discounted. While I hope that men might be encouraged to tell the stories of their academic lives in a more personal way than is usually thought "appropriate," this book is not that undertaking.

~

The other day I woke up and there was a tiny gnat flying around my right eye. I grabbed at it forty-three times without success, waking up my cat and my husband, both of whom looked at me as if I were not the brightest firefly in the yard. Soon Mollie commenced licking herself. Tom did not. Whereas the gnat continued to taunt me like Socrates' gadfly through two desperate showers, Tom suggested I might have a "floater" and should call my eye doctor. Annoyed that this would steal time from my precious summer writing days, I dutifully made an appointment anyway, only to find out that this thing is probably not serious but is also going to hang around for awhile—like maybe for life.

My very nice, very pretty optometrist Nicole, who is sixteen, asked me to look at a drawing of an eye in which the vitreous solution at the back was "melting," allowing the membrane that presumably holds it like a dam from pouring out your eyeball like some trick 11-year-old boys would play on you at a Halloween haunted house. Of course, I couldn't actually *see* this eyeball because mine had yellow dye in it and my pupil was now as big as Jupiter. When I got home I read the warning points—things for which you should call your doctor immediately (for instance, if Hurricane Hugo was happening inside your eye socket or the gnat had turned into a condor)—and things that were "a nuisance, but not dangerous."

The *real* nuisance was that phrase I come across about every hour now, or at least every time I have a medical checkup, read about what I should do with my stock portfolio, or receive that completely unwarranted copy of *Modern Maturity* in the mail: *"As we get older. . . ."* As we get older, apparently, we start to see things that weren't there before. Maybe my hot flashes melted my eye Jell-O and that's why I have this irritating little gnat companion. I am suspicious of this getting older business as a rule, but it is true, I guess, that I see things now I didn't see when I was younger. Some of them are about academia.

I'll try to tell you some things here I see from the vantage-point of a fifty-ish professor who's spent a life in school—as my friend Jane says, to provide "A Room with a View." Like my new floater, it's hard to say whether the things I describe are *really there*. That black spot in front of my eye really isn't, it's in back. What I'll end up describing are my floaters and those of others. Maybe you see some of them, too, and maybe you don't. What seems important is that they're in our fields of vision.

THE MYTHIC LIFE

Outward Bound, the serious boot camp for problem teenagers that believes *Outdoor Living* is therapy rather than a slick magazine, has a phrase for when your foot misses its mark and you end up precariously spread-eagled on the face of a sheer cliff: "The only way out of this is into it." Although I've spent more than a year of my life in tents, thanks to my family's penchant for roughing it in the Rockies, I realized my true essence after I broke ranks for college. It's a little shameful for someone who knows twenty-three different meals you can make in a Sierra cup as well as how to use a wooly worm, but I'm really a little like Rose in *Titanic*, whom Jack figures as "an indoor kind of girl." My perils are precipitated more by crises in meaning than by grizzly scat on the backpack trail, although I have dealt successfully with the latter—you beat the Sierra cup noisily with a spoon. When "I can't find my ego with both hands," as Guy Clark sings, my way into the predicament is to plunge deep into narrative. In *Crow and Weasel*, a sumptuous children's book that surely must have been meant for adults, Badger says, "Sometimes a person needs a story more than food to stay alive."[12]

As much as anything, it is *myths* that have helped me find my existential footing. Myths are the layered legacies of centuries, lifting me out of my small, self-absorbed world, landing me gently in the arms of time. I don't mean by this that myths offer simple answers. The people in them usually suffer, often grandly and with bloody gore that would put any *Aliens* movie to shame—look at Prometheus, or Medea, or the survivors in *The Trojan Women*. But myths teach me to bear the torment—not exactly to wallow in it, but to refrain from *doing* anything right now, to just sit with the dilemma. Mysteriously, if I am willing to do that, a way out of the impasse may come from nowhere I yet know. I become less isolated, for others have been here before.

An enduring myth is also a supremely useful history book with pictures. The great ones may reach beyond time, but they also bear its footprints. If we care to look closely, there are many curious evolutionary tricks and turns in mythology. Myths that center on a female hero get buried and lost.[13] Or they stick around, but in a form that greatly distorts and reduces her importance.[14] A jealous god swallows the mother of wisdom, for example, and gives birth to her child himself, or a sacred ritual of feminine sexuality transforms into the wiles of an outcast whore. A goddess' sacred consort becomes a dominant male hero. A once-powerful goddess is raped or forcibly married to an Olympian god.[15] Perhaps she is relegated to a cave or buried beneath the sea.[16] Or, if the gods really want to do away with her, she may simply be murdered. I have long suspected that the patriarchal bias of American universities is warehoused in myths that, like those of the culture at large, are built upon the grave sites of their more feminine bones. But since the reigning myths are made to seem "natural"—"just the way things are"—the process of rooting out their influence is disguised.[17]

Myths should help us, then, not only as ways into our individual and collective dilemmas as women in academia, but in lighting pathways out of them. If we are unconsciously living a myth, our options are not very many, for we merely follow the timeless dimensions without making them our own. I have done this many times, getting "tangled up in fate," as if trying to fit myself into a template I didn't even know was in front of my nose. I can live the myth *forward* only if I become aware of its grip on me—a spell that typically has historical roots not only in my story but also in my culture's. Then I can personalize it, use and discard what I want, make it my own. Encountered with eyes wide open, a myth mirrors the complexity of a life among others, offering one of the best ways I know to stay alive.

REAPPEARING THE FEMININE

This book calls on myth to help illumine how women live and work within the academy. In particular, I want to explore how women relate to men, and how they relate to academia as a masculine institution. As we know from plenty of research on the subject, women are blessed with a more "relational" orientation than men.[18] Of course, there are exceptions—sometimes howling ones. But as a general rule, this means not only that women tend to emphasize community over competition but also that even their egos are not sustained in exactly the same way as are men's. Here is an example. Tom and I compare notes on our respective classes.

"How was your pop culture class today?" Tom asks me.

"Fantastic," I reply, buoyed up by a loud hour and a half. "The energy was great. Lots of comments. I felt like they were really into it. How did your film class go?"

"Awesome. I was *brilliant*."

Tom thinks that when students speak "it's an interruption in their education." I think when they don't, I've failed. His sense of self seems incomprehensibly independent of how others react to him. I can't imagine a self except in relation to those around me. I put the classroom chairs in a circle to facilitate interaction. Tom leaves them in straight rows to—well, I'm not sure if it's to facilitate his authority, or if he just doesn't think about it. I suspect he just doesn't think about it.

Although I generally believe my way is better, I also have to admit that this tendency toward relationship is a curse as much as a blessing for women—at least within the university and other institutions that do not adequately value a mode that is more collaborative than competitive, precisely because that mode is coded "feminine." Such feminine behaviors "get disappeared," writes Joyce Fletcher, because they are considered "soft" and inappropriate to "a masculine logic of effectiveness operating in organizations that is accepted as so natural and right that it may seem odd to call it masculine."[19]

This disappearing act causes many problems for women. Their contributions to the humane functioning of academia are undervalued because they are not seen, for one thing. For another, women learn not to see their own value themselves, but to regard their too-feminine gifts as extraneous to the mission. Even worse, they learn not to look at the ways men retain their power, and at the ways women depend upon and reaffirm it. Semele, one of Zeus' legion of extramarital mortal conquests, asked to see her lover when he came to her, not in disguise for once, but as he really was. Because he had promised to fulfill anything she wished for, Zeus reluctantly appeared to her in his full glory, knowing her unfortunate fate. Semele was incinerated to ashes on the spot, having made the terrible mistake of seeing his godhood directly. Women may be covertly punished for looking too closely at the power men have.

This book is divided into three parts, based upon how women relate to men and to academia as a male institution, and how they attempt to build selves that are not dependent upon men. In Part One, "The Man-Made Maiden," I recount women's stories of relationships to actual men, exploring how women are molded into projections of a male ideal. Most of these relationships are sexual in fact or in tone. In Part Two, "Fatal Attractions," I look at the close relationship between resisting and perfecting the male ideal within the academy. That is, women often try to gain their independence and success by asserting their own sexual dominance, by hiding their femininity from view, or by becoming toughened warriors who fight for their rights. In Part Three, "One-in-Herself," I consider how women may develop their own selves by lighting a lamp in the rooms that have been closed to them so that they may see their own "dark marriages" to men and to the university. This section poses the possibility of a woman building a self-in-relationship that does not deny "feminine" ways of being and that makes possible the birth of her most creative gifts. Most women do not want to cut themselves off from men, but they would like to depend upon them less for defining themselves.

I have purposely chosen primarily Greek and Roman myths for the journey. I had to think long and hard about this, because there are myths from other cultures—particularly Sumerian, Cretan, and Celtic—that are more hopeful for women. But the Western academy is built upon the bedrock of the Greco-Romans—their philosophy, their drama, their mythology. As many scholars have demonstrated, the Olympian gods and goddesses and the myths related to them represent not only the foundation of Western culture but also the pinnacle of patriarchal takeover of earlier religions that centered upon worship of the Great Goddess in her many forms.[20] All over western Europe, you can visit cathedrals that are built literally upon earlier sites of worship. Close to the Forum in Rome, for instance, the church of San Clemente's top layer is twelth-century Byzantine, which sits atop a structure from the fourth-century Constantine era, which in turn lies atop Mithraic ruins from B.C.E. Below that, as with many such cathedrals, is a stream, site of an undetermined Great Goddess, buried beneath the layers of male-centered orthodoxy who banished her from sight.

And so it is with these most familiar stories from our patriarchal heritage that we begin, not only to get the contours of the foundation but also to provide an X-mark on the archaeological map—a place to dig.

INSIDE PLATO'S CAVE

One day I came across this quote by Albert Camus in the contemplative journal I read every morning: "I know with certainty that a person's work is nothing but the long journey to recover, through the detours of art, the two or three simple and great images which first gained access to his heart."[21] Suddenly, in a vivid daydream, I was back in that room I shared with my sister, as if an electrode had stimulated my soul.

I am gazing at the large unframed poster above my chest of drawers. It is a fabulously detailed drawing of myths and fairy tales; the figures are intricately interwoven, the characters moving in and out of each others' territories, filling every square inch with color and intrigue. As I study the pictures, I mount a white horse, ride onto a bridge, cross the moat, slide down Rapunzel's hair. I find the Holy Grail, wait for a knight to save me from a dragon, rescue Hansel and Gretel from the witch's oven. I am fearful and courageous, tentative and exhilarated. For hours I lose myself in this splendid landscape until my mother calls, and I re-materialize back into "reality."

With a jolt, I realized that much of my scholarly career spent analyzing the myths in popular culture was prefigured in my lost time with that picture, when, to paraphrase James Agee, I was "disguised as a girl."[22] There was my life's work, just a few inches above my "school." All this time I have been working it out, entering the realm of the imagination, what Joseph Campbell terms "the facts of the mind,"[23] and coming out again, finding as I go that the "fiction" of myth and the "reality" of living are not all that discrete. I believe it is the same in the academy, where our myths flow in and out of one another in intricate and indistinct patterns.

Here is the first dream I recorded in my journal, way back when I was a brand new assistant professor:

> I am in my classroom teaching. It is the last day of the semester, and I am anxious to finish. I'm showing slides on the wall that outline the points in my lecture, but they are projected on top of a very intricate handmade quilt in a kaleidoscopic, repeated pattern—like flying bird mandalas—each block a circle of stylized wings. It is in very rich colors—dark blue, red, and bright pink. Most of the time you can see the slides clearly, but occasionally the pattern of the quilt comes through. Someone asks me where I got it, and I say that my grandmother made it.

The next morning I found a picture of this quilt in the newspaper I picked up from the driveway, exactly as I had dreamed it except in black and white. I cut and pasted it in my notebook, soon to forget about it until I saw it there as I was writing this chapter.

~

Apparently there is more on the walls of Plato's cave than the inferior shadows cast by his brilliant Forms of perfection. Some of these figures are woman-made—or even ghosts of the Goddess in her many forms, rising again from their long consignment under the earth. If we look carefully beneath the more visible slides of academic presentation, perhaps the grace of their patterns will show through.

CHAPTER 2

MAIDEN LOVER

He was my most spectacular and cherished fuck-up.

Harper, *Guinevere*

When I was a senior in college, I took an unforgettable honors seminar. We met on Tuesday nights at the cozy apartment of one of the students, where we sat amidst the bricks-and-boards bookcases on floor pillows and a few rickety chairs, saving the one good armchair for the typically late arrival of God, who wore the disguise of a fortyish professor, grayed and balding but impressively pumped up, with a goatee and enigmatic smile that cast an image somewhere between James Coburn and Satan. He had us read and discuss things this good preacher's kid from Texas found devilishly interesting: Betty Friedan's *The Feminine Mystique*, Philip Wylie's *The Disappearance*, Freud's *A General Introduction to Psychoanalysis*, Nietzsche's *Thus Spake Zarathustra* (our group bible), and notes from his own book-in-the-making, *The Marriage Malady.* All twelve disciples were utterly enthralled, talking about the texts during the week, intricately analyzing His every word and gesture, and eagerly awaiting our next audience. These were invigorating times. We were the campus liberal intellectual elite, rebelling against the university's archaic policies toward women, reading the names of the Vietnam War dead from the steps of the student union, debating the era's treatises on free love and alternative education.

Imagine my thrill when He started driving *me* back to my dorm after class, inquiring into my love life, saying he liked the way I looked, accidentally brushing my leg as I gathered my books from the front seat. Best of all, he said I was smart; in fact, he was so intrigued with my ideas that he made my papers the centerpiece of an extracurricular study group he formed with the select of us elects (and his wife) to study things that no one had ever studied before. I quit my voluntary post as leader of a large student congregation at the local church, tried hard to understand Nietzsche, and feverishly wrote weekly papers for our secret society, anticipating his praise. I gave up my dream to marry a minister like my mother did; in fact, I decided that capitalism and traditional education were as culpable as marriage for the deplorable state of Western civilization. Of course, this was before the mall-ing of America was completed; now I blame The Gap. But at age 20 I had found my dark genius, and I sought out my kind and fatherly mentor in my own department less and less. I was in iconoclastic, post-Christian, *Big Chill* Heaven.

So why did I not question my professor's antipathy for the physique of the average woman—wandering hungrily instead through the Union snack bar, eyeing the cheeseburgers with fries but dutifully settling on lettuce, striving to conform to his dictum that I diet down to 92 pounds? I let him tell me how to dress, stopping by his office for daily fashion-and-weight checks. I yielded to his molding of my every insight to his own standard of rational perfection. In fact, I was so enamored with his assessment that I was somehow better than the rest that I gratefully delivered my weekly papers to Him for his own research. But after a few months, I was startled to find myself in a guilty contest with my best friend for his intellectual and erotic attention. Why did he disdain my chosen field as inferior to his own and discourage me from the grad school to which I was headed in the fall? Perhaps I should have thought more carefully about the title of the seminar that unleashed it all: "The Nature of Man."

PYGMALION AND GALATEA

This is one of those times I mentioned that I was living out a mythic template without knowing it. So was my professor. The story is "Pygmalion and Galatea," and you are probably familiar with it in its more modern forms as George Bernard Shaw's play *Pygmalion*, or the Audrey Hepburn–Rex Harrison movie *My Fair Lady*. You no doubt enjoyed it as *Pretty Woman*, even if you had to denounce its blatant male hegemony, and if you are a lot younger than I am, you might prefer *Can't Buy Me Love*, or even the gender-bending *She's All That*. Here is a short form of Ovid's Roman rendering, the one many of you will recognize:

> Pygmalion was a sculptor from Cyprus who hated women. Refusing to marry, he molded all his genius into a statue of a woman—some say it was of ivory and others, stone—so exquisite that no mortal woman could approach its beauty. He then fell passionately in love with her, dressing her in rich clothes and imagining that she was pleased. But she was unable to respond to his touch, for he loved a lifeless thing. Desperately he prayed to Venus, who brought her to life. Pygmalion named the maiden Galatea and Venus herself graced their marriage. We do not know what happened after that, except that their son Paphos lent his name to Venus' favorite city.[1]

Now this is terribly romantic, but also tantalizingly brief, quitting just where it gets good with a happily-ever-after ending characteristic of lots of fairy tales, but not that many myths. Galatea does not exactly have a sparkling personality here; she never speaks a word. No sense going for Meryl Streep—Britney Spears could play the part. But I have learned that when a central female character in a Golden Age myth seems peculiarly docile, there may be more to the story.

As I read pieces of history that have been mostly forgotten, a story spanning millennia began to emerge. "Galatea" comes from *gala* or "mother's milk," and was another name for the Great Goddess in her many manifestations as milk-giving mother, all associated with the crescent moon. She was the Egyptian Hathor—the Celestial Cow, the Phoenician Astarte, the white Aphrodite of Paphos, and the Phrygian Cybele—whom you may remember was called "Alma Mater." She made the wheel of the stars and constellations from her own milk, and you can see it on a clear night, providing you get away from the city lights, as the Milky Way *galaxy*. Celtic tribes from *Galatia* worshipped her as *Galata*, and the *Gauls* and *Gaels* traced their descent from her. Neither was "Pygmalion" a single man, but, as a Greek translation of the Phoenician "Pumiyathon," a common name for Semitic kings.[2]

Galatea was once the Great Goddess? Something big must have happened on her way to becoming a sculpture. Who was this goddess before she changed to stone? As it turns out, the Great Goddess was supremely powerful all over Europe, the Mediterranean, and Eastern Asia. She was Nature, the force of life itself, its creator and destroyer. In early times, it was obvious to people that life sprang from blood, but the role of the male was not so obvious. Thus, he was subject to term limits and she was not. Her earthly stand-in took a divine son-lover consort each year—or in some cases every seven years—in a *hieros gamos*, or sacred marriage, performed at her temple. The people greatly honored this "god-king" or "year-king" and let him live opulently as the queen's lover for a time, but ritually slew him at the end of his short reign and scattered his blood upon the crops to make them grow.[2]

The fertility of the land and the people depended upon the sexual potency of this goddess. Galatea was apparently powerful when her sexuality was hers and not in the service of Pygmalion. Before Christianity abolished the custom, she was worshipped for nearly two thousand years throughout Eurasia, including Pygmalion's Cyprus, in the ritual of "sacred prostitution," a form of the *hieros gamos*. In the temple of Aphrodite, a woman lay with a stranger or with a priest thought to be an emissary of the gods. Some records suggest this was required of all women before marriage, or once in their lives, and others that temple priestesses enacted the rite for women everywhere, *in absentia*. Whatever the case, the woman used her body not to attain security, power, possessions, or devotion from the man. Rather, the purpose was to unite flesh and spirit in a religious offering, to call down the goddess' universal love into the human sphere, to animate the everyday with the dancing flow of life.[3]

Under the Goddess' authority, however, the year-king's role was not enviable. A king in a matrilineal society who wanted to lengthen his reign could do so through an ingenious strategy: he simply married a young priestess, nominally his daughter, who was supposed to be the next queen, therefore preventing another young man from marrying her and taking away his kingdom.

This helps to explain a version of the Pygmalion myth that predates the one from Ovid:

> Pygmalion was in love with Aphrodite. Because she would not lie with him, he made an ivory image of her and kept it in his bed. He prayed to her for pity, and she entered into his image of her and brought it to life as Galatea, who bore him Pathos and Metharme.[4]

This story probably arose from a ritual of invocation that called down the goddess' spirit into her sculpture.[5] When Pygmalion refused to give up his white ("milk" = Galatea) cult-image, he was attempting to extend his reign by holding on to the goddess' authority.

If we consider that Pygmalion was succeeded by Paphos, the son borne him by one of Aphrodite's priestesses, and then by Paphos' son Cinyras, who also married his own daughter, then Pygmalion was the first to replace the matrilinear with the patrilinear system of divine descent on Cyprus. Pygmalion's priestess-wife, his daughter by blood, was called Metharme, which means "change."[6] Indeed, the onset of patriarchy coincided with the demotion of the Mother-Goddess figure and the ascendance of her male consort/son, who eventually merged with a storm-god to become the supreme male Creator, the head of the pantheon of gods and goddesses. Thus, wherever these changes occurred, the power of creation and fertility was transferred from the goddess to the god.[7] In the terms of our myth, Galatea lost her capacity to animate, as Pygmalion substituted "making" for "making love."

Thinking about how much Galatea has been reduced over time offered some clues to the double-edged feelings I have harbored over my early mentoring. The relationship with my professor was both thrilling and distressing, and though it conformed closely to the later Pygmalion myth, I did have a life before him, and must have provided him *something* other than a virgin block of stone to shape. I also knew that sexual-intellectual apprenticeships were—and still are, even in these days of sexual harassment policies—very common in the university. I remember musing one time as I looked up the towering central atrium of the Los Angeles Hyatt Regency at all those guest room doors clearly visible from the glass elevator, "This would never work as a convention hotel!" Professional conferences and meetings are notorious for professor-student flings, but such things also take shape in offices and parking garages, much closer to wives, husbands, and deans than is "safe," as if proximity to watchful eyes only ignites the fires of surreptitious seduction.

I wanted to understand my own experience within a broader contemporary as well as historical context, to hear the complexity of Galatea's voices, what other women would have to say. I never asked outright about such relationships, but it became one of the most prominent themes in my interviews without any prodding from me. The women I tell you about here recreate Galatea as a character who reaches back into her ancestry and ahead into new possibilities. I can only recount a few of Galatea's stories, but you may trust that they are both legion and very much alive at the university.

The creative instinct operated in many of these stories. The Goddess, whether Aphrodite or the early Galatea, can be a force for transformation and the birth of new life. When her spirit is invoked physically, the result can be a literal child. Creative work of any kind comes out of a similar passionate involvement. Jean Shinoda Bolen says this happens "almost as if with a lover, as one (the artist) interacts with the 'her' to bring something new into being."[9] When a mentor and student come together with the passion of Aphrodite, a symbolic or "divine child" often emerges; it might take the form of a musical composition, a manuscript, a theory, or an invention. bell hooks tells of her own romantic relationships with teachers and with a student. She thinks of the erotic as "a space of transgression," asking, "[r]ather than perceiving desire between individuals (let us imagine her teacher and student) as always and only dangerous, negative and destructive, what does it mean to consider the positive uses of that desire, the way the erotic can serve the interests of spiritual growth?"[10] At times the women I talked with spoke of their erotic mentoring as if it glowed with the divine, and at others as if they felt just like a child. But whether left with wounds or with wisdom, most did grow from the experience.

Such relationships typically began with the woman being what Polly Young-Eisendrath calls the Maiden Lover, who reflects Pygmalion's desire for a "soul mate, daughter, or sisterly dream lover who is either the match or the potential match for the perfect relationship."[11] The Maiden Lover is usually only the first phase of such a relationship, the one in which Pygmalion projects upon his Galatea all the nascent potential of the art work he is sculpting. While she is being thus fashioned, the woman feels awakened from slumber by her incomparable creative genius. Like Buttercup in *The Princess Bride*, she waits for her prince to open the flower of her latent beauty. "I will always come for you," Wesley says, as he prepares to ride off and seek his fortune. "How can you be sure?" she asks, her eyes reflecting the dread in her heart. "This is true love," Wesley answers. "You think this happens every day?"

AWAKENINGS

Pygmalion sees his Maiden Lover as innocent, beautiful, and full of the latent talent only he can bring out. The middle-aged photographer Connie in the film *Guinevere* (1999) tells his 20-year-old charge Harper—one of a series of "Guineveres" he loves and mentors—that she can live at his bohemian loft apartment if she works and studies hard, if she "creates something." Not yet confident of herself, Harper whispers softly, "Oh, you're mistaking me for someone with potential." But when she sees herself reflected by an "artist" who adores her, the woman in love with him is stirred to unfold a part of herself that may have been lying in wait. Harper blooms sensually and cerebrally under Connie's sensitive tutelage when she begins to see herself as he does, materialized by the beautiful photographs he takes of her. The first ones he shoots are at her sister's wedding, traditional symbol of promise. But Harper is off to the side, not comfortable with the trite excesses of her dysfunctional family. Connie sees, not the awkward, shy girl, but the blossoming rebel, and she begins to unfurl like a rose; the flowering of feminine possibility—which begins with a *de*-flowering—is to be Harper's, not her sister's. She learns to take beautiful pictures herself, to realize the artist within.

Laura, a 54-year-old ex-professor now flourishing in a second career, described a passionate relationship with her PhD advisor Al, that she considered more the norm than an aberration. We were drinking herbal tea in her study with the tape recorder on, and her story continued to unfold over lunches and walks in her tree-lined neighborhood. Her face and her voice changed often from pleasure to pain as she remembered this episode of her life, obviously one that she had still not completely put to rest. "This was, after all, the early seventies, and all of these professors were having affairs with their students. Everybody was."

Laura had had only one female teacher, who was outside her specialty, and she got constant attention from male professors at conferences away from home. A redhead with a penchant for long form-fitting fuchsia dresses, Laura was noticed when she walked into one of those squashed-bodies cocktail parties at convention hotel suites, the ones with beer in the bathtub and no music to soften the buzz, the soundtrack instead humming with job talk and "my next book. . . ."

Laura perfectly captured the blissful oblivion of romantic love between a Pygmalion and his Maiden Lover as she recounted the "romantic haze" of her relationship.

"This man was only ten years older, but the incredible rush of feeling understood and seen by this power figure—that was pretty heady." She was immersed in the euphoria of feeling different, valued, and adored by a powerful and admired man. Laura had come from a fairly restrictive religious background, and her professor must have seemed like luscious forbidden fruit.

"I was a confidante, I understood him, and we felt, as people in those relationships often do, kind of outside the norm—we don't have to follow the rules—this is special, this is different."

~

"I'm sure you could have a heyday analyzing older man–younger woman," ventured Maggie, as she kindly handed me two Tylenol PM tablets for the cold that had kept me awake for two nights. "Mixing sex with an academic career happens more often than not. In my case he was 39, and I was 19 or 20."

Miraculously, I stopped blowing my nose for a few minutes. I had known Maggie for many years, and had no inkling of this episode of her life. And I was struck with her assumption, so similar to Laura's, that such relationships were more the rule than the exception—though theirs were separated by almost two decades.

Now a very successful 45-year-old chairperson, Maggie was talking to me a year after our first conversation. She had called me up to say "Okay, now you want to hear the *real* story?" She had told only her therapist, her husband, and her best friend, who experienced a similar, but more troubling, relationship at the same time she did. Though Maggie acknowledged that her advisor Rick's instigation of their relationship while she was an undergraduate would today be termed sexual harassment because of the unequal power dynamic, she has no regrets about their nine-year affair, and regards herself as "at least as much the aggressor as he was."

In graduate school Maggie, like Laura, had only one female teacher, who was outside her own department, so she was "completely mentored by males. It was almost as if there was this unwritten rule floating through my national association," she said with a touch of cynicism that she probably didn't have back then, "that men who were fairly well-known figures felt a license to spend as much time, in whatever ways they wished, with the young, dewy-eyed graduate students."

Maggie became devoted to Rick, but she also loved seeing her own potential mirrored by other older men in her field. "Some of these guys were good—they really had the lines down, like 'I want to talk to you because you're smart.' And I'd go like, 'Wow, cool! How do you know?' And they'd say, 'I can just tell.'" At this last part she lowered her voice in a seductive and knowing imitation of what we both had heard many times, and we laughed long and hard. She admitted that she sought out the attention, as did Laura.

"It was so flattering, and, you know, you feel like such a stranger in that setting that any type of affection with somebody that you have some admiration for was enough to make me not think about this as much as I should have."

Maggie was fascinated that Rick's wife was "smart, gorgeous, classy, tasteful, and he was still interested in *me*." I remembered feeling the same way when I met my professor's wife, who had precisely the same qualities—why did he want *me* if he had *her*? She was about two feet taller than me and could have been a super-model, if that's what you called them back then. *And* she was gathering scientific data for her doctoral dissertation. I was a mere senior and not that good at science, if you recall. It was only later that I understood she was more "sculpted" than I. It was more than the fact that she filled out a swimsuit better than I did. I was fresher clay.

I asked Maggie why she was so incredulous that Rich had found her attractive. "Because I'm a dork and a nerd and I was a debater, and I had glasses," she answered with a laugh. This seemed completely incongruous with the photo she showed me of a lithe young woman with long dark curls, but then I thought of how "Guinevere" had actually *become* more beautiful when adored by her mentor. Then, too, I had hung up my more nondescript fashions in exchange for yellow hip-huggers and platform shoes—neither of which I could afford—when my professor picked me out of the crowd. Apparently, Maggie really did not see herself as special until Rick held up to her the mirror of his attention.

For a woman swept up in this kind of elation, the relationship is not just exciting but "heady," as both Maggie and Laura put it, by which they meant something closer to a total emotional-intellectual awakening. Maggie doesn't remember being sexually interested at first in Rick, who was also her debate coach, and who had a "huge crush" on her from the beginning. "But he made me feel smart, and he provided a forum in which I could speak and excel, and he told me I could do it."

Still enthusiastic fifteen years later about this relationship, Maggie related both being "in her body" and becoming more articulate, "finding her voice." She told of getting up at 5:00 a.m. with Rick and her debate partners on trips to tournaments, surfing while stoned, then going to rounds with their hair still wet and "kicking ass." They lived "moment to moment," their lives were "packed," and she loved being "on the edge."

Maggie hadn't planned to go to graduate school for her PhD. Returning again and again in conversation to her first symbol of academia—a visit to a prospective college where she would have had to live in a gray, institutional-looking, high-rise dorm—Maggie mused, "I think part of why I wasn't drawn to academia at first is because I didn't think I could be moved there, I didn't think I could be myself. I don't like to conform . . . I really resist when things are rigid or judgmental. So Rick was showing us a way that we could succeed *and* surf and smoke pot."

A gifted athlete, Maggie clarified that she meant "be moved" in a literal sense, that what she learned from Rick was not to compromise on passion in terms of society's rules. Much like *Guinevere*'s Harper, like Laura, and like me, Maggie broke out of the strict roles she had been brought up with when Rick awakened her. Time and space were not rigid, but fluid. "We weren't bound by the laws of physics and time in a way that linear Western thought wants to tell you."

Maiden Lovers typically experience what Maggie called "an opening up rather than a closing down," especially at the beginning of the relationship. This feeling closely echoes the sacred prostitute's ritual, in which the woman enacts for herself and for the man the transformative side of the Goddess—the urge to break free of what is confining, like the divine madness of the soul in Plato's *Phaedrus*, or water flowing where it will. Such a force transcends the limitations of social constraint and reason. It is ecstatic ("outside of stasis") imploring her to *move*, to become larger than she used to be.[12]

Maggie remembered her early trysts with Rick as transfigurative, and spoke as if she were fluid Aphrodite herself when she extolled being taken out of social constraints, ecstatically riding the waves of the surf and of her winning debates. I recalled seeing Botticelli's "The Birth of Venus" in the Uffizi in Florence, with the ocean-borne Goddess floating ashore on a seashell. Although Maggie eventually married someone else—"Rick was an instigator, not a partner"—she still thinks of him "really fondly," for "he changed my life. He's one of the most influential people in my life." Like Harper in her current relationship and in her career, Rick apparently initiated her in ways for which she is still grateful.

UNDERGROUND GENIUS

Maggie, Laura, and I no doubt saw our Pygmalions as the Underground Genius, the gender complex Polly Young-Eisendrath sees as most commonly projected onto men by women in their twenties and thirties. "He is seductive, sensitive, passionate, full of dark exotic powers. He's also somewhat androgynous and the 'artist type'—good with words, music, painting, film, something that reeks of *culture*, from the woman's point of view."[13]

The Underground Genius is related to the Greek Hephaestus, as un-Olympian as such gods get: dark, rather ugly, and very creative. But because he was the god of fire, especially of the underground volcano, and made beautiful things out of metals, he was worshiped as the god of craftsmen. Fiery and mysterious, he is "the first raw stirrings of a woman's creativity." The Underground Genius also may appear to the woman as Dionysus, the god of ecstasy who is exotic and erotic, attracts crowds of women, and represents the power of being rather than power over another.[14]

Maggie described her debate coach as "passionate," "brilliant," and "incredible," all qualities Laura said she had attributed to Al. And I saw my professor as a dark genius, whose satanic look marked him as more underworld than Olympian. *Guinevere*'s Harper obviously sees her slightly rumpled and not-very-handsome photographer in this way, as did all the Guineveres before and after her. Harper's venomously seductive mother nails the source of her daughter's attraction to him. Asking Connie why he prefers a naive girl like her daughter to an "experienced" woman her age, she answers her own question: "I know exactly what she has that I haven't got," she hisses, blowing smoke in Connie's face. "*Awe*."

~

It may seem that the Maiden Lover is merely raw material for Pygmalion's craft, whether this is beneficent or malevolent. It is true that he almost always had more power, and he did sometimes abuse it. But "[i]t is troubling," writes bell hooks, "when focus on the ways teachers can victimize students, especially via erotic engagement, denies the complex subjectivity of the students and makes them into objects by assuming that unequal power means that they are always acted upon and are without any agency."[15] When I read this, a rather astonishing statement by such an influential feminist, I thought back to my own question about what I might have offered my professor. Then I re-read how the sacred prostitute, by impersonating the Goddess, offered the man a "rekindling of the divine spark of life, a full and complete sense of well-being, perhaps sorely lacking in the world outside the sacred precincts."[16]

~

Elizabeth, a 59-year-old former professor with doctorates in two fields, helped me understand what it is, other than an obvious sexual target, that the Maiden Lover might offer Pygmalion. Women often seek a "magical partnership" with a man, she claimed, one that is intellectually and sexually "aflame"; this is not necessarily "bad," even when the man begins as her superior. She described her long-term relationship with Michael, a teacher and later a colleague, as productive and erotically intense for both of them. She likened it to those of Abelard and Heloise and Marie and Henri Curie. She was the Goddess in the form of the sacred prostitute for him, and he was like Hephaestus or Dionysus for her. Stirring each other's creative spirits, they conceived theoretical advancements that she thought capable of changing their field. They never physically consummated their relationship, but surely they gave birth to a Brainchild (see Chapter 5) that for a time felt divine.

DAUGHTER

When an academic woman willingly plays the Maiden Lover for her Pygmalion, it seems, she is exhilarated, sexually alive. Sometimes this feeling co-exists or alternates with the coquettish flirtations of a young girl, like a grown up and highly educated Lolita. Although, as Underground Genius, Pygmalion can facilitate a woman's break from her parents, and she usually sees him at first as radically different from them, he can transmute into a father figure rather seamlessly. Remember that Pygmalion broke from the Mother Goddess by marrying his daughter. I expected academic women, who need a certain masculine fierceness to succeed, to be closer to their fathers than their mothers, but following the pattern of Lolita, who never knew her father, it was more typically the other way around, particularly when they played the daughter/lover role. Some of these women found father figures, however, in their Pygmalions.

Maggie, who pictures her mother as a best friend and is not close to her father, said that Rick never seemed like a father figure at the time, "but looking back, I'd curl up in his lap and we'd go over papers." I thought of Guinevere draped over Connie's lap in a manner half winsome, half seductive, as he called her his "good girl." Rick taught Maggie how to teach and gave her access to important people she otherwise would not have had.

"It was a really neat introduction to the field," she pondered, echoing the sentiment of several women who had such father/lovers. "I think I was able to gain a certain maturity—in the field and for myself—within the safety of his love and support." When I asked whether Rick ever tried to mold her into what *he* wanted her to be, she replied, "No. He worked against the roles that were confining us. I don't remember him ever disciplining me. I still think of this as good. I am a scholar because of Rick."

~

Carrie fell for Greg while on a job interview at his campus. A promising scientist from an Ivy League school, Carrie was courted by several universities in a whirlwind of interviews. Greg, a full professor and twenty years her senior, was immediately taken with her star potential—so bright and shining, yet still unrealized. Carrie would need to finish her dissertation while beginning her position as an assistant professor.

Carrie got the job. Greg's adoration combined with the excitement of her first academic position was a heavy elixir. Before she moved to town she began a relationship with Greg that rivaled her interview schedule in tornadic intensity, as did Greg's divorce from his third wife, one of his former graduate students. Greg-and-Carrie formed a classic Underground Genius/Maiden Lover pair, nauseating their friends and colleagues with locked gazes that drifted off into eternity. They eloped and had a civil ceremony on the West Coast campus where Greg had spend his S.D.S. years in the 1970s, returning to announce their union to a shocked faculty.

With a faraway timbre to her voice, now modulated with experience, Carrie remembered Greg's "mystery" and "power." "There was something about him I couldn't quite pin down," she told me. "He was just so . . . so . . . *enigmatic*."

Greg tutored Carrie through her dissertation and first publication, introducing her to the movers and shakers on campus and to her "footnotes" at conferences. The two could be seen at conventions, official faculty functions, and parties in complementary profiles: the slightly frail young scholar on the steady arm of her tall and rumpled father/lover, who coached her in academic etiquette and the phallocentric ways of university politics.

Not all these women were so lyrical about their daughter/lover roles, however, and some were angry or confused about how hard it was to resist or exit their relationships. Pygmalion's marriage to his daughter, after all, was not so innocent—it was the power play that ushered in the loss of Galatea's creative divinity.

"It was straight out of *The Mary Tyler Moore Show*—I was Mary and there was a whole club of Lou Grants," said Amy as we sipped margaritas at a Mexican restaurant and she smoked Camels end to end. She had tried to quit for the last twenty years, but today she showed no sign of those efforts. At 51 she sported shoulder-length blonde hair and looked good in short skirts and tights, pulling off Goldie Hawn's magic trick of refusing to age. It was her voice that showed age as she recounted moving through the ranks from graduate school to full professor in the same department. She was a reluctant "mascot" to the older men, she recounted, fending off unwanted sexual advances with placating wit. "I got lots of rewards for smiling, drinking with the guys, not appearing to be a 'feminist,'" Amy admitted.

At Amy's suggestion I talked to another woman in the department, who said "They treat us all like little girls. I've seen them physically pat Cheryl on the head."

Amy explained that, in her college, "You have to be a fat man. It seems to be a symbol of power, taking up lots of space. These huge men feel comfortable with each other. Of course, the department always operates on a paternalistic basis, with Orson Welles and Burl Ives [her code names] vying for the Big Daddy role, in both senses of the word." The two even acted in tandem. Orson Welles would rage at her as the punishing father and Burl Ives would try to comfort her as the "good Dad." In the department the two were known as "the walruses."

Women often left Orson Welles' office in tears, Amy elaborated. "Really—he'd go postal all the time. He can't stand not to be in control of their lives. So far this year, two new faculty women have run in tears from his office to their own, where they lurked, waiting for the halls to clear before trying to get to their cars."

Amy told of being brought in to graduate school when she was about 20 by a 40-year-old "nice gentle chair of the department who wore Mr. Rogers-type sweaters. I became this person's student, and eventually his comforter." Mr. Rogers was like a diminutive pet for the "walruses"—as long as he remained a figurehead only, they protected him in return for his puppy-like fealty.

"His wife was so 'difficult' and all that, so I did research projects and took classes with him. You know, he was so fatherly and emotionally needy." Amy grew up without a father, and saw that as a factor in "this daughter thing I got stuck with."

One day Amy went to Mr. Rogers' home to work on a research project. When she realized Mrs. Rogers was not there, Amy wanted to leave, but felt obligated to stay. When he put his arm around her, she brushed him off politely, but left as soon as she could.

When other women revealed that he had acted similarly with them, Mr. Rogers was dismissed as chair, although he stayed on as professor. Amy interned elsewhere for awhile, partly to get away from him. When she returned, the graduate coordinator, as well as others in the department, all of whom knew about her situation, pressured her into taking another class from him since he was so "depressed" and she was "one of his favorite students." Apparently, the powers in the department considered Amy to be, not just his daughter, but a sweet and dutiful one at that.

According to Young-Eisendrath, the Father, Brother, or Guide to the Maiden Lover "feels enabled to be special or unique in assisting, supporting, or encouraging the woman. He may feel that his worth or future depends on her agreement to his plan."[17] Certainly, Amy felt responsible for Mr. Rogers' sense of worth, but also trapped and guilty herself. And, rather than protect *her* from his inappropriate behavior, Mr. Rogers' colleagues protected *him* from feeling his own humiliation.

~

Whether Underground Genius, Father/Lover, or both, the mentor who guides may desperately attempt to keep his precious Maiden Lover for himself, as Pygmalion stole the Goddess' icon and kept it in his bed. We will return in the next few chapters to some of the women we have met here because their stories sometimes took this turn. For now, let's look at how the Pygmalion and Galatea story often ends—an abrupt halt painted over with a golden varnish in Ovid's version, in which the principals ascended to Olympus.

LEAVING

Wrapped in this myth is a paradox that neither character can see when enveloped in the raptures of a fresh start, even if they have been there before. Pygmalion fervently desires Galatea to come to life as a match-mate for him, but when she does, he loses the thrill of creation. Either she seems stale to him now, like a hardened medium no longer yielding to his sculptor's tools, or she surpasses him in his own artistry. In this second case, a star is born, and he in danger of being overshadowed by her brilliance. As *Guinevere*'s Harper becomes a skilled photographer herself, his alcoholism drowns her adoration, and she realizes she no longer needs him. Either way, he moves on to another Maiden, who can revitalize him with her youth, beauty, and malleability.

Two years further into my interviews, Carrie was stunned when Greg announced he was divorcing her. They had been a perfect pair—love that so brimmed with brains and heat—how could he give it all up in a heartbeat? What Carrie did not know at that moment, but learned soon thereafter, was that, as her first major publication was getting her noticed in the scientific circles that Greg had opened to her, Greg's heart was beating fast for a new graduate student. Carrie had lost that "new car smell," as I've heard it crassly put, and he was looking at the new models. Carrie was due for her third year review. Greg didn't have a vote, of course, but he was influential. How would their split affect the rest of the faculty? Carrie was terrified.

One day when Elizabeth and Michael were at work, a younger researcher entered his office. When she left, he remarked "She reminds me of you when you were young." Their relationship—beginning, middle, and end—flashed before Elizabeth's eyes, the drama of her predecessors and her successors compressed into one excruciating eternal now. Not wanting to stick around for her own irrelevance, she left him and their research, never to return to either.

"I lost fifteen years of my work," she said flatly.

An unusually reflective person with an immense knowledge of

mythology, she believes that the symbolic feminine is the ingredient that makes the elements "fire" for the alchemist when he is trying to make gold. Then it is discarded. She agreed when I suggested that the woman's innocence, beauty, and intelligence is offered up as a sacrificial fire that allows the rebirth of life for the celebrant. What seems to begin as a sacred marriage may end up sacrificing, not the small egos of the initiates, but the woman's very sense of self.

CHAPTER 3

MUSE

> You are a pioneer woman. Your function is to create a man. Some women create children but it is greater to create a man. If you create Murray you will have done something very fine for the world.
>
> C. G. Jung, to Christiana Morgan

Romantic love between Pygmalion and his Maiden Lover can easily evolve into a Genius-Muse relationship, in which she labors as a "midwife to the man's creativity," investing her own artistry wholeheartedly in his development.[1] You might think that Pygmalion and Galatea have shifted roles when this happens, for it is *he* who is being "made" now, not *her*. Certainly, being a Muse can be intoxicating, especially at the beginning of a relationship. Visitations by the Muses, or "mountain goddesses," were highly prized in ancient times, for "[t]he man they inspired was sacred far beyond any priest."[2] In paintings, these bestowers of *mus*ic and a*muse*ment are usually seen in flowing robes and hair, dancing and singing with the grace of lissome fawns. The great man's Muse is a numinous figure in literature, from Dante's Beatrice to *Faust*'s Margareta. Lately she has appeared in the seductive blonde form of Sharon Stone in the movie *The Muse*. In countless stories, the tortured artist lives or dies according to whether his Muse appears in his dreams or on his shoulder. Indeed, the Muse seems to have the power to make or unmake the artist, for in myth she appears at her will, not his.

But it is really the man who remains at the center, whether his lover is Maiden or Muse. When Pygmalion chisels a perfect woman to his own specifications, it is his creativity that is satisfied. When a Muse inspires a man, though he may be dependent upon her for his vision, it is still his creativity that is fulfilled. For in both cases he is the artist.

A mortal Muse is in danger of resenting the ruin of her own talent, inspiration, and ambition, of feeling empty and inferior. Feminist biographies are unveiling how many women gave up their own Genius to their male partners in art and in science—Camille Claudel with Auguste Rodin, Marie Bonaparte with Sigmund Freud, Toni Wolfe with C. G. Jung. Even though feminism has greatly illuminated the problem, contemporary Muses still delay, or even forfeit entirely, their own creative ambitions while they financially support their partners' schooling or art.[3] The Muses in myth frequent places with wells and springs. We might say they are creatures who yield up insights from the unconscious depths to the struggling poet. The question for academic Maiden Lovers, as it must be for those in any milieu, is whether they give all their pearls away, or whether their visits to the wellsprings of the spirit benefit themselves as well.

The nine Muses were originally a triad, the very Triple-Goddess herself (Maiden, Mother, Crone) in her orgiastic aspect. They were the source of in*spir*ation, meaning to breathe in I*deas*—deities or Goddess-spirits. Historically, they are part of that feminine underworld upon which the academy is built. The Alexandrean shrine of the Muses was the *Muse*um, an ancient forerunner of the modern university, and still a place of culture and learning that is often located in a central place on campus.[4] But the Museum in Alexandrea was destroyed by Christians, who rejected pagan learning. Likewise, the Muses' origins, echoing Galatea, are obscured by an Olympian co-optation. Zeus claimed to be the Muses' father as the result of a tryst with Mnemosyne (Memory), who enabled the poets to remember their sacred sagas. But this, like many of his claims to paternity, was a late one; Hesiod calls the Muses daughters of Mother Earth and Air.[5] By the time of the Greek pantheon, they sat near Zeus' throne, and sang of his exploits as well as those of the heroes.[6] And a goddess who was once both orgiastic and spiritual, like the one the sacred prostitute enacted, inhabits a woman vulnerable to losing her voice as it is ceded to a man.

FROM DAUGHTER TO MUSE

I arrived for lunch at Jessie's office in another part of the country, a bit apprehensive because I knew what a busy health professional she was. She looked at me with incomprehension rather than pleasure over seeing me for the first time in a year. "Oh no, aren't you tomorrow?" she exclaimed, but then remembering herself, gave me a hug and looked at her calendar. She had one hour, minus time to get to the deli and back. Disappointed, knowing fragments of her rich background, I grabbed a quick cherry-romaine salad, hoping to get at least a shred or two from her life that I could use. So much for the tape recorder.

But as we talked, it became clear that Jessie knew her own story well, probably from years spent in analysis and a long struggle to make it cohere. She launched into her life with little prompting from me, and soon I was quickly absorbed.

Now a 49-year-old publishing mental health practitioner who left academia after obtaining a PhD at a famous university, then teaching for five years, she related a series of early incidents that delayed the development of her own voice. She called herself the "fourth child in a silent family," where her intellect and ideas were not encouraged. She was "tight" with her mother, whom she adored, but saw her father as an "impediment" who did not have time for her. She eventually fell in love with and married a fellow graduate student, who became the intellectual genius she wanted to be. Her story illustrates the struggles of an un-fathered girl whose drift into daughterhood injured her independent self when it should have been nurtured by the very men who mentored her.

Jessie fought much of her adult life to reclaim the intellectual she now thinks she has always been. She was an avid reader as a child, and always analyzed what her teachers taught her with an inquiring spirit and often a dry wit. In graduate school, she fell into playing daughter for her advisor. Although he looked like "Jabba the Hut," she "had a warm place in her heart for him" because he was crippled from polio like her beloved mother. But his wife was not at home when she responded to his invitation to watch opera at his house, and when he tried to push her into sex, she abruptly left. Much like Amy, whom we met in the last chapter, she continued to avoid his advances in a slippery high wire act as his advisee, balancing on the line between placation and self-protection.

Jessie studied hard and by all accounts was a star graduate student with a promising future as a scholar. Her comprehensive exams were a series of original papers that she thought should have received encouragement for publication. But Jabba "came after her" in the orals, criticizing her theoretical orientation, her methodology, her execution. Other committee members were "stunned," she recalled, and, although they passed her, no one verbally came to her aid. Nine years later, someone published a paper very similar to hers. It wasn't stolen, she lamented, because her version had never been published. "It was just an idea whose time had come." This framework "became the paradigm" in her subject area, but it was too late for her to participate.

At 45 Jessie had a "mid-life crisis" centering on her continuing failure to write or publish her burgeoning ideas. She never valued herself as an intellectual because she hadn't gotten a publication—the magic totem of intellectual legitimacy in the rites of academia. During this time she became passionate about heroes, such as those in *The Last of the Mohicans* and similar stories, who were "young and boyish." She needed to develop her "warrior within." Jessie discovered C. G. Jung's concept of the *animus*, the masculine figure in a woman's unconscious who crystallizes the culture's stereotypes of the masculine and is especially concerned with matters of work and reason. This *animus* can anesthetize her with listless inactivity or brutal criticism, or he can galvanize her by focusing her on the work at hand. Usually, the first source of the *animus* is the woman's father or other significant male figures in her early life, but it later takes on aspects of patriarchal institutions and their personal representatives.

Jessie had a series of dreams that symbolized the conflict between her *animus* and her own feminine creative instincts. The first one went like this:

> There was a pregnant pig in a farmyard without a shelter. There was no place for her to go to give birth. Then I noticed there was a partial wooden structure that might do; I just had to finish it. So I led the pig into it.

Jessie had been quite disappointed in her Dad's failure to nourish her intelligence and budding accomplishments when she was a young girl, and attributed much of her difficulty in claiming her scholarly voice, including her search for father figures who repeated the injury, to that lack. But in this dream, she realized that her Dad *had* given her a "partial structure"—by which she meant a masculine framework in which to house her feminine creativity. She associated the homeless pig with the animals her father gave each of his children to raise, care for, and sell through 4-H to make money for college. He had indeed taught them crucial lessons about ambition and worldly practicality, about finishing a task.

The female pig, or Sow-goddess, is a common form of the Great Mother in her Devouring form—in cults of Astarte, Demeter, the Celts, the Teutons, and Tantric Buddhism.[7] But, of course, the other side of the female Destroyer is the Creator. Perhaps this dream, as simple as it seems, expresses Jessie's need to give birth to her own ideas within a "masculine" analytical framework, as well as the other side of the Goddess' duality—that all could be destroyed if there was no "room" for the birth.

Energized by this dream and others, Jessie's work began to take shape in the idea for a book. "I was successful," she said wryly, so "I tried valiantly for several years to get my *husband*, the 'brilliant intellectual,' to write the book I wanted to write." She and her husband evidently had an unspoken contract that she would inspire him, and both would revel in his fame. Eventually Jessie was visited by another dream:

> My Dad had bought a boiler to warm the house. But he put it right in the middle of the living room—where it was inconvenient and inappropriate. I realized that I would have to move it to a better place.

She interpreted this as a sign that she had inflated her *animus* passion—that is, that after her dream about the pig, she had attributed too much to her father's beneficence, and assumed she was now equipped with a "workhorse" within. In fact, though her Dad had been more helpful than she'd remembered, he hadn't done *everything* that was needed. He had admirable instincts—to provide "warmth" for the family. But he certainly lacked subtlety! There was still much she would have to do on her own—making the finer distinctions that would fit her theory to specific contexts, for example. This dream helped Jessie realize that she could not depend on her father, or intellectual father figures, or the generalized world of the fathers, to produce her work for her. She began to claim her book—and her voice—for herself. She recently authored the lead article in the most prestigious journal in her field. It was the blueprint of her master work in progress.

STEALING THE GODDESS' ICON

Laura played the romantic Maiden Lover for her advisor Al, not the daughter, as did Jessie. Only after she left graduate school for a job at another university did Laura realize the extent to which she had served as her advisor/lover's Muse. Perhaps she couldn't have recognized this until after the romantic phase was over. Many women told stories of what one called a "partial blackout" during this falling-in-love stage, in which they willingly gave away their ideas to their lovers for the power of playing the *femme inspiratrice*. Only after the romance faded did they "come to" and recognize what they had forfeited. "I cannot believe how exhilarated I was that he liked my ideas," another woman winced. "I let him have them with no thought I might want them back some day." I remember how I willingly surrendered my papers to my honors professor—how I was *grateful* that he asked for them.

Several other women told of their mentors' appropriation of their work. Common forms included having her write sections of a book or a teachers' manual for a textbook without credit for authorship; having her write a grant proposal with him as the primary investigator; "co-authoring" a paper that was really hers, ostensibly because he had advised her on it or his name would help get it published; assigning papers in a course that he then used for his research; having her do the "dirty work" of a research project, then "authoring" it by himself. In fact, these practices seem to occur in all combinations of the sexes. When students or young professionals worship or feel beholden to their mentors or are afraid of their retributive power, whatever their sex, they often fail to confront inappropriate uses of their work.

But when a sexual relationship between the two is consummated or implied, the less experienced person—who most often is female—

seems particularly vulnerable to rationalizing the theft, or even to not recognizing it as a theft. That "romantic haze" spoken of by Laura, Maggie, and so many others obscures it as such, because she is enamored with his adoration of her. Or she is so ashamed of the relationship that she shrouds herself in silence.

A year after graduating, Laura attended a convention at which Al presented a paraphrase of one of her dissertation chapters without her knowledge. Although they were no longer lovers, she still cared for him, and she was torn between feelings of outrage and inferiority.

He didn't expect her to attend the panel. "I sat front and center, and he stood up and did this incredibly awkward referring to his colleague. But my name was not on the paper and it was my work."

"Were you shocked that he did that?" I asked.

Anger tinged her voice decades later as she remembered: "Not only could I not believe it, I *didn't* believe it. I didn't believe that it was my work. I did a little mind game and thought 'Well, we've talked about these ideas, and I got these ideas from other places' . . . but I didn't have enough confidence in my own authority and voice to be able to claim that synthesis as mine. I thought 'It's really common domain, I guess.' And it had been so exciting when I told him my thoughts, and he said that they were brilliant. But he used my phrasing, my citations, my points, and my applications.

"He came up to me immediately afterward, ashen-faced, and said 'I didn't know you were going to be here. I'm going up for promotion and I need every *vita* line I can get; I *hope* you understand.' . . . He said something like 'I should have put your name on it,' and he *implied* that he couldn't put *my* name on *my* goddamned work, because people knew we were having an affair."

Doubting whether I would have had the courage in a similar circumstance, I asked if she had confronted him.

"No," Laura replied. "I said, 'that's all right.' I was 28 or 29 years old, I was already ashamed about the affair, I was not sure that I had anything original and good. And so, by stealing my work, which I now see *was* stealing it, he also was helping nail down the idea that it really *wasn't* mine. But at the same time *he* was ashamed."

"I get the impression that you couldn't sort out your own self-image from all that relational stuff," I offered. "What comes to me is that it was so mixed up that you couldn't recognize an actual theft."

"I didn't know what was rice or millet or barley. I didn't know the difference. I didn't know what was my work, his work, common domain, should have been shared, should have been separate," Laura agonized. "I thought it was kind of just desserts for having gotten involved. I didn't have any real rights. I had anger. But what would I have done? Who would I have gone to?" Although the department chair "adored" her, she thought he would have protected Al because he was his "rising star son." Besides, the chair had a crush on Laura too. "And so here his boy had had an affair with the grandkid—who he was attracted to," she said. "It was incestuous."

I suggested it was "sort of like getting your pot stolen from your own house—who were you going to go to?"

"Exactly!" she confirmed.

When Pygmalion steals the priestess' icon and takes it to his bed, her own creative divinity is diminished while his is enhanced. She can no longer speak in her own voice, or even recognize her likeness.

FROM ROMANCE TO MUSE

One woman recommended a biography that helped her understand cultural pressures for a woman to give away her Muse to a man, Claire Douglas' *Translate This Darkness: The Life of Christiana Morgan, the Veiled Woman in Jung's Circle*. I put off reading it for a year, mostly because C. G. Jung has long been one of my heroes. But the book is an even-handed, if passionate, treatment of how the woman Lewis Mumford once called one of the three best minds he had met at Harvard let herself be plundered by famous men who loved her.[8] Douglas sees her biography of Morgan as recounting "what befalls a woman who strives to create a life of her own while remaining in thrall to the idea of Romantic love." Christiana was brilliant and powerful, but never at ease with her strength.[9] She "yearned for a larger life than was allowed a woman and for the expression of orgiastic sexuality, all the while restraining herself and subjecting her force of will to self-frustration."[10] Although Morgan lived before Second Wave feminism nurtured the voices of many contemporary women, her story casts in bold relief the risks of turning the romantic love of a Genius and his Maiden into the aesthetic love of the Genius and his Muse.

Born in 1897 to a Bostonian Brahmin mother and a Harvard Medical School professor of pathology father, Christiana was her father's favorite child. Reversing the pattern of Galateas who were closer to their mothers, she idealized her unconventional and intellectual yet earthy father, and adopted his view of her mother as a superficial servant to moral strictures and social codes. She later remarked that her father "created her" with his early devotion and by introducing her to a world outside her mother's. But he "allowed her only a temporary glimpse into the masculine world he would have opened to a son," and in fact, expected Christiana to be conventional as she grew up and to remain within the very social circle he mocked.[11] Preferring her father's iconoclasm, Christiana thus remained un-reflected by her father's attentions, and, like so many other Maiden Lovers, sought adult affirmation from Genius men who were a bit outside the pale of polite society.

Morgan consulted Jung for analysis in the 1920s. In the early twentieth century, both Freud and Jung turned to their patients, and especially a circle of women around them, for inspiration. These women often were extremely creative in the analytical and artistic realms; perhaps because they were not held to the strict rational standards of men of science, they were able to call up images from the unconscious and explore its depths in a way that fascinated the founders of psychoanalysis. They formed bridges between their own creative energies and their analysts' latent creativity. Jung valued women and their analytical ideas as few of his contemporaries did, and greatly encouraged Morgan, as well as others, to delve into her inner life. However, instead of cultivating the women's creativity for their own good, Jung encouraged them to project it onto a series of talented men and to subordinate their own gifts in order to advance the men's work. Morgan was perhaps the least known of these women, but she had trance-induced visions, which her artistic skills allowed her to translate into luminous paintings. Jung imposed his own conceptual scheme on Morgan's visions; in fact, he mined them for a four-year series of seminars. But "Morgan herself vanished under the veil of his interpretation of her reality."[12]

Morgan also worked alongside Henry (Harry) Murray as a lay analyst, research associate, and co-author at Harvard's Psychological Clinic from 1927 into the 1960s. With Murray she co-authored influential works on personality theory and the Thematic Apperception Test (TAT), for which she drew six of the nineteen pictures still in use today. When the article was published on the TAT, Morgan's name preceded Murray's as chief author, but it was inexplicably dropped from all later editions of the test. Reconstructing Morgan's work was a challenge, writes Douglas, because:

> Morgan gave her ideas so freely to others. She did not take her creative work as seriously as she would have done had she been a man or had she been born a generation or two later, when the curriculum vitae became acknowledged as the sine qua non of academic achievement. . . . In going over the psychological clinic's files, I found her handwritten notes and research strewn through almost every project Murray undertook.[13]

Morgan's patients, lovers, and friends recall her beauty, style, creativity, and analytical skills. However, while her close friends Jung, Alfred North Whitehead, Mumford, and Murray still are remembered, Morgan is not. "She remains at most," Douglas writes, "a footnote in other people's history."[14] Toward the end of the clinic's productive life in the 1950s, Murray had at least eleven unfinished books, pieces of which he began giving away to new people who caught his fancy—"work on which Morgan and other co-authors had staked the meaning of their lives."[15]

Both Christiana and Harry consulted Jung for analysis, and were deeply impressed by his theories and personality. The two were falling in love, and sought Jung's help in dealing with the trouble, for each was married. Jung encouraged both to face the issue squarely, and Christiana was at first elated by Jung's close attention to her inner life. But he may have been infatuated with her himself. Whatever the case, he did not adequately differentiate her from his own extramarital "lover, mystical sister, and muse," Toni Wolff, and advised both Harry and Christiana to engage in a similar relationship.[16]

With what Douglas calls "nineteenth-century hubris," Jung's psychological theory divided women in terms of the roles they played for men. Although Jung's wife Emma was involved in his psychological work and became an analyst in her own right, Jung classified her as the wife/mother type who cared for the family, while he looked to the *anima*-type—the female counterpart in the man's unconscious to the *animus* in the woman's unconscious—to inspire him. Jung found his own romantic muse in a series of other women, most importantly Toni Wolff, who resembled Christiana Morgan physically and temperamentally. Harry Morgan's wife Jo, the practical and extraverted sensate opposite to Christiana's dark and introverted intuitive, fell easily into the wife/mother category as well, while Christiana seemed perfectly suited to act as Harry's muse.[17]

Harry openly proposed that Christiana become his lover. This flattered her ego and she was excited by the idealism of inspiring a great man, but she also became further exhausted and depressed. Mirroring both Emma Jung's and Toni Wolff's pain and dissatisfaction with the dichotomy used to define them, neither Harry's wife Jo nor Christiana accepted the idea at first. Nor did Christiana's husband Bill, who seemed the least powerful of the four principals. But perhaps yielding to the twin inexorable forces of their passion and Jung's theories, Harry and Christiana did become lovers and collaborators until her death in 1967.[18]

Christiana recorded in her notebook what Jung told her:

> You are a pioneer woman. Your function is to create a man. Some women create children but it is greater to create a man. If you create Murray you will have done something very fine for the world.[19]

She wrote of her elation about Harry:

> To me the world is Harry—he entirely surrounds me and I feel that although I am more alive when I am with him than I ever could be alone, so alive that I feel greater than myself, still I have peace.[20]

Yet in the same passage, she expressed an uneasiness:

> However there is this about him. I feel him to be clutching and tearing at me for something—as though he would tear the secret of his own love out of me—and at times with him I feel absolutely exhausted and drained dry.[21]

Her disquiet then spread to encompass her attempts to fit the template of Jung's theories and men's demands of women in general:

> A strange oppression has been on me for the last two days. . . . It is like gazing at something full in the face—the fact that to my child to my husband and to H. I must be a mother and that nothing will ever stand between me and the forces which are around me—that I will be eternally alone—looking at these naked things always unprotected, and then measuring them to the capacity of these several individuals—veiling them and transforming these things that I see to meet the needs of each one—while I see them in the raw. I have the feeling that this may be the real awakening consciousness of woman. It makes me feel appallingly alone.[22]

Indeed, Murray used Morgan's visions, which he didn't have, for his own development. She struggled against his attempts to retrofit her into an impossibly one-sided ideal, but at the same time was captivated by his admiration of her. She also felt the heaviness of Murray's exaggerated expectation that she "could carry the entire archetype of the transformative feminine."[23]

Jung, Murray, and Morgan all had one handle on the power of the Goddess' transfiguring sexuality. What they did not understand was that in the ancient *hieros gamos* celebrated in the sacred prostitute's ritual, the woman called down the spirit of the Goddess herself—an impersonal force that transcended any one individual. The purpose of this rite was facilitated by the utter other-ness of the celebrants. They were strangers to each other; by impersonating a god and a goddess, they could not project their own individual needs upon another person and demand that they be fulfilled. The *Goddess*, not an actual woman, carried the weight of the collective "feminine." The ritual was intended to accomplish what we are seldom able to do in these more enlightened times—to free the participants from the selfish needs of their egos in order that they might love the other as a mere mortal.

MUSE VS. WIFE

The theoretical dichotomy that pushed these women into accepting one of two roles—wife/mother or muse—certainly sounds like nineteenth-century draconianism. But thinking over what I learned from academic women, as well as what I know of many professors' wives, I am not at all sure that we have put a stake in its sexist heart. Recall that Amy's "Mr. Rogers" confided in her about his "difficult" wife at home. Jessie's "Jabba the Hut" had a stay-at-home wife whom he considered necessary, but dull. Laura did not know Al's wife, but suspected she was essential to his domestic, but not intellectual, welfare. Maggie's advisor Rick had an attractive and capable wife with a career of her own, but Rick considered her not quite his equal in matters of the head. Greg lied to Carrie that he was "separated" from his professional wife, whose competence he admired, but whose inability to match his academic prowess he insinuated. Elizabeth would not consummate her relationship with Michael because he had a wife at home, but this wife was conventionally religious and not very inquiring—Michael's reason for seeking his Heloise at school. Another woman I spoke with said she does most of the "leg work" on the essays and books she and her husband write together; although both have PhD's, her laborious groundwork allows him the freedom to "think great thoughts," to present them in public, and to receive the adulation of his peers.

In James Hynes' supernatural, though hysterically incisive, novel of academic manners, *The Lecturer's Tale*, the head of the English Department, Anthony Pescecane, carries on with another faculty member, the gorgeous, smart and seductive Miranda de la Tour. He hosts a dinner for a job candidate at his home, where the "gray-faced housekeeper" welcomes the faculty guests and serves them at his table. As the candidate Jennifer Manly skillfully entertains the faculty with her stories, the protagonist Nelson Humboldt watches the gray woman, who keeps her eyes on her work, clearing plates and fetching water and wine.

> "Coffee, please, Maria," said Pescecane expansively, giving her a name toward the end of the meal. Then to his guests, "Tiramisu next." He kissed the tips of his fingers. "You'll fucking die."
>
> Maria left the room silently, with an armful of salad plates. Nelson rose to empty his bladder before the dessert came.
>
> "Um, *habla Ingles?*" Nelson ventured to the gray woman as he passed from the toilet through the kitchen on his way back to the table.
>
> The woman was drawing on the cigarette at the moment, so she just nodded.

"Wonderful meal," he said, still uncertain how much English the woman might know.

"Thanks," she said. Nelson wasn't sure if he detected an accent or not. He lay his hand on the side of the door. He couldn't think of anything else to say, but Jennifer Manly still had not reached the end of her story.

"Will, um, will Mrs. Pescecane be joining us later?" he asked.

The woman had just inhaled, and before she spoke, she widened her eyes and held up a finger for Nelson's patience. Then she gasped out a huge cloud of smoke, the same color as her skin.

"I *am* Mrs. Pescecane," she said.[24]

Although Hynes' caricatures may exaggerate the split roles, they also evoke a sharp bolt of recognition. The gray Mrs. Pescecane gets our sympathy, whereas Miranda gets our blood boiling. The wife keeps the home fires burning, whereas the Muse fires up the man's inert eloquence. But there is a downside to Miranda's "tour de force" sexuality as well.

Upon starting her affair with Harry Murray, Christiana Morgan wrote in her journal: "I wish that with Harry I didn't have this feeling of a snake in the grass somewhere."[25] This snake does all too often rear its disturbing head, an unwelcome guest at the picnic of romance that the Muse inspires. We will next get a look at its colors.

CHAPTER 4

MISTRESS

> O that this too, too solid flesh would melt,
> Thaw and resolve itself into a dew!
>
> *Hamlet*

Christiana Morgan's snake rears its head when Galatea descends from pedestal to property. The Maiden Lover is a luminous potential as Pygmalion shapes the beautiful soul that only his creative touch can animate. Even if the figure who emerges becomes his Muse, at least she has some value within the university because her reason for being is of the spirit, not the flesh. But as we have seen, when Pygmalion steals the Goddess' icon, he possesses her voice. If she becomes his Mistress, he also lays claim to her body. The academy has Hamlet's attitude toward embodiment in general. Absent the light of rational clarity, the solid flesh—Hamlet's "unweeded garden, that grows to seed"—is assigned to the "feminine" and considered outside the pale. The Maiden Lover is up on the block, waiting to be materialized, but the Mistress has been around the block, and is too corporeal for the Ivory Tower's purity. Is it any wonder, then, that she will feel like used goods?

A woman becomes Mistress when her utility to the man shifts from soul to spirit to body. Romantic or aesthetic love may turn to sexual dominance. Sometimes the man and woman exchange currencies for mutual profit, although each usually ends up sacrificing what was once so precious—he loses his potential match-mate and she loses her creative catalyst. Or perhaps the woman will not submit, and Pygmalion retaliates against her for threatening his virility. Whatever the case—whether she is a "willing" partner or not—she is likely to suffer a loss of self-worth, often accompanied by illness and despair. In the worst cases, the relationship descends into violence.

Some of the women we have met thus far did not evolve from Maiden Lover or Muse to Mistress. Maggie, our Venus-on-the-half-shell champion debater, went on to other relationships, remaining fond of the initiation provided by her advisor. Elizabeth, if you recall, got left by Michael when a younger researcher took her place. Jessie, who married her Genius, spoke not of becoming his property, but of maturing into a more equal relationship. But others did come to play the Mistress, or were cast involuntarily in the role by men at work. We will come back to Amy, Laura, Carrie, and Christiana Morgan as Mistresses, and meet a couple of others along the way.

But first let's revisit an ancient ritual to get a perspective on how the Maiden or Muse can transform into the Mistress. As prostitution lost its connection with the sacred, the women who practiced it turned from priestesses into whores. The Goddess disappeared, to be replaced by mere coins.

CORRUPTING THE SACRED PROSTITUTE

By the middle of the first millennium B.C.E., religious and commercial prostitution flourished in proximity to one another in or near the temples in Babylon and elsewhere. The relationship between these two professions is not completely understood, but there are signs that sacred harlotry may have been corrupted when temple prostitutes kept the gifts meant for the temple (or the Goddess) for their own profit.[1] Galatea's or Aphrodite's life-force cannot be bestowed when there is an exchange of currencies. Like grace, it is freely given when the celebrants surrender their personal power to her, not subordinate her power to themselves.

Commercial prostitution also prospered when women were enslaved in the process of consolidating social classes. Military exploits made captive women readily available for private sexual use by kings and chiefs, who displayed their wealth in the form of servants, concubines, and harems, symbols of power to be emulated by aristocrats and wealthy men.[2] Such a woman in bondage was not a soul to be contoured but a sign to be exhibited.

PROPERTY RITES

Since she is now a professor in the same department where she began as a graduate student, Amy is a bit unusual. Unfortunately, her experiences are not. In fact, her long career there is almost a textbook case of a woman who attempted to dodge Galatea's roles and refuse sexual involvement, but was pushed and shoved anyway into playing Maiden Lover, not realizing the men would treat her more as Mistress as she got older. Although their personalities and backgrounds are radically different, her story closely parallels that of Theresa, who entered the department years later as an assistant professor. Pairing their stories reveals a boys' club that they found impossible to get around—a situation made more difficult, both said, because women were so few in number.

Amy dodged sexual harassment for at least fifteen years. But she did play daughter to Mr. Rogers, returning to his class at the insistence of the walruses, and she did play mascot to the men, drinking with them after hours, fending them off with humor and good will, and failing to register any official complaints. She didn't think she had a choice, since she needed the job and their support, but she was both bitter and ashamed about trading in her freedom for professional "safety," which turned out to be more like their entitlement to her.

Amy stayed single for years. "The Old Boys were convinced when I came here that I was gay because I didn't have a boyfriend," she laughed. If she didn't want one of *them*, she must have been a lesbian.

She felt free to start a relationship with someone else only after getting tenure. Since the walruses didn't approve of him, she kept it secret for a long time. Clearly resentful, Amy divulged, "I almost had to ask their permission. I knew they'd be angry that 'Marian the Librarian'—me—betrayed them by getting a life."

She described going to a football game with her new boyfriend, not realizing that her tickets were close to where the boys' club sat.

"And I look down from me, about ten rows, and there are the walruses—they're sitting in these little seats, so they have to sit almost stomach to stomach. The wives sit on the outside. And as soon as I saw them—it's horrible—I started to cry."

Amy's voice broke as she recalled the scene, perhaps innocuous to anyone else, but obviously loaded with meaning for her.

"They're sports fanatics, and I associate the school sports with them, and with the provost, and I thought, 'I can't stay here.' Of course I did, because there's nowhere else to go. I needed a Valium or something. They're everywhere I go. They take up so much space. I can never get away from them."

She recalled that when she was in grade school, she "got in trouble a lot for mouthing off." She had an abusive brother, seven years her senior, who would hit her if she didn't do what he said, and then she would get in trouble with her mother for wisecracking back to him. Her mother expected her son to be a father since Amy did not have one, and thought it was appropriate for him to "discipline" Amy because "it proved he wasn't gay."

"In high school I did better," she said. "I needed to get a scholarship so I learned to shut up."

"So that's what it means to 'do better'?" I remarked, "to shut up?"

"I guess it is," she replied, "and I must have still been trying to do better here at the university. I needed their protection so I tried to keep quiet."

Amy eventually began speaking out more, especially in support of others who she thought were being treated unfairly. "I knew it would catch up with me eventually. And this is when all this getting in trouble in school came back to me. I can only be nice for so long, and smile, and I knew that, deep down, they knew I was insubordinate."

A scholar visiting the campus for a lecture, who she had only just met, congratulated her on the grant she'd just received. "'So this should help you with your problem,'" he remarked.

"What problem would that be?" she asked.

"You know, the problem you have with the faculty."

Amy lit into him. "*I'm* not the one with the problem, the only problem I have is that I don't have a penis!"

The walruses anxiously calmed down the scene by saying, "'You know Amy, she's all right, she's just a little hysterical.'" Apparently, they felt justified not only in passing judgment on her relationships and preventing her from "getting a life" but also in interpreting her personality to their peers.

Theresa was less accommodating to the walruses than was Amy, not just evading their pats and hugs and sexual suggestions but actually telling them to leave her alone. More assertive in her personal style, she would not play Daughter to them, even at the very beginning when they expected her to seek out their patronage. She came to the job "not so young," and with several years of experience in private industry and an admirable track record. "There wasn't a sense that they could mold me," she explained. After just four years at her job, she was already bitter.

"No one there has ever actively engaged me in discussion about my work. I find that appalling. Hasn't happened in a formal evaluation or in conversation. They let me know it's my fault they don't understand what I'm doing."

"What do you think they want you to do?" I asked.

"Suck up."

"If you asked for the Daddy-type protection, would they like you?" I wondered.

"It's too late, they've seen me as I am. They thought I had an agenda for the department, but I didn't. I just wanted them to get out of the way and leave me alone. I'm a workaholic. But being a female and not sucking up, and taking students away from them, was a threat."

"What if you did all the stuff that you did *and* sucked up?" I probed.

"Well, I don't think it goes together."

"Is this right?" I ventured. "They see you seeing *them* mess up. So it's 'The Emperor's New Clothes.' They know you see them naked although they're pretending to look good?"

"Yes!" she confirmed. "I'm not this strategic person trying to manipulate them, that's not me. But I do observe people's behavior—I'm pretty good at that."

As they did with Amy, the walruses psychoanalyzed Theresa to others, calling her "crazy," complaining that "she doesn't play well with others," and, "We've tried with Theresa, but you just can't talk to her."

~

Kate, a diminutive and vivacious musical theorist, passionate about her art, was trying to decide which faculty member to ask to be her PhD advisor. Her department was very social, hanging out together in coffee shops and bars around the campus, and giving frequent parties that almost everyone attended. Ted had published several well-received books and achieved a reputation as one of the best in their field.

Before she settled on Ted, he said to her, "Temporary advising is like dating. If you commit, it's a more serious relationship."

"Ted told me he loved me on several occasions," Kate remembered. I asked her how she felt about that.

"Good and weird," she replied. Although theirs turned out to be a very troubling relationship, she still admitted the advantages of a Maiden Lover/Daughter role. "There are worse ways to break away from Mom and Dad than to be Ted's advisee."

The two of them went to an outdoor opera together. She was excited about the event and about being with him. At a break in the performance, he turned to her and said "I don't think I can be intellectually close without being physically close." He asked her to have an affair with him.

Flattered and nervous, Kate fidgeted before she replied "I'd rather be colleagues and friends." She knew she didn't want the affair, but obsessed about the fact that they had talked about it. Afterward, she sent him a note to make it right. "Everything I said was wrong, and I kept trying to make it right—what it should be. But it could never be right."

Kate chose Ted as her advisor anyway. The intellectual give-and-take was wonderful; they "clicked" on their subject matter, and Kate produced a dissertation she was proud of. But she still felt that she could never really please Ted. He asked her to contribute to his research several times, but each time he criticized her work and "dumped" her, forfeiting her contributions and giving the work to someone else.

When her beloved sister was dying of congenital heart disease as Kate was writing her dissertation, grief compounded the depression she felt over her increasingly strained relationship with Ted. "He didn't think I was going to make it." She contemplated dropping out. Echoing the walruses' psychologizing of Amy and Theresa, Ted said Kate was "too sensitive."

He ridiculed her lack of fortitude. "Do you think this world is fair?" he demanded. "Work doesn't just stop when shit happens! If you can get through this thing with your sister and still give eighteen hours a day to your dissertation, then I'll know you're worth something."

"Ted owned me, in a sense," Kate said sorrowfully.

When she started dating someone, Ted immediately found fault with him, just as Amy's superiors had criticized her boyfriend. All traces of romance with Ted now vanished for Kate, although he still treated her like his Mistress. "I didn't flirt with him," she insisted. "In fact, I changed the way I dressed. I bagged out to keep from attracting him or anybody else. I wouldn't even engage in playful repartee. I built this really serious and professional persona."

"Did that work better for you?" I queried.

"It makes me want to cry, because I'm a fun-loving girl. It's only now [twenty years later] that I've discovered I can be flirtatious again and it's fun. I can do that now and still keep my boundaries."

Apparently a Mistress may still signify wealth and power to other men, even in the non-worldly arena of academe. As Kate neared graduation, she and her best friend, who *was* having an affair with her advisor, were both looking for jobs in the same area. Ted and her friend's dissertation director acted as if the women were in a "horse race" to get the best job. Kate remembered how, at a convention party, Ted introduced both women to prospective employers at the same time.

"He really played up the rivalry. This was the 'macho Ted,' because I was his student and she was his friend's. It was like setting up a cat fight."

Yet the competition between the men was overshadowed by a camaraderie that bound them to protect each other's ownership of their Mistresses. Kate tried to get another mentor when she realized Ted was not facilitating her independence. But all of the possibilities in her department were men, and none of them would encroach upon his "property." What was probably even worse for her career, Kate saw this male support club extending to her field at large. Though they were not having sex, Kate and Ted had been seen frequently together at conferences, and she had been junior author with him on several papers.

"I could not join the community as a scholar in my own right because everyone considered me 'his.'" She appealed for help to an older man at a different university whom she considered wise and trustworthy, but he was friends with Ted, too, and proved to be unhelpful. "He washed his hands of me."

Kate winced when she recalled the last line of Ted's letter of recommendation for her job hunt. It expresses Pygmalion's quintessential proprietary attitude toward a woman he regards as his Mistress: "This lady is a charming commodity."

When we last met Laura, she had discovered how she unwittingly played Muse to her advisor/lover Al when he presented her work at a convention as his own. Laura had also been Al's Mistress, as she painfully recognized during the writing of her dissertation.

"I wanted to write on feminism, and he wouldn't let me," she explained. "That was my real passion."

"Why wouldn't he let you do that?" I asked, incredulous until I realized how much things had changed since the early 1970s.

"It wasn't considered a topic of study. I had five men on my committee and none of them thought it was a good idea. So I worked in his area, but in a totally different way. I was developing a theoretical synthesis that later became the model for my book."

I knew this book had become a major success, still in print and widely consulted twenty years after it was first published, so I was amazed when Laura revealed, "I didn't believe in what I was writing. I had doubts about myself, of course, being a young woman in the academic world. It was new ground. But I was afraid that the other men would decide that this dissertation proposal, which Al had passed, was not good enough."

"Did you undervalue your work because of your relationship with Al?" I inquired, thinking that her perspective must have been badly skewed and her dissertation had been better than she thought.

"No. Even now I really don't think it was as good as it should have been. I am proud of the book, but not my dissertation."

Al kept telling her to rewrite, she remembered. But by then their collaboration had become a contest of wills, as she guessed he wanted to keep her in school as long as possible, yet still would not demand the kind of high quality he would have from a man.

"I was passive-aggressive. I would change words and phrases here and there, but not really rewrite, the way it should have been. But he wouldn't make me do it. He should have made me redo the whole thing, and the committee knew that, too. But they wouldn't make me do it either because they knew I was 'Al's girl.'" Just as the other men did with Kate, Al's colleagues practiced a "hands off" policy with Laura.

Laura's suspicions that Al was trying to keep her at his school and "be a disciple" eventually turned into the nightmare she dreaded. At conferences she attended, representatives from three universities revealed they had been interested in hiring her, but when they called Al and asked "What do you think about Laura?" he had replied, "She's not ready."

By this time the affair had ended, and Al was missing it. Another university was interested in hiring Laura, but Al had discouraged them. "I had a panicked feeling that if I didn't leave then [with her dissertation not yet finished], I might not ever finish, that I had to get out, I had to escape. I was afraid that he wouldn't pass me, that the affair would become known, and that the men on the committee would have decided I was no damn good."

Desperate, Laura went to the department chair, who was also on her committee, and pleaded for help. "I am in trouble," she pleaded. "I don't think Al is going to let me through because he wants me to stay around."

The chair intervened for her by talking to Al, "partly because Al was one of his rising stars and he didn't want any problems. He also thought I was good. It was mixed. He recognized my competence, but he was protecting his son." At his chair's bidding, Al called the university to reverse his assessment, and Laura got the job and left. But she was saddled, as are so many brand-new assistant professors, with finishing her dissertation while starting up new courses and a heavy load of service. She was also fearful of returning for her orals because she did not know what Al, or her other members, would do.

"Did it feel like ownership to you?" I suggested. I knew better than to pose this sort of leading question. I should have said something more open-ended, like "How did you feel about this?" But I had already encountered this aspect of the Mistress relationship several times, and was fast formulating my own ideas.

"Yeah, it did," she answered. "He owned me and my work."

Laura was not by any means the only Mistress to escape a sinking ship. Not all had the option, and so they remained to be treated like "used goods" or retaliated against for ending the affair. Some fled because they were forced to, often to lesser positions or out of academia for good—whatever first popped up as an avenue of escape. Not one wanted to remain in thrall to a man once she realized she was his "possession."

RETALIATION FOR RESISTANCE

There is a double-bind inherent in the Pygmalion-Mistress relationship. If a man presses you into the Mistress role, your two "choices" are to play the Mistress, or resist. If you play along, you're a whore. If you resist, you're a bitch. Either way, it's your fault. Either way, you pay.

Men tend to get tired of their Mistresses, and sometimes subvert them professionally for being "used goods." This is what Greg did to Carrie. On the other hand, if a woman is a man's "property," he won't like it if she refuses his "rights" or leaves him. According to Kate, Ted made her pay for her sexual refusal by criticizing her competence and dedication. Al attempted to stall Laura's dissertation progress and undermine her job prospects. And, as we will see, the walruses made Amy and Theresa pay dearly for rejecting their seductive patronage.

~

Carrie, the new assistant professor who "got married in a fever," was last seen reeling from Greg's sudden ardor for divorce, and frightened as a cornered animal to face her third-year review. As it turns out, she had reason. Greg critiqued her research record with the powers in the department and planted rumors that her teaching was suspect. When he found out she was dating someone not in academia after their divorce, he threatened to use his legendary political connections to get *him* fired. He opened her mail, sent her insulting e-mails, and generally made her life, as she put it, "bloody hell." This was his course of action within their university and town.

To those outside their milieu, however, Greg showed a different face. He spoke highly of Carrie's competence as a researcher and teacher. A job at a distant university came open, and Carrie grabbed it. Greg was free of a woman who could have become a "problem" for him. Within two years she had quit academia altogether. Meanwhile, Greg was busy getting the graduate student with whom he had since taken up dropped from the program. With dizzying efficiency, Greg was disposing of the waste materials of his love life.

~

Amy went up for promotion to Professor after she thought her record more than warranted it. She had been given a university-wide teaching award, her classes were overflowing, and she had earned major awards in scholarship. "I had been getting 10's in research, but I was turned down," she said angrily. She appealed her case, partly because she believed the walruses had tampered illegally with her promotion file. She hired the university attorney to represent her.

"He was good," she said, "but I was turned down at the president's level, and he backed out."

"Why?" I queried. "Didn't he think your case was solid?"

"He plays golf with the president. He wasn't going to get involved in a lawsuit against the university." Amy was still heavily in debt after taking out a loan to pay this attorney.

"The worst thing is, I really feel that these men are having fun with this because here I was, doing all this work for the appeal, having all these witnesses lined up. It was like the *Twilight Zone*, where all along, people are just looking down at you and having fun watching you, and thinking 'Look at her, she's a fool.'" Amy said she indeed was a fool to spend her own money on the appeal. "It's been one indignity after another."

Theresa fared no better. When she went up for her pre-tenure review, although she had been ranked highest in her department in research the final year and had over one hundred papers and publications, she was told to look elsewhere for a position.

Both Amy and Theresa remarked that men with lesser records got wholehearted support from the walruses. Amy recalled that when she won an award for a major publication, one of the walruses demanded, "Do you really think you're the equal of T. J. and Lance [the second and third authors]?"

Amy told me she responded, "Of course I do. Why would I be here if I didn't?"

"But," she said to me, "they couldn't even process that. They just stared."

She was bewildered when the walruses organized to protect a guy in his tenure case who only had one publication. "They don't even respect him, but they like him. They'd never do that for a woman."

Amy recounted a string of incidents in which she and Theresa were intimidated—she is pretty sure the culprits were students. One time Amy found a lewd drawing of a female teacher being gang-raped by a group of male students in her briefcase. Another time Theresa received pornographic poetry in her e-mail from an unknown source. Amy went to Orson Welles, explained the situation, and asked him to look into it.

He couldn't help her, he replied. "The problem is you—you're attracting this kind of attention." Even though Amy had resisted playing Mistress to the Old Boys sexually, they had typed her as one, probably for what they saw as flirtatious behavior.

Theresa, on the other hand, was a "bitch." She had heard about some of the Old Boys' "handsy" behavior before she took the job. It wasn't too long before the provost began grabbing and hugging her. Graduate students were starting to say things about how he "handled her."

"I didn't say anything," she recalled. "I had to be really careful."

But not long after that, another "seasoned female" applied for a job and called to ask about this man's by-now-legendary conduct. Theresa told her that he had indeed been inappropriate. Unfortunately, the woman revealed in her interview that Theresa had complained to her of sexual harassment.

"Burl Ives went ballistic," she said. "He's been caught in these things, too. Earlier, he had thrown something at me. I became in fear of my life."

Theresa went to the provost and "cleared the air." Neither apologized, but she thought the provost heard her. "But Ives has never forgiven me." It was soon after that that she received her negative review.

LOSS OF WORTH

Perhaps you have seen the long-running series of commercials for L'Oreal, in which gorgeous women like Cybill Shepherd and Andie MacDowell finger their luxurious hair, turning to coo haughtily into the camera, "L'Oreal. The most expensive hair color in the world. Because I'm worth it." Here in the space of about 30 seconds are all the indelible marks of the Mistress: she is beautiful; she is coming on to the viewer, whom we may think of as a man but is more likely a woman who identifies with the model in her fantasies; her worth is tied to her looks and her sexuality; and she is equated with money. The expected response from the viewer is a kind of defiant right to commodification: *Yes, by God, I am worth it! I want my expensive beauty products!*

Although it might be great to be as demanding and beautiful as Shepherd or MacDowell, what this ad doesn't tell you is the costs of such equations. If a woman is valuable for her sexuality, what becomes of her when she is "used"? If she sees her worth as residing in her beauty, what happens when it fades with age? And, if she is treated as a man's property—which also means his currency—of what value is she to herself? I have not consciously identified with the Mistress role, but I once had this dream:

> I receive a letter from some professor announcing lectures that I and another person will give at a university. The flyer has pictures of the two lecturers. The man's picture is a typical professional studio shot. The one of me is in a lace teddy lying on a bed. I am shocked! I don't know how the professor got hold of it, and I don't even know where it came from.

This flagrant depiction of my own eroticism was to some degree titillating, but it was also unsettling. If I were approaching the presentation "like a man," I would not have been on display. And as one woman warned, "A sexual relationship with a mentor can be damaging because it really does ingrain you with the idea that the only way to succeed is in bed."

I was struck by how few women who reach the Mistress stage come away unscathed, not only in terms of the men's retaliation but also in the way they think about themselves. All of those with whom I spoke struggled with their self-esteem, usually for a very long time. Guilt, shame, loss of voice, depression, and illness were common, as was disaffection for academia.

~

Kate felt shame over the relationship with Ted when she was a PhD student. Even though he was the aggressor and she did not comply sexually, she took the responsibility herself for letting it "get out of bounds." When Ted seemed to lose faith in her intellectually as she was struggling to complete her dissertation amidst her sister's tragedy, she felt that "there was no hope, my career was a bleak wasteland." She considered dropping out of academia, and even took steps to get a job in business before she redoubled her efforts to finish her degree.

Once, when she was driving, she recalled "I almost let myself hit a tree."

It was not obvious to others, because she secured a good academic position and became quite successful, but Kate had struggled hard to regain her self-esteem in the two decades that had passed. As she did after Ted's attempt at an affair at the opera, she kept trying to make things right. When she recalled this encounter to Ted several years after she had graduated and moved on, he denied that it had happened.

"It was all in your mind," he said, to her bewilderment.

As if trying to undo Pygmalion's self-projected sculpture, she has written him on several occasions, saying "I'm not the person you think you created." Ted stoked her emotional chaos by writing back "It's you who have created this perception of *me*."

~

Both Amy and Theresa attributed their depression and physical illness directly to their treatment by the walruses, especially in their promotion and tenure cases. Both had sought psychiatric help, and both were so jaded about academic life that they were considering leaving.

Amy was in the midst of her appeal during one of our conversations. "It takes so much energy to take care of yourself, to look out for your mental health," she complained, "that I draw back from things that I care about, like teaching, because they're connected to the hostile working environment. I don't want to do that."

Amy said that when she had family troubles at the same time her job was falling apart, she got "clinically depressed."

"There's a point of depression . . . I come home, and I can't move, I'm so tired. I do aerobics, have a big glass of wine and watch [the] O. J. [trial]. I thought I was picking up all these legal tips," she laughed at herself. "I got this great two-hour massage one afternoon, and I walked into a grocery store, and I looked around at the people and thought 'I have been going around with my head down for so long'—it was the strangest thing—not making eye contact.

"My friend said 'You know, you've been watching too many American movies. In Europe we would know that you're going to lose, but you honestly think that you can stand up on a table and there'll be these men cheering for the underdog, and everybody will come to your aid, and you'll win.' But it only matters who's at the top—that's all."

She described having been in a bad car accident that killed her dog. "My experience in the department wasn't exactly like that, but in a way it was, because my self-esteem was so damaged. I wonder, am I just a natural loser?"

Theresa's tougher shell did not seem to shield her from the pain any more effectively than did Amy's softer one. She, too, was in the midst of her pre-tenure appeal when we talked.

"They have made my four years there such Hell. I have been to the employee assistance program for psychiatric help, and I've almost used that up." She clung to her other interests and previous careers to reassure herself that academia was not her life.

"If that had been my one role, I'd have been dead by now."

"Are you serious?" I asked.

"Dead serious. I've had more stress-related illness since I've been here than I ever have before. This performance review pushed me right over the edge. This is my only source of income, so what do you do?"

I asked Theresa if her voice had been affected. "Do you speak out—do you monitor yourself, or do you let it out?"

"No, I try not to speak at all. I minimize my communication as much as I can. I have no voice."

Having resisted the walruses' come-ons for so many years, Amy mentioned aging more often than seemed appropriate for one who looked so young and seemed so vital. She wondered aloud whether things would be any different once these men retired, then answered her own question.

"No, I'm already considered the Old Guard. I see these new whippersnappers, and they look like babies." I thought that turning middle age may have rattled the roles she played in relation to the men, and that even though these were always uncomfortable, growing out of them was also disquieting.

"So when you turn middle age," I proposed, "you're too old for them to take you under their wings?"

"It's like they don't know what their role is, if they can't be 'Daddy' or sexual, what can they be? And, if I were a full professor, how could they protect me any more? It's threatening to them."

When a woman plays Maiden Lover and then matures away from the Mistress, it seems, the man may be confused as to how to categorize her, which in turn may make him uneasy about himself. I heard many comments from women about how they thought men had difficulties relating to them as they developed into middle age and beyond. Some thought the men were afraid of women's power when they grew beyond the need of protection and were not interested in seduction. Others saw men's denigrating remarks as payback for resisting both personae altogether.

~

These tensions related to aging affect women whether or not they once enacted the Mistress, partly because the Mistress is such an expected role for younger women to play. I meet with Christine in a coffee shop or bar at the same convention once a year for an update on our lives and careers. It's a little like the movie *Same Time, Next Year,* because we don't talk much or see each other during the year, and then we check in to see what has changed. She became an assistant professor at age 51 after an amazingly successful career that was no longer fulfilling her creative needs. The first year we met, Christine was full of excitement about her work, and eager to publish it. The second year, she seemed a bit chastened, as she recounted the difficulties of balancing her penchant for service with the need to publish. The third year, at 54, although her other interests in volunteer work like hospice were fulfilling her, she was desperate and depressed about academia.

"There is no place in the university for a post-menopausal woman," Christine stated starkly. "I am not seductive at work, so the men can't relate to me on that level. And, although I'd like their mentoring to help me get published, I don't seek them out as Daddy. In a lot of ways, I know more about life than they do. So they don't know what to do with me."

I was sadly touched by how her demeanor had diminished in three short years. My annual conversational partner is a vivacious woman at a peak of creativity and spiritual development, who wants to be of service to others in a meaningful way. And now she is wondering whether she can stay in this vocation that called so powerfully to her at the beginning.

Amy discussed several women in middle age who had "just given up." Theresa agreed that "this is not unique to us." One colleague quit her tenured position at a midwestern university to come to their college for a job specifically related to her interests. Another was a very successful chair of a department.

"Either one of them should have been considered for dean," Amy said. Both loved their work, published influential research, and were wonderful at administration. But the woman from the Midwest was told she was "too outspoken," and "dressed like she was on Wall Street," which Amy interpreted as "not sexy enough." She was also informed in her performance evaluation that "Graduate students are concerned about your biases against the male students. What do you intend to do about this?"

This woman was, as Theresa called herself, a workaholic, but was so demoralized that she was thinking of quitting. As Amy saw it, she was being punished for *not* fitting into the Mistress role. Amy was also considering another job, but had not taken steps to find one because she felt that "there would be another can of worms elsewhere, I know that."

I wanted to know how Amy felt about academia in general at this point in her career.

"I just feel really old and tired. I just don't think academia is the place where interesting things are done any more."

This morning I told my husband Tom about this motif of the aging Mistress that I was writing about. He told me a saying he remembered from his hunting days with his buddies in the marshes of Wisconsin: "An old woman is like Australia. Everybody knows about it. Nobody wants to go there." It came as a total surprise to me when I started to cry, since I don't think I ever played the Mistress role. Of course, Australia is now a rather desirable vacation spot. But the culture that produced that phrase was equating older women with the outback before it was glamorized by Crocodile Dundee and the restaurant chain: a dry wasteland—ugly, unproductive, useless. I wept for the women—and, yes, even a bit for myself—all brimming with the creative spark of Galatea/Aphrodite, who had struggled against internalizing this ruinous American attitude that, of course, far transcends academe. Somewhere, the Goddess, the one who owned her own sexuality and did not need a man to create her in his own image, must be seething with the insult.

Laura's anguish over having become Mistress to Al surfaced as one reason she eventually left her university job. Like Kate, she suffered guilt over the relationship. "I took all the responsibility for several years in that blaming, shaming way. But he's the one who took me to lunch and kissed me and said, 'We should meet.' But I blamed myself because I was married—never mind that he was married, too. We didn't talk about those things then in terms of power like we do now."

To complicate matters, Laura had another affair toward the end of her graduate career with a professor at another university. "Sebastian was in my field but didn't seem dangerous. He seemed marvelous because he was not involved in my career. He was one of the three or four great loves of my life."

But Sebastian never read her dissertation and didn't know what she was doing professionally.

"That's the thing, here was this man in my field who was in love with me, but who really didn't have a clue what I thought or who I was, other than personally. So here I had all this respect for him and people were seeing him in this special way, but we didn't talk about ideas. And I was not interesting to him for that reason. So that was another split."

"Can you clarify that split?" I asked.

"I didn't feel that my primary currency to anybody was my intellect and my career potential. My primary currency was my personal self. My sexuality. The professional Laura was not very interesting to anybody else but me." Laura's words aptly illustrated that what happened to the sacred prostitute long ago—when the temple took coins for her services or the man used his collection of mistresses as social currency—is still an everyday event.

Sebastian wanted her to move across the country where he lived, but she finally realized that he hadn't really taken seriously what she would do—for a living or with her time. And he made no plans to divorce his wife.

"I got it," she said.

"So he didn't get it?"

"Looking back, I think he was just stoned."

Laura learned not to take herself seriously in an intellectual sense, while at the same time overworking to compensate for her loss of self-esteem. "I don't think I've been free of that until five years after I left academia," she reflected. "It's been a major, major pain and loss of self in my life."

Clearly having agonized about this for many years, she declared "I ended up with a degree that felt tainted." Now brilliant in a non-academic career, she made a stunning disclosure: "I know that I persevered to get a second PhD because I devalued the first one."

A TURN TO VIOLENCE

A Pygmalion-Mistress relationship can harm a woman's body, as well as her self-respect, if the man perceives her as a powerful threat, or if each blames the other for the loss of romantic or aesthetic love. Young-Eisendrath thinks a man projects the Mistress onto a woman when he fuses sex with aggression, turning women into objects in order to reaffirm his control.[3] Or, he may become violent with a woman he *wanted* to be his Mistress if she refuses him.

The case of Harry Murray and Christiana Morgan is more tragic than any that women have related to me, but its extremes underscore the injurious instincts embedded in a Pygmalion/Mistress relationship.

Recall that Harry considered Christiana his Muse, and used her visions and trances for his own development. Although she craved his admiration, his inflated image of her power also weighed her down.[4] When Harry failed to finish his books, Christiana lost respect for him. When she also denied the responsibility of her own genius, "then she tried to compensate by getting him to 'thrill her and make her afraid,' by mastering her with whips and chains," writes Douglas. The two of them began experimenting with sadomasochism "as a way to bring some heat into a relationship that was growing increasingly empty and cold."[5] The orgiastic aspect of the Muse descended into violence.

Although Harry promised to marry her after his wife died, he never did, and although Christiana promised to give up her drinking if he married her, she took it up again at their last fateful encounter. In March of 1967 the two vacationed on the island of St. John at the cottage of friends. Christiana was intoxicated with the bracing air and the hopes of revitalizing their love, but Harry was intoxicated with Nina Fish, his latest lover, twenty years his junior, to whom he was sending flowers.

Sensing defeat, Christiana awoke one morning from an alcoholic stupor to a disgusted and abusive Harry Morgan.[6] The subsequent events remain in a fog, partly because Harry obscured them with differing reports. "What is clear is that on that sweet and sun-drenched morning, Christiana died," writes Douglas, who obviously interprets her death as a suicide.

> She had taken off the emerald ring Harry had given her thirty years before, wrapped it in her little beach bag, and placed it carefully on the sand. Then she had walked out into the sea. She drowned in the lagoon just below their cottage, the outline of her lifeless body floating unobscured in the tender ripples of the waves.[7]

What Harry and Christiana never grasped was that the Maiden Lover, the Muse, and the Mistress, all of which they both expected Christiana to play, are not persons, but types. There is no way that a woman who identifies exclusively with these roles can see herself as whole.

Christiana apparently went through with the suicidal instincts that I had only glimpsed. Locked into these "agreements" with a man who expected her to fulfill him, she was locked away from her self. And so she destroyed it in the oceanic tides of her despair.

CHAPTER 5

BRAINCHILD

> There is no mother anywhere who gave me birth, and but for marriage, I am always for the male with all my heart, and strongly on my father's side.
>
> Athena, *The Oresteian Trilogy*

My parents always expected me to be good in school. But they didn't notice my efforts much, at least not apart from the equally good performances of my sibling-pack. We were a very "we" family, and it was against the unspoken rules for anyone to stand out. My straight-A report cards typically evoked a bland "That's nice, Janice," not the dollar bills or excessive crowing my peers got for achievements I dismissed as feebly inferior to mine. To get big people to notice my brainpower required some ingenuity.

So at age 6 I learned how to spell *antidisestablishmentarianism*—not because I knew what it meant, but because someone told me it was the longest word in the English dictionary. I targeted unsuspecting male guests in our home with "Want to hear me spell *antidisestablishmentarianism*?" The assaulted man (for it usually *was* a man) always nodded bemusedly, so I would plant my feet and, gathering courage and volume, fire off letters with a staccato delivery that would make a winning debate coach proud. Applause generally followed as I retreated to my room with the sweet taste of success half-compensating for my parents' indifference. Early on, I learned the power of "text appeal" with older men.

Thus formed the shell of a heavy linguistic armor that I am still trying to shed. It works as well in the conference panels and journals of academe as it did in the living room of my childhood home. This armor gains me entrance into the academic contest halls where the discipline's progenitors tilt at theoretical underpinnings, even if holes appear where my softer parts show through, "revealing" that I might not have the Right Stuff to joust with the true initiates after all. But the yearning to be accepted by those who do has goaded me all my years in school, for this manly arena is where the action is, and it is where I earn whatever acclaim can come to an academic.

Like the Maiden Lover in one of her guises, the Brainchild is her father's daughter. But her connection to a father-lover, or to "the fathers" in general, is more intellectual than romantic. The Brainchild is not a soul-mate who complements a man with her feminine radiance, but one who mirrors his masculinity in a perfectly rational reflection. She is Henry Higgins' dream come true: "Why can't a woman be more like a man?" Rather than inspire the man to the heights of artistic passion, as does the Muse, she carries his standard and speaks for his principles. The Brainchild is the despoiled Mistress' pure sister, unstained by the curse of emotional embodiment.

I explore here not only the Brainchild's relatedness to a man or men but also her *dependence* on them—particularly on one who stands in for the father. Perhaps this father is supportive, taking great pride in his smart and capable progeny. Or maybe he is disparaging, berating her for not living up to his standards. She may or may not be entangled sexually; her "purity" can be more her resolve not to identify with things "feminine" than to maintain physical chastity. At times a man may employ a sexual relationship like a weapon to increase her dependence on him. What is crucial is that she wants to receive his praise and avoid his criticism.

The Brainchild is related to Galatea, for it is a Pygmalion-like man who materializes her. But she is more centrally Zeus' daughter, so let us turn to this story.

ATHENA

I have called the Brainchild chaste. Hers was indeed an Immaculate Conception, although it was a man, not a woman, who gave birth to her. The Brainchild's prototype is the Greek goddess Athena. Athena sprang, fully armored with a mighty shout, from Zeus' *head* after he tricked his consort Metis, the Titaness whose name meant "wise counsel," "practical wisdom," or "female wisdom," into becoming smaller so that he could swallow her. He did this because an oracle of Mother Earth declared that his rape of her would produce a son who would depose him. Zeus later claimed that Metis counseled him from his belly, and it was indeed her advice that allowed Zeus to succeed in overthrowing the Titans. He incorporated her into himself and took her attributes and power as his own, including the ability to give birth.[1]

Predictably, this version of Athena's birth was a patriarchal adaptation, for Plato identified her as the Libyan goddess Neith, who belonged to an epoch before fatherhood was recognized. Virgin priestesses of Neith annually engaged in armed combat for the position of High Priestess. After Zeus' co-optation of Athena, she became his favorite child, trusted to carry the awful aegis, his buckler, and his devastating thunderbolt.[2] She retained her warrior persona and, although she bore no arms during peace, once engaged in battle she never lost the day. But she preferred to settle disputes peacefully by upholding the law—for example, by casting the tie-breaking vote to liberate Orestes after he killed Clytemnestra, and to send the avenging Furies back to their underground abode.

Athena was independent, active, nonrelational, achievement-oriented, strategic, and practical—all qualities coded "masculine" today, as they were in Athena's time. "Athena values rational thinking and stands for the domination of will and intellect over instinct and nature." In trials she always sided with the patriarchy, and was typically pictured with a male.[3]

As Zeus' daughter, not his lover, Athena was dedicated to chastity and celibacy, even though various gods, such as Hephaestus, tried to trick her into intercourse or marriage.[4] In her popular book *Goddesses in Everywoman*, Jean Shinoda Bolen sees Athena as one of the three virgin goddesses, along with Artemis and Hestia. As such, she is "that part of a woman that is unowned by or 'unpenetrated' by a man—that is, untouched by her need for a man or need to be validated by him, that exists wholly separate from him, in her own right."[5] Bolen is using Esther Harding's sense of *virgin* as one-in-herself—belonging to no man—and she regards Athena as a feminine archetype, not as "acting like a man."[6]

But I think it is significant that Athena eventually forgot that she had a mother, employing priests, not priestesses, in her service, and functioning as Zeus' obedient mouthpiece.[7] Metis' feminine and earthy wisdom, literally consumed by Zeus, was recreated as a daughter hatched from his brain. As Bolen also points out, her adaptation to virginity was *identification with men*—"she became like one of them."[8] Athena was "the archetypal father's daughter," rather than a sister to other women, and Bolen does notice that "[t]his stance begins to wear thin as a woman approaches the third stage of her life. . . . "[9]

ALMIGHTY FATHER

Athena-type women gravitate toward authoritative men. They may seek power as a companion, wife, executive secretary, or ally of an able and ambitious older male mentor. In college, Bolen claims, they are drawn to the star in the department.[10] I have found that many, if not most, academic women are drawn to such a "star," whether or not he exists as a particular man. That is, our culture provides so many experiences that most of us have internalized this man's voice with enough detail that we may not even require his embodiment in order to hear it.

The Brainchild is somewhat similar to what Maureen Murdock calls the "daughter of the father."[11] Daughters of the father are ambitious and high-achieving, seeking the approval and power of their first male role models. They often have fathers who nurtured their talent, and they organize their lives around masculine rather than feminine principles. Murdock sees such women as having "confidence that they will be accepted by the world. . . . They have an inner masculine figure who likes them just as they are. This positive inner male or *animus* figure will support their creative efforts in an accepting, nonjudgmental way."[12] Whereas Murdock's description of such women as ambitious, high-achieving, and approval-seeking fits academic fathers' daughters, however, I have not found that many of them have this inner masculine figure who likes them. I think it is often precisely the opposite.

Every morning when she sits down at her computer to write, Anne Lamott has to contend with "radio station KFKD," or K-Fucked, which, if you are not careful, "will play in your head twenty-four hours a day, nonstop, in stereo." The right speaker of your inner ear spews forth an endless stream of self-aggrandizement: "the recitation of one's specialness, of how much more open and gifted and brilliant and knowing and misunderstood and humble one is." So far, so good. The problem is the left speaker: "the rap songs of self-loathing, the lists of all the things one doesn't do well, of all the mistakes one has made today and over an entire lifetime, the doubt, the assertion that everything that one touches turns to shit, that one doesn't do relationships well, that one is in every way a fraud, incapable of selfless love, that one has no talent or insight, and on and on and on."[13]

Actually, for most academic women, the left speaker is a good deal more clamorous than the right. Folk songwriter Iris DeMent sings of this speechless ghost in her song "The Way I Should":

A cold wind against my shoulder woke me up in the middle of
the night
An autumn leaf was scraping against my window
Like it was tryin' hard to get inside
And then a ghost that I had met before kept me up till dawn
And everything I thought was right was suddenly all wrong
He said, "Your score is lookin' pretty bad"
Then he asked me what it was that I had to show
So I went runnin' down a list of things
Some were real, but on some of them I lied
'Cause I felt I had to justify each breath that I'd been breathin' in
this life.[14]

The same silent ghost was there when I tried breathing through a meditative exercise suggested by Buddhist teacher Jack Kornfield to help develop a sense of compassionate kindness for yourself: close your eyes and breathe, and recall two good deeds you have done in your life. Just two. "Some people find this exercise very difficult," he warns. "No good deeds will come to their mind, or a few may arise only to be rejected immediately because they are judged superficial or small or impure or imperfect." In fact, when I first tried this I was astonished to find I could think of only one, and I had fifty-two years to choose from! "We judge ourselves so harshly," Kornfield concludes, "only an Idi Amin or a Stalin would hire us to preside over their courts."[15]

You may remember that Jessie, who served as a muse for her husband, "the brilliant intellectual," referred to the father figures in her dreams in terms of C. G. Jung's *animus*—the figure in a woman's unconscious who personalizes the culture's stereotypes of the "masculine," especially in relation to matters of work and reason. Although most contemporary feminists reject, as I do, Jung's assumption that the *animus*' qualities are fixed and "essentially" masculine, assuming instead that they reflect our culturally variable patriarchal preferences, this *animus* seems to me alive and well in the subterranean depths of academic women's psyches—like Lamott's radio announcer and DeMent's ghost.

Polly Young-Eisendrath identifies the Terrible Father as a "Dream Lover" (or psychological complex) within the woman's psyche that criticizes, attacks, belittles, and diminishes her worth. Zeus is a good example. "He is remote and judgmental. His greatest interest is in keeping his own power. He is never interested in seeing something in a new way nor in hearing any opinions differing with his." Women frequently attach the Terrible Father image to language and achievement, she finds. "If they don't get the right words or get their words right, they attack themselves mercilessly."[16]

Shandra, a 27-year-old assistant professor just out of graduate school, referred to academic mentorship as "medieval and abusive." When I asked her what she meant, she twisted her six-foot frame in her armchair, growing increasingly animated. "You know, it's like, you are of my loins, you *spring* from me as my student." Although she referred to the traditional form of procreation, her words echoed Athena's spontaneous delivery.

Shandra spoke of a certain "evil character" from her undergraduate years, Cameron Rush, who was "fifty-something, very European." She took a class she called "fantastic" from him, in which he lectured eloquently in a traditional style. "He speaks five languages," she recalled with more than a touch of awe. "This is a sign of an intellectually accomplished person to me."

Shandra talked to Professor Rush about going to graduate school in his field and asked him what language would be most useful to her.

"Don't worry about it," he replied. "Women mostly aren't cut out for grad school. They're not confrontational enough.'"

Shandra started to cry, "the absolute worst thing I could have done. I tried to pull myself together because I knew I was proving his point, but I couldn't. I've gotten better about it now. This was 1992. I'm a child of Title IX—this wasn't supposed to happen!"

She went to the university ombudsman, who helped her keep records, but she decided not to bring any case against her teacher. Instead, she learned to bring the case against herself. She asked Professor Rush if there were any women he thought *were* fit for graduate school in their field.

"Cokie Roberts," he answered.

Shandra considered Cokie to be "Amazonian," assertive, outspoken. "But I was affronted by that, because I thought I had those qualities too. My height apparently didn't even help me in that situation."

We spoke of our frustration that a woman sometimes cries when she is angry, but that if she does, she is considered "not able to hack it." "There's no crying in baseball!" I remembered manager Tom Hanks shouting to his female charge in *A League of Their Own*. Even more than that, Shandra was angry with herself for not having completely shaken her need for approval from male authorities.

"How did this affect you?" I asked.

"Very deeply," she responded. "It shaped me a lot. I still think of him—maybe not weekly any more, but probably monthly. He shaped me, not necessarily for the worse, because I learned some assertiveness from it. But he did place some doubts in me. I still admire him. I think he's a bastard, but he's an excellent teacher."

"If a female wanted to take his class today, what would you tell her about him?"

"I would say he's a very smart jerk."

Shandra's answer reflects the ambivalent attitude many women have toward their authoritative mentors, whether in the flesh, like Cameron Rush, or in their fantasies, like the large collection I have inside my own head. It also demonstrates how an actual figure can live on as an *animus*, shaping a woman's work and opinion of herself long after her contact with him has faded away.

A similar thing happened to my friend Carolyn Ellis, author of *Final Negotiations: A Story of Love, Loss, and Chronic Illness*, a narrative of her nine-year relationship with Gene Weinstein, a sociologist and her teacher, who was ill with emphysema when they met. His intellectual, metropolitan, Jewish-influenced culture at SUNY Stony Brook presented "a formidable but exciting challenge" to her as a young graduate student from a Protestant, rural, working-class region in the Blue Ridge Mountains. Apparently, Carolyn played Maiden Lover to Gene's Pygmalion in the early part of their relationship. Here is a passage describing her attraction to and ambivalence toward him shortly after they met:

> Since Gene epitomized this world, I was more than willing initially to let him play Pygmalion and mold me into his version of a "cultured sociologist." Gradually, through talking about my insecurities, I became comfortable with our teacher-student exchanges, and I learned more formal sociology around the kitchen table than I encountered in classes. Gene didn't seem to mind that it was one-sided. "Nor," he assured me, after my confession, "do I think you are dumb."[17]

Gene both intimidated people and drew them to him with his self-assurance and intelligence:

> Always ready for a good discussion and intellectual argument, he took up a lot of space—both physically and psychically. He earned attention and validation for his intelligence by listening closely and asking probing questions, allowing others to proclaim their wisdom. Challenging every statement with his darting, alert eyes, he was in control, directing the story even when someone else spoke.[18]

Eventually, Gene took on the qualities of what I am calling the critical *animus* for Carolyn, one whose voice could resonate in either ear of radio station KFKD:

> I became intellectually dependent on Gene, my toughest critic, needing his approval of my ideas. If he said my work was good, I believed him. If he didn't, I worked until he approved. This feedback offered an invaluable push then; later I would see it as holding me back.[19]

Carolyn married Gene and cared for him as he grew gravely ill. She relates this scene that occurred just before his death:

> Crazed from drugs, lack of oxygen, and loss of control during the last stage of his disease, Gene yells, "I made Carolyn. Without me, she never would have gotten her PhD." . . . I shudder now at how costly his approval had been; at the same time, I appreciate the contribution our interactions with and feelings for each other made to the person I have become. My relationship with Gene in some ways symbolizes my relationship with the orthodoxy in social science, an elite who have determined how and what I write.[20]

It is far too simple to call Carolyn "Brainchild" to Gene's "Terrible Father"; her account richly documents a complex and multidimensional relationship. Yet his influence lived on in her evaluations of herself long after he died, and colored her views of herself in relation to her field in general.

Earlier I identified my honors professor as a Pygmalion upon whom I had a powerful Maiden Lover's projection. Although our relationship lasted less than a year, it soon took on characteristics of Zeus and his Brainchild. Like Cameron Rush and Gene Weinstein, my professor held me to a ruthless standard of intellectual perfection. As I mentioned, he thought the field of speech communication to be beneath me. He made a fetish of contrasting "elite" with "non-elite" disciplines and research topics—a demarcation that also extended to people. I wanted desperately to measure up, knowing I would be rejected if I failed.

I was shocked to find out that my best friend Margo was another of his Maiden Lovers. He pitted her against me in a sort of intellectual writing competition, and she lost. I remember my dismay when he belittled her papers and held mine up as the standard she should emulate, as a parent often does with siblings. Margo, a strong and beautiful person voted top scholar in *his* field (I was only top scholar in my own, "inferior" one), once collapsed in tears in front of our entire study group at his relentlessly disparaging remarks, which reached beyond the intellectual to make even her body and bearing seem inadequate. Egotistical triumph battled with empathic humiliation in my head and heart. But, like Tom Hanks' manager and Shandra's Professor Rush, he continued to debase her for crying, in his view a sign she wasn't "elite." This marked the beginning of the end of my respect for him, as it finally dawned on me that being his Brainchild could mean the loss of my friend. I graduated, went to the graduate school he cautioned against, maintained my relationship with Margo, and never spoke to him again.

THE FATHER INSIDE

My professor was a prominent Pygmalion/Zeus/Terrible Father for me, but he had simply materialized a figure that took root in my head long before college. We might as well take a look at some of these "ghosts that I had met before"—not because mine are unique, but precisely because I know from talking to other women that many of them are strikingly similar to figures in their dreams. I have *animus* figures for all seasons, but I'll give you some idea of the Terrible Fathers that have gotten inside, keeping me up until dawn with disturbing frequency.

I begin with a dream I call "Lost in the Halls of Science" because it is a fairly complete crystallization of my own entrapment within academia with my critical *animus*. It even offers a way out that, as an assistant professor in my late thirties, I didn't quite understand at the time. Later I will come back around to such paths for myself and for others, but our task here is to get a clear picture of the problem.

> I am trying to make it to a class within a very large building, but I can't find my way through the many halls and floors. I have to take a test and I need some time to study. I see a big, empty classroom, and decide to leave my books there while I do something else. When I get back to the classroom, I'm horrified to see that it's got a big class in

it, with a professor up front teaching. I'm desperate to get my books because time is running out to study for the exam. I watch the teacher (it's a chemistry class) and decide that if I walk behind him to the table where my books are, and leave quickly, he may not see me.

So I start toward my books, but he catches me out of the corner of his eye, stops the class, and tells me I can't take them. "Why not?" I say. "They're mine!" "How do I know they're yours—you might be stealing them!" he retorts accusingly. I say, "Look, these are on Jung and Eliade, and I know a lot about these people. Just ask me any questions you want and I'll answer them, and that will prove these are my books!"

Somehow I escape the classroom, trying to find my way out of the building. Again I go up and down the halls, looking for a way out, but I can't find one. I don't even know what building I'm in, much less what part of it. I think if I could just find my way outside I'd recognize where I am.

I wander around looking for an exit, and eventually come to what feels like a dark and very deep basement. There are women in cubbyholes practicing vocal music. Each person is by herself, but when each one sings, it sounds like an entire choir. It's beautiful in an eerie sort of way.

Eventually I find my way to a door that leads outside, climb some steps, and am on the ground. I look around and see that the building I was in is a part of a very large complex—a huge institution. I seem to know more where I am now, but it's still not crystal clear.

Here I am in a mazelike labyrinth with my very own minotaur; you may recall that science is not my forte, and so it figures that my Terrible Father would take on the voice of a chemistry professor. This is one of at least a thousand dreams in which I must take a test or get another degree, even though I passed all the necessary exams and I already have a PhD. Many women told me that, along with arriving at a class unprepared or signing up to take or teach a class and forgetting about it until halfway through the semester, these are their most common dreams about academia. It is like we forget we passed, and must prove ourselves again.

In this dream I feel I must sneak around this accusatory man, just to take what is rightfully mine. I don't want to be seen, for then I might be found out. "Found out as what?" you might ask, and I can only answer "as unspecifiably unworthy." I head for the door, but like a good monster he keeps one eye on me. I try to rise to his challenge, playing on his ground of argumentation and debate, even though he has ludicrously accused me of stealing my own area of expertise. I do realize I'd better get out of there, and I even seem to intuit that I will only know where I am (*who* I am?) if I can get outside this institutional structure. I can't see where I'm going—I can't be objective—as long as I am lost in its maze. As luck would have it, and as often happens in myth when the fool or "dummling" stumbles accidentally upon the hidden treasure,[21] I wander unaware into a place of mystery that could have spelled liberation from this Terrible Father. In this deep and dark space, each individual is whole within her *temenos*, or sacred circle—unbound from the collective institution above, and singing the parts of an entire choir. The basement is often literally and/or figuratively where we put the arts in academia. This is happening as I write at our own university, the recent recipient of the largest single monetary gift in the history of public higher education—most of it designated for the sciences and technology, and thus destined to make an under-funded graveyard of the arts and humanities.[22] It is also, as we have seen, the burial site of the deepest feminine mysteries, which we rarely glimpse at the academy except by lucky accident or determined excavation.

Had I stayed a bit longer in that cellar and fully absorbed its sacred music, perhaps I could have eluded further evisceration by my critical *animus*. Instead, the insults continued. Four years later, I was visited by "The Armless Maiden":

> I am sleeping, and in the middle of the night the lights in the house go out—there is a complete cessation of electricity. Apparently this affects my life systems and I stop breathing for a few seconds. The next thing I know I wake up in a hospital. A doctor has cut off both my arms at the shoulders, and has replaced them with prosthetic devices. However, he has saved my hands and has sewn them back on at the ends of the fake arms. I can see the seams and punctures where the needle has been at both the shoulders and the wrists.
>
> It is evident that I will still have full use of my hands—I don't seem to be seriously handicapped, and perhaps this will be all for the better. But still I am shocked and very sad at the loss. I go shopping and

try on a sleeveless dress, and realize that I'll only be able to wear long sleeves from now on.

When a person goes to sleep in a myth or fairy tale, we can pretty well assume that he or she has gone unconscious, like Dr. Frankenstein immediately after he creates his monster.[23] Or she may have been enchanted, like Sleeping Beauty, or in a trance brought on by repetition of the same empty routines, like the heroine of "The Handless Maiden."[24] In this fairytale, a miller makes a bargain with a man he does not know is the devil to give him whatever is behind his mill in return for untold riches. Thinking there is only a flowering apple tree—not realizing his daughter is there mindlessly sweeping the yard—this "fathering function of the psyche" who does not know about issues of the soul sacrifices his daughter in a disastrous bargain.[25] "By choosing whatever appealed to her as riches," Clarissa Pinkola Estes writes, any woman who has allowed her internal father to thus sacrifice her, has "surrendered, in return, dominion over some and often every part of her passionate, creative, and instinctive life. That female psychic slumber is a state approximating somnambulism."[26]

Although I wasn't to read this story until years later, my dream is a contemporary update of "The Handless Maiden" in which today's culture plays a role, for my very breath is sustained by electricity, much like the astronauts unplugged by the computer HAL in *2001: A Space Odyssey*, or any number of other movie travelers in hypersleep aboard their spaceships, and I wake up in a hospital after undergoing modern surgical techniques. It is the masculine-dominated culture of *techné* that both gives me life and takes it away long enough for me to undergo a frightful dismemberment. And, although I didn't choose it, I do accept it, as does the maiden in the tale, when the devil orders her father to chop off her hands because her voluminous tears have washed them clean, making it impossible for him to take her away. The maiden is only able to repel the devil because she has bathed, dressed herself in a white gown, and drawn a circle of chalk around herself, reminiscent of an old Goddess ritual of drawing a circle of magic protection, or sacred thought, around oneself when one descends to the underground[27]—much like those women singing anthems in their self-contained cubicles beneath my Halls of Science. But I have not paid enough attention to these mysteries.

Like the maiden, I have made a "bargain without knowing," trading in my soul for the "untold riches" of academic success. Thus, my "psychic hands" cannot do their real work—they cannot grasp my own life. In the original story, a benevolent king—emblem of a higher masculine consciousness than the father in the maiden's self[28]—finds her wandering in the forest, marries her, and fashions silver hands that work just fine until she is able to grow back her own. Although she is still to undergo more terrible descents, she is fortunate to receive these silver hands of the spirit, as delineated in many myths as well as in Jane Campion's 1993 film *The Piano,* in which magical prostheses are forged and fitted for the hero or heroine. Silver is one of the precious metals of Hephaestus, the underworld Olympian craftsman who was thrown down a hillside by his father Zeus, shattering his legs. But he fashioned new legs out of silver and gold, and thus became the patron of things and humans who were split, sundered, or dismembered.[29] The handless maiden carries with her, then, the Underground Genius who enables her to function in the world with prostheses until she can do it on her own.

My predicament is a little bit different. I retain my *own* hands, and thus am able to do my own work, which I was still accomplishing just fine, thank you, at the time of this dream. I was, indeed, publishing up a storm and accomplishing the requisite steps of promotion, just as I should be. What is cut off and replaced are my *arms*, that part of me that connects my doing with my being in the world. I can accomplish my academic tasks with the best of them, but my hands are not connected to my torso, where my heart lies beating. I cannot "put my heart in my hands." Although a part of me is sad, recognizing that my femininity is sacrificed and that the loss must be covered up with long sleeves (or maybe a long *vita*), "perhaps this will all be for the better." After all, it is a doctor—one who is trusted to heal—who has performed my surgery.

It was about three years later that I had the "mid-life crash" I have referred to, which was the beginning of my disenchantment with academic sterility, and which necessitated my concerted attempt to quiet the critical fathers inside my head. This is when I slowed my frenetic pace in order to sit, to garden, to just *be*. This was a descent of sorts, like the one in which the handless maiden chooses to leave the familiarity of home, where her parents promised to take care of her. She wanders in the wild forest alone, dirty, and unkempt, more like a beast than a human. I began to weave more feminine themes into my writing and my life, working a tapestry that was more sew-as-you-go, not predetermined by a patriarchal pattern book.

But the Almighty Father's is a hard voice to still. Fully ten years after "The Armless Maiden" (last year, as I write today) I was assailed again by his vitriol, this time in a series of dreams in which, not just my books, but my *office* is not my own. Here is the worst of the batch—hard to digest since it occurred in a convention hotel room the night after I won a surprise award in the Southern region of our discipline for career achievement as a teacher and scholar:

> I unlock the door of my office at school and, unbeknownst to me, someone has completely redecorated it. There is a big, ornate antique desk and there are curtains on the window. My chairperson is sitting behind the desk glaring at me. "Where did you get this?" he demands, curling his lip and looking sinister. He implies that I got it deviously, by doing things behind the scenes that aren't legitimate. A young male minion of his stands nearby. I don't know what he is talking about because this is all a big surprise to me. But he keeps yelling at me. I am furious—enraged—and I yell back. I am absolutely livid that he has appropriated my desk and my office. I wake up shaking and crying.

Perhaps I really had earned this beautiful office with curtains softening its hard, institutional lines, just as some in my profession must have thought I earned their recognition. The antique desk seems an appropriate symbol for my excavation of ancient myths, its graceful curves a fitting site for my more feminine work. My Critical Father—this time in the guise of my chairperson—obviously thinks not, though, and in a kafkaesque scene accuses me of exactly what the chemistry prof had fourteen years earlier—that I got it furtively, by sneaking behind his back. Here, in a tidy twenty-four hour period, I re-constellated a radio station KFKD broadcast as the capstone to my career. At high noon I sat around the banquet table with my advisor from Southern California, my star student who won an award himself as a young professor, his student who won an award for top undergraduate honors paper, my husband, and my friends.

KFKD's right speaker told me how "gifted and brilliant and knowing" I was. At night with the lights out, however, the left speaker shouted out all the mistakes I had made today and over a lifetime, that I was "in every way a fraud," that everything I touched had turned to shit.

At least I was mad this time, and instead of sneaking out of the building I yelled back at my tyrant. I also cried, and as I will eventually come around to, there *is* crying in academia. Perhaps my tears were not that bad a sign.

"I TRY MY BEST. . ."

A woman can become a Brainchild even without a specific male to "conceive" her. In fact, I suspect from talking to many women that academia is chock full of such cerebral daughters, whose nagging apparitions are just as vociferous as Carolyn's, Shandra's, and mine. Without benefit of actual Critical Fathers, they drive themselves on mercilessly to one accomplishment after another, never stopping to savor their successes any longer than it takes to berate themselves for not doing the last one with pristine perfection.

It doesn't take an extant man to deliver the verdict. I think of my 5-year-old niece, who used to pick herself up quickly whenever she stumbled on the backpack trail, blonde pigtails flying, skinned knees bleeding, tears of self-reproach forming. Rejecting her Dad's helping hand, she would announce defiantly: "I can do it *myself*!" Although, mercifully, she did not grow up to be a Brainchild, this is the cry of women who are always on probation, as in one of my recurrent dreams in which even a 4.0 is not quite good enough to take me off the list.

I felt an instant rapport with Claire, an extremely articulate associate professor who plays tennis, loves medieval literature and children, and speaks passionately about her work. Her father was a Protestant minister who was too radical for his congregations, she was small for her age, she moved every three or four years while growing up, she spent her summer vacations camping in the mountains with her family, and in college she became involved in political action groups concerned with feminism and racial justice. We must have been twins separated at birth.

Claire's parents were "broad-minded intellectuals," although not scholars, and they always encouraged her in her academic pursuits, at which she excelled early and often. "I had frizzy hair and I was skinny and I never fit socially until college," she mused. "I hung out with my parents and their friends. I was kind of an 'adult's child.'"

"What were your mentors like?" I asked.

"I had good ones," she replied. "In junior high they encouraged my writing of poetry and they lent me books. I was just intellectually different from the other kids, and some of the teachers recognized this. At Bryn Mawr [her undergraduate school], I had a very influential instructor who thought I had talent and pushed me to become a creative writer. When I went for my masters' at Brown, I had really good teachers."

"How about when you were working toward your PhD?" I asked, more than impressed with her *vita*. "Did you have good mentors there?"

"Absolutely. I kept thinking I'd be found out."

"For what? You have an amazing pedigree."

"Yeah, but I did feel all the way through, especially when I arrived at Yale, that sooner or later I was going to be found out. *You don't belong here.*"

"But it sounds like you had a great deal of intellectual confidence," I probed.

"Well, that confidence sort of wanes when you find out how much you don't know. I knew I didn't really have the proper background. Most people enter the PhD program at Yale without an MA, which I had, but still, I wasn't really prepared in the theories that everybody else seemed to know about. I didn't know then and I still don't know some of that basic stuff."

"How did your feminist background enter in? Did that help you to believe in your abilities?"

"I never had any female mentors, which is kind of funny from a feminist perspective. My feelings of inferiority never had anything to do with thinking that women were inferior—not at all. Friends who wanted to do a quick pop psychological analysis said, well, this had to come from somewhere in your childhood, but I never thought so."

Claire did think that perhaps her feelings of intellectual inadequacy were related to her "social scarring" in junior high—that is, she wasn't beautiful or popular. And now, in her early forties, she was still unpartnered, which was a disappointment to her. Still, she insisted, "I can't entirely trace that back to childhood."

"So there's a disconnect between the abstract idea and the feeling about who you are?" I asked, trying to understand the smudges in this very bright woman's self-portrait.

"Yeah. I don't think it's that we weren't smart enough—well, maybe it was that. At Yale it was very supportive, but rigorous. We were being taught by gods. I think maybe men and women react to criticism differently. Even if the negative remark—on a teaching evaluation or from a prof—is something I know is factually wrong, I still react so strongly from a gut level."

"So if it's not your childhood and it's not your mentors, what is it in the culture that would do that?"

Claire picked up her recently published book on a medieval poet. "I have this book published with Oxford University Press," she mused. "And what do I think? 'I'm never going to produce another one.' I don't have any ideas in my head right now. I just have this huge capacity for guilt, and people will say, 'Oh, that's because you have a preacher as a father.' And it's just not! My parents didn't even believe in Hell!"

Claire related how she often "gets quiet" in groups of academics. "Of course, the 'smart thing' is a big pressure in academia. Having interesting conversations with people means being witty and tossing off comebacks that are worthy of the academic mind—or having literary allusions, or New York wit, I don't know. I'm just not quick with that kind of stuff."

"Is that with all kinds of groups, or just mixed-sex ones?" I queried.

"It can happen with all kinds. It's the anxiety of influence—I have to produce a dissertation, or a book that's as good as Derrida's! There are always two thousand more books you have to read before you can put words on paper without blushing."

Though Claire does feel that she can express herself creatively in teaching and writing, and is glad to be in this profession, she is currently torn about whether to stay at her current institution or to try to land at a really prestigious one.

"I have a lot of respect in the field," she admitted. "My first article won an award. People know who I am. But if I get a job somewhere I might get eaten away with feelings of inadequacy. Maybe not, if I were at one of the top twenty. But definitely at the top ten."

I was reminded of my own Almighty Fathers—in the flesh and in my dreams—and also of Tom's gentle chide, a repeated refrain to my songs of self-loathing over my last imperfect achievement: "You try your very best, but sometimes your best is just not good enough."

AILING ANIMUS

In *The Wounded Woman: Healing the Father-Daughter Relationship*, Linda Leonard writes of "the man with heart," a figure who appears in some women's dreams when they are able to face the negative male images within. Her own inner man, hard won and not appearing until later in life, is "caring, warm, and strong," a man who sees beyond her bewitchment and artificial defensive appearances and loves her as a woman.[30] Maureen Murdock also sees this "man with heart" as a necessary corrective to the "cold and inhuman" masculine figure in women's psyches who is "combative, critical, and destructive," and who "demands perfection, control, and domination," declaring that "nothing is ever enough."[31] This inner figure helps her do her own creative work, not his. Apparently not all inner men are judgmental jerks.

The Brainchild needs this more loving *animus* in order to soften her hard edges, to quiet the Critical Fathers, and assure her she is OK as is. In my experience, a woman who identifies with the Brainchild indeed has other men within, but they are seldom men with hearts. The flip side of the Almighty Father is the Ailing *Animus*—a sick, driven, artificial, or depressed young man, or a man who might be the woman's inner lover, except that he is dominated himself by her more demanding Old Man.

On my thirty-ninth birthday, I had this dream, which posed the problem of my inner sick male:

> I am in a dark apartment. An older man and I are doing an experiment—we have made our own Frankenstein's monster from spare male parts; he is lying on a table. He is grotesque-looking, with a

> huge head—a couple of feet in diameter—and no internal organs, such as a heart or a liver.
>
> All of a sudden this being we made comes to life. We had not expected this to happen. He starts to chase me and clutch at me. I am terrified. The man says I should wait there—he will go get help. I protest and say there's no way I'm going to stay in that apartment, it's obvious our monster is out to get me. The man insists I must stay, and then he leaves. The monster chases me and I'm again very afraid.

At this point in my life, I was still going strong as an academic Athena, not having yet gone into mid-life descent or realizing that much was awry inside. I had been working with Tom on an article about the Frankenstein complex in contemporary films, but as has often been the case, I had no clue that this had anything to do with me—it was all "academic." In the dream I seem to intuit that I need a "new" man—one I make myself—but I am collaborating with my familiar older *animus*, and so it's no wonder that our creation has no heart. I am trying to put together this needed new counterpart from pieces of other men lying around like detritus—that is, I don't know how to "make" this being except from masculine energies that are used up and there for the taking.

Our monster has a hideously large head; like many of the mad geniuses in science fiction who make artificial creations, his body is incomplete or atrophied, and the emphasis is on the cerebral—mirroring Dr. Frankenstein's obsession with scientific creation and the neglect of his body and the feminine (his monster eventually kills his new bride). My creation can't have a heart because he is artificial, not an organic life-form sprung as a partner to my more feminine self. And although the older man who is helping does not belittle me, he does abandon me here to our own devices. In the 1986 remake of *The Fly*, Geena Davis' character Ronnie says to the prostitute hired by her lover (played by Jeff Goldblum), who is slowly turning into a fly because his genetic transporter machine has gone awry: "Be afraid. Be very afraid." I am right to be afraid, for this figure we have co-created does not love me and will no doubt try to kill me.

The split in my *animus* is evident in my Frankenstein dream—the more experienced Father figure and the sick or unnatural "young" man (in this case, not even a day old). In "The Bull Dance," a dream that occurred two years later, this schism takes on higher definition:

> I am half-watching, half-participating in a bull dance. My partner is a young man, and we are performing for a very sadistic and sinister man. There is a feeling of deep mystery surrounding the event. We are graceful and skillful, performing acrobatic leaps. I am totally in tune with this man, body and soul. We outlast the bull, he tires, and the dance is over.
>
> Afterward, we talk to the man who has been watching us, and he identifies himself as a Nazi. I think about the fact that Nazism doesn't fit the time frame of the bull dance, which was in ancient Crete, but that this man is like the Cretan men who ordered these dangerous dances for their own pleasure.

I do have an inner man who, as Leonard puts it, brings me "heart and glowing feeling," who "dances with life's rhythms" and accompanies me on my adventures. Unfortunately, however, our duet is not liberating for, as it turns out, we are being watched by a Nazi. Leonard finds the "perverted and sadistic old man" to be a common figure in the dreams of women she has analyzed. She sees perversions like this as sick and twisted forms of a potentially healing archetype. In this case, it is the Wise Old Man—who has turned nasty because he has been neglected; "the father has not functioned as a father."[32]

But what of the fathers' daughters I speak of here, including myself, who are so closely bonded to a father figure, singular or collective, that we speak for him, carrying his thunderbolt and his mission to the world in a way that appears reasoned and thoughtful? Haven't our men—inner and outer—worked overtime for us, functioning as more, not less, than the average father of a less fortunate girl? But what we do not have, I think, is the wise inner man who watches over *our* pleasure rather than directs us in a dance of death for his *own*. The dirty secret is that the Brainchild's father, like Zeus, is not interested in her performance unless it brings him gratification.

If my "man with heart" and I are performing for a sinister old man, it is no wonder that my potential inner lover is depressed. Three months after "The Bull Dance," I had this dream, in which the younger *animus* is himself split in two:

> I am in high school or college. I, as well as the others, am younger than I am now. A boy comes up to me, along with another who seems to be hanging back and subordinate to him, and tells me I

need to do something for his friend. I think he is trying to get a date with me for his friend, who seems to be shy. I don't want a date with the second one; I find the intermediary much more attractive.

But the intermediary tells me that his friend doesn't want a date with me, he wants a drug, and they think I can get it. I then talk to the shy friend for the first time and ask him what he wants. He says, "PRO-DOS"—and indicates he desperately needs one pill. I am surprised that they would ask me for it. Anyway, I don't have any.

So the first boy asks me if I'll give them the money for the drug. I don't really think I should, but I agree to, and get out about three dollars in cash. But the first boy says that won't be enough—they'll need twelve dollars. I think that's awfully expensive for one pill, but I write a check for it anyway.

At first this shy guy's request for "PRO-DOS" seems cryptic, but if we consider that the dream occurred soon after I got my first personal computer and most of my friends got on Prozac, it is not that hard to decode. This adolescent man wants Prozac, probably for his depression; perhaps he is overworked using DOS programs at his PC. He doesn't know me well enough to ask me for help himself (he is too "shy"), so he sends his friend who, since he is apparently not depressed, is more attractive to me. Perhaps *he* can be my lover, my dream self thinks.

Neither of these boys is sinister, but neither can they help me, which is what a "man with heart" would do; rather, I have to help them. I must keep the primary one sedated and his companion mollified. The "shy" one is, in fact, in dire need—he doesn't want to feel his pain—so he begs a drug from me. I'm surprised about this, which suggests I'm unconscious of my role in providing the "cure." Maybe this unattractive, ailing boy will leave me alone if I just buy him off cheap. No, says the friend, it will cost you much more than that. I don't want to give it this much effort—I seem to wish the whole thing would just go away—but the dream testifies that it is costing me a great deal to make this young inner man not feel anything.

After years of pacifying this young man who is depressed from my unabated Brainchild drivenness, I had this dream just last year:

I am watching television, although it also seems like "reality." An official airplane—perhaps government or military—is flying and a

> newscaster is announcing what is happening. All of a sudden the airplane develops major trouble and one of the passengers, a man in uniform, bails out with a parachute. However, the parachute doesn't open, and he is headed toward a dangerous-looking rocky beach. I am terrified as he gathers momentum, surely to hit the rocks and die. But instead he lands on a patch of sand right next to the rocks and close to the ocean. He gets up and walks away. I am so relieved. I try to find Tom to show him what happened, because I think they will replay the event.

This one starts out with ordinary "military" precision; I'm getting my usual work done, so my airplane is flying. This dream wants to get my attention, though, because it's on the news, and it's even going into instant replay. When trouble develops, my "man in uniform"—the one who has heretofore accomplished all that work—bails out, and I, as semi-objective observer, am terrified he's going to "hit the rocks" and die. But instead of being curious about what really happened up there in the heights and horrified at his close call with death, I am merely relieved that he made it. Maybe he'll just walk right into that ocean of my unconscious and I won't have to deal with him any more, just like my shy guy on Prozac.

I have come to call this my "On Your Feet, Soldier!" scenario in honor of Sarah Conner of *The Terminator*. Toward the end of this movie, Kyle Reese, her mentor/lover, who has tried desperately to save her from the death-force of the relentless machine that wants to kill her because she carries within her womb the creative antidote to future technological destruction, is mortally wounded. He simply can't go on any more. She forces him to his feet and, with the energy and tunnel vision of a combat warrior, commands: "On your feet, soldier!" He obeys her orders, gets to his feet and moves, but eventually succumbs to the Terminator's onslaught. My own inner Kyle Reese, who appears in endless variation, is still standing, but just barely. In one dream, a macho-man forces a weaker man to dive headfirst into an icy-cold rocky stream from impossible heights. Periodically the taskmaster pulls the other man out of the water and lays him on the rocks to dry off and warm up in the sun. Then he forces him to dive in again. I am amazed that he is still alive.

AVOIDING THE MOTHER

I began this chapter with Athena's grand statement that no mother gave her birth, and that she is strongly on her father's side. Of course, she had conveniently forgotten that her father swallowed her mother Metis, that his miraculous cerebral conception would have been impossible without her, and that she continued to counsel him from his belly. The Brainchild may or may not have had a good relationship with her own mother. Whatever the case, it seems most important that she exclude the Mother's influence—personal and collective—from her performance in the university.

Although many academic women do successfully integrate raising their own children with their careers, fear of the Mother induces profound ambivalence in others over the choice of whether to have children. Shandra, for instance, mentioned at one point that she liked spending time with her sister's children and that she enjoyed "creating things—gardening, growing herbs and flowers." I asked her whether she and her husband planned to have children, and she replied wistfully, perhaps weighing her ticking tenure clock against her biological one, "I'm interested in it, but I don't have time." I thought of the button I used to wear occasionally when going out with my female academic friends, most of whom had heard the tenure clock above the other one. It read: OH GOD, I FORGOT TO HAVE CHILDREN!

Time for both is scarce enough. But whether or not a woman becomes a birth mother, the Mother represents biological embodiment and emotion, the polar opposites to "the life of the mind" and rationality. Thus, few successful women allow the motherly aspects of themselves to show in the halls of learning. At all costs, the Brainchild must avoid getting slimed.

One night in 1986 Tom and I saw the movie *Aliens*. I had turned off its predecessor *Alien* whenever it came on TV because its motif of an Amazon trapped on a spaceship with a hideous monster that its creator admitted he modeled after his mother[33] was too frightening. Though I was bothered by the way this James Cameron installment represented everything biologically maternal as yucky, it got my blood surging in ways I couldn't quite reconcile with my feminist ideology. And so I undertook another in a long line of critical essays in which I hadn't a clue why the film was so important for me.[34] Perhaps it had something to do with the hideously comic inversion of the Zeus-swallowing-the-mother motif, in that the mother monster's phallic offspring bursts through the stomach of the human male who had disturbed her lair. The night I saw the film I had this dream:

> There is a terrible monster at school—it is the Mother Monster from Aliens, but it is long and slimy rather than crablike—more like a deep-sea monster. People at school have caught and sedated it, and it is supposed to be harmless for a long time—maybe even a year. However, it still has its eyes open, its pulse continues rather loudly, and I get the impression it is not completely harmless or asleep. I am terrified of it and would rather not go near. The problem is that it is lying in front of the desk in my office, and there are some books in the bottom drawer that I must have in order to prepare a class for Monday morning. So I have to go in the room where the monster is. I go in very carefully, but am horrified that I will get some of its slime on me, and that will mean I will be irreversibly adulterated.

This dream recapitulates several "ghosts that I had met before." As in "Lost in the Halls of Science," my own books are being guarded by a "monster" who keeps one eye on me—but this time it is the contaminating mother rather than the Critical Father. She must be severely unconscious, for she has come from the ocean's depths. Unlike the situation in my former dream, in which the sinister professor operates freely within a university structure, this very structure has captured and sedated the mother monster—much as I had tried to sedate my depressed adolescent with Prozac. The school is supposed to be safe from the aberration for up to a year, but I know better and, as in my Frankenstein's monster dream, I am afraid. So I try to sneak my books out, as I did in the first dream, without being seen.

The fact that she is lying in front of my desk should tell me something. As long as she slumbers I will have to be stealthy, and such surreptitious behavior is not conducive to the free flow of creativity. Perhaps I could do my work better if I talked with her rather than try not to wake her. This *Aliens* monster is my own version of the Terrible Mother, which the hero must slay on his mythic journey and from which the heroine must separate. Murdock regards such separation as the first step of the heroine's journey, since the mother represents body, soul, and the unconscious, all anathema to a woman's achievement and recognition in the outer world. "The image of the ogre who neglects the daughter or holds her captive," writes Murdock. You might think here of the neglectful father or the devil in "The Handless Maiden," "projected onto the mother who in turn must be slain. The stepmother, as in Hansel and Gretel, becomes the Wicked Witch, who meets her demise in the oven."[35]

At some level I do "know" that the Mother's pulse still beats. She is just so very hard for an achiever like me to acknowledge. As Marion Woodman notes, "No other era has so totally divorced outer reality from inner reality, the matrix of which is the Great Mother. Never before have we been so cut off from the wisdom of nature and the wisdom of our own instincts."[36] The slain Mother's vengeance is the Furies, who avenge all mother-murders, such as that of Clytemnestra by Orestes—the very same crime settled in the son's favor by Athena. These Furies hound the mother-murderer to his grave unless Athena sends them back to their cave, as she does in the play. As a good Brainchild, I have staved off these Furies for much of my career—or at least I think I have.

But my night dreams have betrayed me for as long as I can remember. This mother-monster is graphically dreadful—yet a much more common motif in my dreams is poignantly grave. I have a whole zoo of starving animals appearing in a plot as inexorable as *The Terminator*'s. Within the dream I wake up startled, either from night slumber or from a handless maiden-like trance, and realize I have precious pets I have forgotten to feed. I rush out to my back yard to find them sick, spotted with the plague, or almost dead. I quickly feed them, but it is never quite clear whether they will make it back to life. I am absolutely distraught. Most of the time, these pets are precious puppies or kittens. But it is my sentence as a movie critic to have sequels, in which the puppies of one night are followed by full-grown dogs, then hippos, elephants, and whales. The swallowed mother goddess has not disappeared but has gone into my body and continues to counsel me from my belly: do not forget your embodiment, my child; do not forget to feed your precious instincts, or the flow of your life-feeling will one day run out.

SEX AS PURGATION

If the Brainchild denies her body, represented mythically as a mother monster, it is not surprising that she would be "chaste" or a "virgin goddess." Athena's chastity is psychological, not necessarily physical.[37] She must be free of any influences that would interfere with her unstained and rational armored personality. Her father/mentor can, however, use sex like a weapon to keep her within this frame of perfection, and to lay claim to her as an intellectual emissary.

Joan is a 41-year-old writer who employs mythic themes in her fiction. Joan quit her masters' program before finishing because her advisor wanted her to be his cerebral surrogate, as well as his sexual conquest. He approached her before she completed her BA, remarked how intelligent she was, and announced "I want to wash you clean of your former mentor." Joan's undergraduate mentor was a woman feminist whose influences, like the Great Mother's, the advisor considered to be contaminating.

This man was the only person who taught Joan's specialty, and so he became her advisor when she entered the MA program. When he suggested that she study "under" him, the sexual connotations were quite clear to her. "I know I could get you into Stanford," he offered.

"I remember looking at him, pondering the costs, imagining the possibility. And being tempted. Was it a good thing or a bad thing that he was so unattractive to me?"

Joan's recollection of her advisor's phrase, "wash you clean," made something click for me that I hadn't understood before. Although fueled by mutual desire, my honors professor's approach to sexuality had seemed "clinical," not really romantic or orgiastic. It was more like a purgative, something to be gotten out of the way so that our minds would be free of interference. I thought of Socrates' notion in Plato's *Phaedrus* that one could use this unruly black horse of desire to ascend to the pure heights of reason, where the white horse and the charioteer himself could tame it, keep it in its place.

I think this orderly orientation to sexuality is related to the Brainchild's compulsion for perfection and avoidance of the Mother's embodiment. "Perfectionism means that you try desperately not to leave so much mess to clean up," Anne Lamott points out, and although she is talking about writing, not sex, the analogy seems to fit. "But clutter and mess show us that life is being lived. . . . Tidiness makes me think of held breath, of suspended animation, while writing needs to breathe and move."[38] Recall that the last time I held my breath I lost my arms. This "breathlessness"—both in the sense of merciless efficiency and suspended animation—is a dangerous business for a woman with a Zeus-like *animus*.

The Brainchild's Father figure may enjoy her body, but she is not supposed to enjoy her own. Here is a dream in which my Critical Father is revealed as "dirty" himself, but demanding cleanliness of me.

> I am at some large public gathering—perhaps a party—and everyone begins to dance to rock 'n' roll music. I dance, too, and eventually discover I don't have a shirt on. I am mildly embarrassed and wonder if I should cover up, but I keep on dancing.
>
> Later, I'm in a large building with a gymnasium that has an old-fashioned bathtub with a shower at one end—with no curtain. I am waiting in line for a shower. An older man finishes his, and as he comes out, he reminds me not to forget the shampoo. I go in and start my shower, and then notice this man standing over in one corner, watching. I'm very annoyed, because this means I'm going to have to find my suitcase (which is in another room) and rummage through it, dripping wet, for my bathing suit. I wish the man would go away.

This one begins as "The Bull Dance" did—although I have no partner, I am enjoying the music and my body, unconcerned about my performance. But it turns, just as the earlier dream did, for there is someone taking his pleasure from gazing at me. He wants to make sure I get clean after my libidinous dance (was he watching that, too?), as is made evident when he reminds me about the shampoo. Apparently, it's most important that I wash my *head*! He gets clean, too, but then becomes a leering lecher.

At least I am irked, if not fed up enough to banish him, and resent having to cover up to meet his demands. I'm seeing the critical *animus* for what he is—not only demanding but also a dirty old man, as was Zeus. The kind of relationship I had with my professor, as well as with the collective academic *animus*, has a cost, which is not only the diminution of my free intellect but also the denial of my embodiment. The Brainchild inherits Athena's practical reason, but also her tolerance of her mentor's privileges. As a classical version of the story goes, Athena the Weaver turned Arachne into a spider when she wove a cloth that was superior to hers. It depicted the love affairs of the Olympian gods.[39] As long as she carries her father's banner, Athena remains invested in protecting Zeus' licentiousness from exposure.

CONTROLLING FEMALE HUNGER

If the feminine body is threatened by rationality, there are more ways than sex to control it. Susan Bordo points out that, throughout the dominant Western religious and philosophical traditions, the control of desire has been the province of males, whereas females, considered excessive and irrational, have been in need of control. Female hunger, as a metaphor for the appetites in general, is especially a "problem" in periods of change in gender relations. Thus, the hungry, devouring female is often imagined as monstrously out of control in literature and popular culture. The late nineteenth century spawned sphinxes and blood-sucking vampires that, although often nominally masculine, nevertheless had sylph-like bodies, blood-red lips, and dark-shadowed eyes.[40] The twentieth century saw *Jaws'* bloody-mouthed shark, an update of the mythic motif of the *vagina dentata*, or "womb with teeth," and the mother monster of the *Alien* series fame.[41]

By contrast, the ideal mass media goddess has jettisoned Marilyn Monroe's size 12 body for the 1960s' leggy Twiggy, the 1990s' waif-like Kate Moss, and the look of starvation called "heroin chic," resulting in a dangerous epidemic of anorexia nervosa and bulimia, mostly among young women. It is not the whole feminine body, just its soft, protuberant parts, like abs, thighs, and butts, that represent uncontained desire and must be mercilessly attacked as "alien." Breasts are an exception because they are associated with nurturing, not birth, and it is the birthing womb that readily turns into the devouring hole when the Mother is feared.[42] This combination results in what one woman, who deals with many eating-disordered women in her clinical practice, calls the supermodel ideal of "an anorexic with implants." As Michel Foucault notes, whereas Western culture used to impose external constraints such as corsets and girdles to keep feminine flesh under control, such constraints have become progressively internal.[43] With constant assault on the bulge from "fat-whackers," "butt-blasters," and "abs of steel," the body shapes up and now acts as corset itself to protect the woman from eruption from within.

Marion Woodman associates the goddess Athena with the "addiction to perfection" that I have ascribed to the Brainchild, and she shows how it often leads to eating disorders in women. She retells the Greek tale in which Medusa, once a beautiful woman, offended Athena, who changed her hair into snakes and her face into a horror story that turned all who looked upon it to stone. "Athena is chained to Medusa as surely as Medusa is chained to Athena," Woodman writes. She sees Medusa as "the negative mother, which her feminine body naturally rejects."[44] Also as the witch "whose snaky locks twist and writhe in constant agitation, reaching, reaching, reaching, wanting more and more and more," and that stands for the woman's addiction to food, alcohol, or perfectionism.[45]

I see Medusa as angry and vengeful because of our culture's murder of the Mother and burial of her beneath the structures that support our perfectionist machine. It is worth noting that older versions of the swallowed Metis were really Medusa, whose Gorgon face and snake hair symbolized female wisdom; Medusa-Metis was yet another version of the triple-headed Goddess among the Libyan Amazons, who worshipped her as the Mother of Fate.[46] No wonder Medusa is angry—Zeus, who claimed sole authorship of their child Athena, consumed her.

Woodman's words of caution about perfectionism, especially as tied to eating disorders, emphasize the lethal implications behind Lamott's KFKD: "Addiction to perfection is at root a suicidal addiction. The addict is simulating not life but death. Almost inevitably a woman addicted to perfection will view herself as a work of art, and her real terror is that the work of art, being so absolutely precious, may in one instant be destroyed."[47]

The Brainchild's Father sometimes shows an obsessive interest in the perfection of her body, an ideal that erases rather than enhances her more feminine characteristics so that she will more closely resemble a man—for example, by dieting away her rounded features. As I related in the chapter on the Maiden Lover, my professor demanded an eating regimen that reduced me to my adolescent size. Viewing a picture from a few years back of my professor's wife, also his graduate student, I marveled at what a bony ghost of her former self she was when I met her. And I now wonder whether his acclaim of my work over my friend's was at least partly due to her refusal to submit to his dietary demands.

But eating disorders, whether in the attempt to stay rigidly thin or to become out-of-control fat, are not only a capitulation to patriarchal demands to control the feminine body. There is a puzzling paradox embedded within them of autonomy and dependence, of the production of a "desirable" feminine body and the rejection of this ideal. The Brainchild's corseting of her own body through unyielding self-control, for example, is in one sense a surrender to the demands of the Critical Father, but is in another a resistance to his control. If *I* keep myself under such strict surveillance, the thinking goes, then *he* can't touch me. As experts now know, the anorexic's rejection of food gives her dominion over her own body, however much she may be dancing with death. This was brought home to me in terms of overeating rather than under-eating when Joan told more of her story.

~

Early in Joan's program, her new advisor started making remarks about her body: "You still have a pretty good figure for a woman who's had three kids." Joan recognized not only the sexual connotation of his remark but also the implied criticism of her full-figured body. She eventually reacted, not by molding her form to meet his ideal, but by gaining thirty pounds to confound it, "eating candy bars, which I never do." If she controlled her own body, she explained, then he couldn't.

Joan's advisor began punishing her with grades and negative comments to other professors when she did not respond to his attempts to "build her up" by trimming her down and making her his Mistress. He encouraged her to submit a paper she wrote for an award, then lobbied against it. Her undergraduate feminist mentor advised her to bring the case to the judicial board, but when she heard what it would take, including the disclosure of specific comments, she felt her only option was to drop out. She didn't want to be seen publicly as a "complainer" and a person who couldn't handle it on her own; apparently, his attempt to make her into a tough Brainchild had at least partly worked. But she dropped out of her MA program and, though she is intellectually active and committed to many writing projects, she never got an advanced degree or an academic job, thus sacrificing her original goal.

"How has this experience affected you?" I asked.

Joan bit down hard on her memories to answer. "It changed my life."

THE BRAIN AT THE BOTTOM OF THE STAIRS

Playing my professor's Brainchild didn't exactly change my life. As my performance of *antidisestablishmentarianism* implies, I was probably headed in this direction by about age 6. But it did gel the ingredients and set a course for my academic success. After all, I got rewards for using my head, and assiduously avoided thereafter anything that would bring me down like my friend. When I wrote earlier that I sometimes live a myth without knowing its grip on me, as if fitting myself into a template I don't even know is in front of my nose, I don't think I fully realized even then how much this is my myth. I am a Brainchild, and a very good one at that.

The Brainchild is often a huge success in school. With mentors inside her head or out who know the ropes, with most signs of the messy Mother kept securely out of sight, and with a mission to speak for the Fathers who are running the show, she is best positioned among the man-made maidens to accomplish great deeds and achieve recognition for them within academia. Her problem lies not in her external world, but within, and it is that her brain is detached from her body.

I close with this dream I call "The Brain at the Bottom of the Stairs" that epitomizes her dilemma pretty well:

> I am at church, and my family has invited a bunch of people to our house for snacks afterward. It is the house I lived in during high

> school. I am anxious to get home because people will be there soon and I haven't done any preparation.
>
> But I am diverted by a friend who points out a gigantic house she lives in. I see it off to the side, as if in a vision. It is very tall and looks quite mysterious. We can see inside it as if the walls are glass, although nothing is very clear. We go inside the house. It is awesome, with tremendously rich and ornately carved dark wood walls. Part of the house is still being constructed, and there are stacks of wood pieces lying around.
>
> She points out her father's study at one corner of the house, and says it used to have a simulated "outdoor" reconstruction of a pond with trees, rocks, and shrubs, but that this recently collapsed and had to be removed. She asks me if I want to see the study and I say yes.
>
> We enter the study, and it is gigantic—about three stories high, with walls full of books, like an old English library with its rich dark hues, carved wood, and heavy draperies. I am surprised to see that her father is working behind his massive desk. But I see that behind him, rather than books, the huge wall is stacked high with beer of every variety. He is a large man with a big shock of silver-gray hair.
>
> He welcomes us, points to an ice cream case on the side, and asks us if we want some. I decline, because I know I have to get back to my own guests.
>
> The man seems to be Don Tyson, the wealthy chicken magnate. This "study" is apparently more a place for him to manage his business and entertain guests than a real place to read books.
>
> The girl and I leave and walk down the stairs. When we get to the bottom, I am shocked to see the man's hair on the floor. It looks like a scalp with some of the brains attached. I wonder if he has been killed.

This dream begins at church, the scene of my upbringing as a preacher's daughter, and a symbol that this scenario has significance for me that borders on the religious. The fact that I want to get back to my high-school house locates the action within adolescence. My anxiety about serving food, aside from the fact that this is a constant demand on church families, gives the plot a people-pleasing tone—that is, I am not on my own mission, but one of others.

But this girl, my sidekick or "shadow," who knows about things I don't when I am so busily operating out of my scripted maiden-like trance, wants to show me something. She wants me to see inside the numinous house of glass she lives in, and I am willing to follow. The house is still under construction, indicating that I am not yet through with what this dream represents. The father's study (and if she is also me, it is Our Father's study) used to have more of the Goddess—its rocks, pond, and trees are more her environs than his—but "it collapsed and had to be removed," just as did the Goddess realm within academia. Now it is a distinctly masculine-looking place, with orderly, upright walls made out of raw-wood natural materials (materia = mater = Metis = mother). This place where things are "studied" is quite impressive, as is the man behind the massive desk, at least at first glance.

Although Our Father seems to do the right thing—he welcomes us and tries to make us comfortable—he obviously regards us as children, because he offers us ice cream instead of beer. He is also a bit of a sham, in that what looks like shelves of books are actually cases of beer—like those designer "books by the yard" ordered by interior decorators to make a home seem warmly literate. He's not really reading or studying anything—he is, in fact, a powerful business tycoon who uses this "study" as a place to entertain. Since he is my Father, the "beer-for-books" motif probably also indicates the addictive quality of my attraction to the father's "study."

A maiden on a mythic descent is often offered something to eat or drink, as Persephone is offered a pomegranate seed by Hades after her abduction. If she consumes it, she will not be able to return to the upper world—or at least not full-time— and so there is generally an injunction by a god or goddess beforehand against doing so. My dream is an ascent to a sort of perverted Ivory Tower rather than a descent into an underworld, but the tower is a fake, and in that sense not a place I want to stay. My refusal of the ice cream, even though I just want to get back to my trance, may mean that I don't want to be trapped in this pseudo Hall of Learning, just as I didn't want to stay in the Halls of Science. If I eat it, I may never get out.

As my alter ego and I "get to the bottom" of this house, I am startled to see her father's scalp on the floor. If he is *my* Father, my academic Brainchild's *animus*, then my white-haired, masculine intellectual faculty—the one I've been carrying as a flag for him who conceived me—like my maiden arms is severed from my body. It lies on the floor at the entrance to my Father's house, waiting to be claimed.

PART TWO

FATAL ATTRACTIONS

The man-made maidens—Maiden Lover, Muse, Mistress, Brainchild—are essentially roles women play in a man's search for his soul. As we have seen, they have both payoffs and pitfalls for the academic woman, but they are not the result of her own search for self. Unless she progresses beyond them, she tends to remain dependent upon the man—or upon the patriarchal structure of the university.

The "Siren," the "Veiled Woman," and the "Amazon" move us into more ambiguous territory, for in each one the woman asserts her own power but still may capitulate unknowingly to men's expectations, or may become an even more enticing target for their domination. The Siren openly uses her sexual powers to seduce, the Veiled Woman covertly employs her hidden femininity to charm, and the Amazon separates from men and becomes a warrior. These three roles—Siren, Veiled Woman, and Amazon—thus occupy a sort of middle ground in our larger story of the academic woman's search for her soul. She breaks away from the plots men write for her, but often ends up acting just as surely according to their scripts. These are "fatal attractions," then, for they offer the woman a pathway to power that may in the end prove a mirage.

CHAPTER 6

SIREN

"My sexual preference is undergraduate," she had been known to say.

Penelope O, *The Lecturer's Tale*

The Siren is related to the Mistress, for both embrace their own corporeality, using sexual enticements for personal gain. Whereas the Mistress' body is the man's possession, the Siren possesses her own body, which she freely employs to gain power over a man. She may be successful at this, flaunting the prohibitions against feminine sexuality and bewitching a man with her irresistible magic. She may even cause his undoing upon the craggy rocks of her aquatic allure. But as her mythological history shows, the Siren is also a manifestation of men's worst fears about women—that they set fatal traps, if not to eat them like the Mother Monster, just as surely to bring about their demise by drowning them in a sea of sensuality.

MYTHS OF THE SIREN

The Siren is one of many "beautiful witches" who ruin men unable to resist their seductive charms. Homer's *Odyssey* teems with such sorceresses, who come forth from caves or the sea to tempt Odysseus and his men: Circe, who drugs Odysseus' advance guard and turns them into swine; Calypso, who detains Odysseus in her bed for seven years, trying to make him forget Ithaca; and the Sirens, the magic women of Cyrene, with girls' faces and birdlike feet and feathers, who threaten to dash the sailors to smithereens if they succumb to their ravishing voices.[1]

Although any of these mythic enchantresses could serve as our prototype, I have chosen the Siren because she charms with her *voice* and she resides in the *sea*. Both of these motifs are relevant to the story that is unfolding here, for words carry a magical force in the Ivory Tower, which we have already pictured as a fortress built atop the womb symbols of cave or sea. One who "professes" lives or dies by the pen, not the sword, and thus how "voice" is gendered in academia is rather a matter of life and death.

The Siren charms with a much more potent song than, let's say, Disney's Little Mermaid, who gives up her lovely voice and home under the sea for her prince. But it is telling to look at the origins of the word *charm*, from the Old English *cym*, a hymn or choral song, after the Latin Carmenta, inventor of alphabets and "words of power." A "charm" reflected an ancient belief among men that women could exercise power over them by mastering spoken spells or songs invoking the help of the Nature Goddess. It was she who was responsible for sexual attraction and penile erection—all that rendered a man helplessly subject to forces he could not dispel through logic. "Therefore everything that made a man feel attracted to a woman came to be synonymous with witchcraft," writes Barbara Walker, "charm, enchantment, bewitchment, spellbinding, witchery, moon-madness, or glamour—in the old sense of a spell cast by Morgan of 'Glamorgan.'" Women's singing was especially suspect as a method of casting spells. "Enchant" came from *incanture*, or "incantation," which meant "to sing over."[2]

A woman whose voice is too charming—especially if she is also beautiful—can be suspect as a witch. "Well aware that witches have power to enervate and destroy their lovers by secretly drawing off their blood in little bladders," notes Robert Graves, "Odysseus exacted a solemn oath from Circe not to plot any further mischief against him."[3] Jean Markale decodes such winning little metaphors as this, as well as Odysseus' lashing of himself to his ship's mast to escape the Sirens, as man's knowledge that, despite his pride and potency, he will be conquered in the act of love. "For him orgasm is almost death, the temporary sapping of his strength, whereas woman is triumphant, regenerated by the act." Odysseus fears Circe's and Calypso's power to "'make him weak and unmanly,' to send him back to the marvellous [sic], timeless world of infancy."[4]

Woman's freedom to use sex as she likes is thus terribly threatening to masculine authority.[5] This is nowhere truer than in academia, where feminine sexuality endangers the search for transcendence of life through the abstractions of cognition. "Throughout history and around the world, men's clubs have sought to create a 'pure' place, undisturbed by attractive, wild, and chaotic Feminine energy," writes David Deida. "Historically, the academic 'ivory tower' was a men's club where the pure forms of ideas, mathematics, theories, and concepts reigned supreme."[6] If a woman's voice is used to enchant rather than profess, she is automatically suspect and is best brought under control.

As we have been doing all along, however, we should look at what these women used to be before the "men's clubs" turned them into witches. Sometimes their physical attributes serve as a clue. Homer referred to "Circe of the Braided Tresses," implying that she manipulated the forces of creation and destruction by the knots and braids in her hair, like Oriental goddesses. Pliny said she was a Goddess who "commanded all the lights of heaven." Indeed, "Circe" comes from *cirque* (or "circle"), which was related to Omphale of Lydia and her cosmic spinning wheel. That is, she was a fate-spinner, weaver of the destinies of men, ruling the stars that determined men's fates.[7] Recall that Medusa was also once the beautiful and wise Metis, mother of Athena, and yet another version of the triple-headed Goddess worshipped as the Mother of Fate. Just as Circe descended from a great Goddess to a witch who turned men into hogs, Medusa was transformed into the Gorgon, whose gawking mouth and snaky hair had the power to turn men into stone—her symbols of wisdom and healing having become instruments of terror and impotency.

The Sirens may not have been the Great Goddess herself, but they were originally more noble than their later seafaring occupation would suggest. One story is that they were girls playing with Persephone when she was abducted by Hades, and Demeter gave them wings so they might search for her. In another, Aphrodite turned them into birds because, out of pride, they refused to yield their maidenheads to either gods or men. They lost their wings when the Muses defeated them in a musical contest and pulled out their wing feathers to make themselves crowns.[8] Whatever their origins, the Sirens were apparently once air-borne, later to descend into the waters as fish-women. These bird goddesses were finally reduced to Mother Goose, who flies through the air on a large goose in children's nursery rhymes.[9]

All mythological traditions, Markale points out, refer to treasures to be found at the bottom of the sea, for they all confirm the role of water in the genesis of life. The primeval mother—the Virgin of the Waters, the Siren or the invisible being in its depths—fertilizes the sea, and this belief in the ocean as mother of all life has survived into our own times. "Its mystery and depth made it the supreme feminine symbol, and as patriarchal ideas gained predominance its secret and forbidden aspects were increasingly stressed."[10] As we have seen, the deep sea is where the Mother Monster can be found—she who must be assiduously avoided by any good Brainchild, not to mention by her Father. Simone de Beauvoir articulates well the dangers: "'The Woman-Mother has a face of shadows: she is the chaos whence all have come and whither all must one day return; she is nothingness.'"[11]

And yet men are compelled to draw near. Markale explains the paradox of attraction and repulsion toward such deep-sea females. She sees Celtic myths as transitional, for they are essentially patriarchal, but retain much more of the old Goddess traditions than those of the Greeks or the Romans. Celtic mythology is full of legends of the "submerged city" or "submerged princess" that express a conflict between the established religion, Christian or Druidic, and a "marvelous woman who comes to fetch the man of her choice." She is a remnant of an earlier age when women had powers lost to them even in Celtic societies, including their right to sacred prostitution. Although banished to the depths, "she retains her wonderful beauty and her power to attract men even as she alarms them. In this way, the fiction of the beloved witch, the *femme fatale*, begins to take shape, and develops through the witch burnings of the Middle Ages and Renaissance to the commercial exploitation of the vamp in modern cinema and its fantasy world."[12]

I do not find the Siren as plentiful in academia as any of the man-made maidens; the very nature of the institution discourages such a woman's success or longevity. However, she does arise from the depths often enough that anyone who resides for long in the Ivory Tower has encountered her. The Siren is not afraid to express her sexuality, or to use it to her own advantage. Let us look at some of the forms the beautiful witch may take, as well as how men may react to her. The women you will meet here are ones I have observed over my years in academe or that others—both men and women—have told me about. Women typically do not talk about themselves as Sirens.

SIRENS IN TRAINING

When I was a new assistant professor, I knew Lisa as a twenty-something undergraduate seeking her BA before the days that sexual harassment had been defined. With startling blue Keane-painting eyes a tad too big for her head, light brown hair that brushed her bare mid-riff, and a leggy frame just slightly more plumped out than Twiggy's, she could fill a professor's office door frame just so. She resembled a fawn barely emerging from its awkward stage into grace, and bore a perpetual look of chary come-hither-ness. Several of her male professors remembered her after she graduated with a mixture of desire and wistful amusement. All described her to me as totally irresistible.

Lisa intuited that her professors were erotically fascinated with her and as up-tight about it as a Buckingham Palace guard. A good student but not a great one, this was the source of her power—although she didn't try to parlay her dexterity into better grades. She just seemed to like playing with her superiors, like a cat with mice, enjoying their discombobulation in response to her moves. In the course of an oral presentation by a fellow student named Kevin to a senior seminar my husband Tom taught one evening, Lisa managed to liberate herself completely from her bra without taking off her sweater.

"What on earth are you doing!" cried Tom when he realized something very out-of-the-ordinary was occurring on his watch. Tom is not easily undone by outrageous behavior, given that he considers this his own God-given mission in life, but this was over the top, even for him.

"Do you have any idea how one of these things feels?" she asked, in feigned exasperation, pulling the lacy contraption triumphantly through her left sleeve. "There, that's better," she said, as Kevin decided to trash the rest of his seminar report. "I learned that from Jennifer Beale in *Flashdance*."

Only a few years older than Lisa, I marveled at her flamboyance, which I couldn't decide whether to respect or resent. She actually *did* things I would only imagine while deeply asleep. But she could also deflect men's attentions from me and my words merely by absent-mindedly chewing on the tiny strand of her hair that she would braid in front of you right down to the end.

Decades after her *Flashdance* performance I sat in a convention hotel bar with a covey of professors from around the country, several of whom had long since migrated away from the university where Lisa had performed her amazing feat. Among her "catches" and others who witnessed her pursuits, The Legend of Lisa still survives, burnished to a fine gloss from years of retelling. Kurt began the tale this time, familiar except for whatever embellishments would be added this year for the benefit of newcomers.

Once their school hosted a famous behavioral scientist for a guest lecture followed by a reception in his honor. Lisa found him enticingly stuffy, so the story unfolded; he stood by the bar discoursing on his latest publication to whoever stopped by for a glass of Paul Masson burgundy poured by the department's indentured servants, the graduate students. After sizing up the luminary and his bow tie from a safe distance, she soon pounced upon him as a worthy, yet relatively untaxing, prey.

"On a good night I can have fifteen orgasms in thirty minutes," she purred, fingering the belt on her hip-hugger jeans.

"That's a career for me!" he retorted, demonstrating perhaps a slightly steadier center of gravity than she had expected. The small throng around His Eminence and the half-emptied bottles grew noticeably. He double-clutched nervously, fantasizing escape even as he grasped that it was futile, given the audience of peeping sycophants curious as to whether he could hold on to his decorum.

Lisa gathered grit from the crowd. "Did you ever have a Binaca blow job?" she ventured intrepidly, upping the ante in hopes of a crack in his composure.

"Can't say that I, umm, that I'm sh. . . sure what that is," he said, beginning to falter as the flock tittered, and taking a long, measured sip of his drink. "But I have a feeling you're going to tell me."

"I'm more into show than tell," Lisa cooed. "Maybe later." Then she reached out and touched his member, which was fast retreating into the recesses of his nattily pleated khakis. "Sssszzzzz!" she hissed, shaking her middle finger as if to cool it off and refusing to dislodge her eyes from his.

"At this the Greatest Behavioral Scientist in America swallowed his swizzle stick," Kurt finished with a flourish, and by now the bar gang was thoroughly challenged to top his story. Several rose to the occasion.

Showing little to no interest in her fellow male graduate students, it seemed, Lisa slipped in and out of her professors' beds with no discernible rewards or punishments. These men seemed to appreciate her skills at luring them into play without demanding the commitment of a relationship or a badge of academic accomplishment. It is just as well, however, that Lisa did not go on for her PhD or stay in academia. The central recurring motif in the Legend of Lisa is a bedroom mystery that Bill, now a distinguished behavioral scientist himself, perpetuates—that of her amazing "athlete's foot" technique. Thus far, as if he knows revealing the climax would render his performance defunct, Bill has declined to divulge the details.

I have also noticed a subtle change over the years that puts the storytellers more wittily at the helm than no doubt was true if you prefer your stories straight. And I am not sure that Lisa would like hearing them as much now, pushing fifty, as she seemed to like evoking them when she was not much more than a farm girl from the Western plains.

~

Melody got her MA well after sexual harassment rules were firmly in place at American universities. If she had gone to graduate school in Lisa's era, she wouldn't have worn denim and hippie beads, but hot pants and go-go boots. She had an artistically highlighted shag, a salon tan that looked a whole lot better now than it would in fifteen years, and an impossibly curvaceous yet fine-boned body. When people complimented her on her size 2 frame, she liked to say "I'm petite for my size." She was, as the Eagles say, "terminally pretty." She had learned just enough feminist theory that, when mixed with her Tri-Delt undergraduate training, she was hell on heels at the Thursday night gatherings of graduate students and self-selected faculty from my department.

Lucas Jones knew the same feminist theory as Melody, given that they were taking the same seminar from me. Actually, he probably knew it a little better than she, since he needed it for his thesis on "Postcolonialist Subaltern Identities in Trans-Mediated Latin American Cultures: Trajectories for Future Scholarship." Melody seemed more interested in harvesting whatever vocabulary she could use to stun the sexist beasts who pawed her at every opportunity in every conceivable site of cultural contestation. However, Lucas did not know much about Melody, and that put him at a disadvantage the night I witnessed their conversation.

Lucas sat across from Melody, who was flanked on her right by her admiring best grad-school buddy Jill, who did not have an artistically highlighted shag or an impossibly curvaceous yet fine-boned body, and on the left by several male graduate students who couldn't decide whether getting Melody between the sheets was worth enduring a voice that was strangely grating for such a delicate beauty. All of us attending the Thursday night brainfry were in advanced states of lubrication due to the masterpieces of the local brewmaster—himself a graduate from our department and a more prominent university Back East. All of us, that is, except Melody, who I noticed held back somewhat, preparing her moves.

Inevitably, Melody caught Lucas looking at her in what she deemed just the wrong location. It was a supreme opening for one of the "Enlightened Sorority Sister as Oppressed Other" riffs she was perfecting this semester.

"Lucas, are you looking at my breasts?" Melody taunted him. Clearly, Lucas couldn't decide whether she was being indignant or flirtatious. He banked on the latter, boldly going where quite a few men had gone before, and cueing Melody to home in on the former.

"Did you get that blouse from Victoria's Secret?" he ventured. "It goes well with your eyes."

"Why don't you keep your own off my tits?" Melody rejoined,

quickly activating her best Code Red plan in case of Male Chauvinist Pig Attack.

"You're wearing a *corset*, for godsakes, Melody," Lucas bellowed, assuaging his injured pride. "You can't tell me you don't want men looking at you!"

"It's my right to wear whatever I want and not become just another reified victim of the objectifying male gaze!" Melody screeched, as Jill gave her a "Thumbs up, sister!" sign and the male graduate students sat dumbfounded, not sure who was ahead on the scoreboard.

Melody sat forward in her chair. "I do Pilates and I'm proud of my body, but that doesn't mean I have to sit here and take your infantile, narcissistic fetish fantasies!" The left bank consolidated behind Melody until she added, almost as an afterthought, "and the same goes to you babies, too!" as she waved off the gaggle of mute boys, driving their decision toward permanently evading this Wicked Blonde Witch of the South.

Lucas wasn't caving in that easily—especially not in front of his stunned brethren, not to mention his professors. Feeling he must rally if he were to save any atom of dignity, he dug deeply into his memory of the seminar reading packet and pulled out his best Laura Mulvey by way of Jacques Lacan.

"You can't have it both ways, Melody. If you want to be the subject of your own pleasure and not just an excuse for men to remain within the plenitude of the Imaginary, then don't dress like you work at Hooters." The brethren perked up visibly, defecting toward Lucas as a dazed look passed over Jill's face. Given that I'd taught Lucas the theory from whence he spoke, I couldn't help being a wee bit proud.

Lucas' bravado was poignantly foolhardy, however.

Melody settled her rear end back in her chair, but kept her chest out there in the lead. "You'll never escape your own Imaginary into the Symbolic world of the Fathers, Lucas, because if you'll bother to check out what's not there when you stand up to piss, you'll find that your phallic signifier is distinctly hypothetical."

Here I was blown away. I admit I hadn't realized how closely Melody had been paying attention. Far past any sense of competition at this point, I was still, as with Lisa, torn. At this pace, Melody could be a force to be reckoned with in my own field. However, poor Lucas had not really deserved what he got, and he appeared to me mostly a convenient foil for Melody's performance. I also wondered what would happen when Melody went after a more seasoned prey. Would he feel compelled to punish her insolence?

Lucas proceeded to drown in his local lager, while Melody advanced nicely toward PhD school as a Siren-in-training. After all, she had been practicing.

THE SIREN AND THE YEAR-KINGS

Circe's isle of Aeaea was a funerary shrine, whose name meant *wailing*. According to Walker, the fact that she turned Odysseus' men into swine was "a mythic picture of the transition from human to porcine sacrifices during the Hellenic period."[13] As we have seen, the Great Mother did once require human sacrifices to regenerate the land. Since men were thought necessary for recreation but not procreation, her representative on earth took a son-lover consort each year in a sacred marriage. The year-king lived well as the queen's lover, but was ritually slain at the end of his short reign, to make room for a new consort and to fertilize the crops. If Circe was once the Great Goddess, then it makes sense that she would demand sacrifices.

Serious academic Sirens are sometimes ruthless magistrates. Men, particularly the young ones, are often drawn to them as irresistibly as were Odysseus' crew. Those of more practiced erudition or ego may also sail near, but know to tie themselves to the mast. I relied on James Hynes' *The Lecturer's Tale* to show how the allure of the collegiate Muse frequently outstrips that of the Wife. I think he is equally dead-on when he turns to the sexually bewitching academic woman. Reading his chapter called "The Story of O" prompted me to tell you about Vanessa. But first, here is an excerpt from Hynes' story. I pick it up as the hero, Nelson Humboldt, tries to savor the eight-ounce supernal hamburger he had bought in honor of being granted an unexpected three-year lectureship. His private celebration at the Peregrine, the fashionable grill frequented by the tenured literati of the English department, disintegrates as Miranda de La Tour, Penelope O, and Penelope's "latest young person" are seated at the next table.

Professor O's chair was held by a stunned-looking but handsome young man in undergraduate kit—threadbare sweater, billed cap, goatee—and she sat, twining her calves together in their tight black leggings and gesturing for the boy to sit next to her.

"Does anyone mind if I smoke?" Penelope's red fingernails twitched before her as she lit a cigarette. . . .

"Lunch is on me, James," Penelope gasped, clutching the young man's wrist. "You may order anything you like."

"Um, it's Jake." The boy scratched his head under his cap.

"Whatever, studmuffin, you've earned it." Penelope dragged on her cigarette. As the current holder of the department's chair in Sexuality Studies, Penelope taught a wildly popular class called "Lord Rochester to Larry Flynt: A Cultural History of Fucking," which featured showings of grainy stag films, European snuff videos, and regular guest appearances by a porn star turned performance artist who encouraged the students to view her vulva through a jeweler's loupe. The reading list alternated between impenetrable theory and smudgy old copies of *Hustler* and *Oui*, on reserve in the graduate library; students were encouraged to masturbate if they got aroused while reading the assignments or even if they got aroused during class. The course drew more students than Introduction to Chemistry, and the vast lecture hall, the largest on campus, was usually standing room only, an improbable mix of earnest young lesbians and awe-struck fraternity boys. Every semester, once she had worked her way through the graduate assistants who taught her discussion sections—"my bitches," Penelope called them—she began to sample her students one at a time, alternating genders. "My sexual preference is undergraduate," she had been known to say. One poor boy had had the temerity to bring her up on charges; and in her appearance before the university's sexual harassment panel, Penelope had delivered a passionate explication of the erotics of pedagogy.

"Teaching *is* seduction," she'd declared, climaxing her presentation with the argument that, since sexual harassment was an instrumentality of the oppression of women, no woman could be guilty of it.

"And ain't I a woman?" she had declared to the harassment panel in her posh accent, fingering the laces of her leather bustier.

> The chair of the panel, a blushing, matronly classics professor in her sixties, had abruptly declared the matter closed. . . .
>
> Nelson lowered himself to his seat and stole a glance at the next table. Miranda was shaking out her napkin. Penelope was coughing with surprising force into her fist. The boy slouched in his seat with his cap pushed back, staring slack-jawed at Penelope. If I move now, Nelson thought, it would be obvious that I'm listening.
>
> Penelope continued to cough, and the boy gingerly patted her on the back.
>
> "Not *now*, Jason," barked Penelope, recovering. She stubbed out her cigarette and lit another. "Bloody hell, can't you think about *anything* else?"
>
> "It's Jake," he said, and then the waitress came.[14]

I first encountered Vanessa at a publisher's party thrown in honor of her third book at one of the many conferences loosely associated with English. Her c.v. was impressively long for her 38 years, and her challenging—some would say impenetrable—prose was eagerly deciphered and debated in graduate seminars all over the country. Her theorizing relied upon a penultimate mix of obligatory classicists and *avant-garde* provocateurs, so that it was difficult for Old Guard professors to dismiss her or fervent young scholars to resist her, although none of them understood her.

Having read several of her works myself, I wasn't sure whether to be intimidated, repulsed, or amused, for she used her brilliance like a hard diamond to cut through her forebears' legacies until they bled. I introduced myself hesitantly, given I did not want her sharp wit turned on me. But then I remembered I wasn't really a "player," so I might as well relax. Which I did when it became clear she was capable of unexpected warmth. We had a short but stimulating conversation resulting in an exchange of e-mail addresses and footnotes. I decided I liked this woman.

Vanessa was dressed in something resembling what Olivia Newton-John wore when she turned bad in *Grease*. She had the electrified mane, except it was dyed to "black cherry" with a white stripe on one side that she kept pushing away from one eye; when she tucked it behind her right ear you could see the six earrings graduating up the fleshy lobe, starting with gold rings and ending with infinitesimal diamond studs. On a less beautiful woman, you might have thought of a skunk who had found its way into a piercing parlor, but on her, it somehow all worked. The next day she attended panels and posed piercing questions—more like speeches—from the audience in a pin-striped Madonna suit leaking a black lace bra, right out of "Express Yourself." Vanessa was the kind of teacher about whom students were inspired to write on their course evaluations: *The professor is hot.*

She held court with four graduate students, who followed her from party to party like ducklings imprinted on a serendipitous mother. It was pretty easy to tell she was "with" Grayson, who lit her cigarettes and produced one for himself from his rolled t-shirt sleeve, although they didn't exactly touch. Unlike Penelope O, Vanessa did give at least a nominal nod to proper deportment. Grayson was just this side of emaciated, but his upper arms were incongruously pumped up, as if he had forgotten his Ritalin and obsessively repeated just one exercise at the gym. Another male seemed a particular pet of Vanessa's, but not quite interested enough in her, so I guessed he was not in line to be the next year-king. The female looked to be an aspiring Vanessa, although I wasn't sure she had the panache to pull it off; she would have to tone down the synthesized vamp Goth look and lose the black fingernails and about half the metal—it was all just a little too gruesome. The Third Male laughed at Vanessa's witticisms and competed with Grayson's pithy observations about the postmodern condition. He was good-looking, a little more Leonardo di Caprio to Grayson's The Artist Formerly Known as Prince. A definite contender.

Vanessa and Grayson performed lover's quarrels for their entourage about whether Michel Foucault or Judith Butler was the true father (or mother) of queer theory, or if, actually, using these familial terms wasn't just buying into the patriarchal construct of the nuclear family, and which was *the* quintessentially American cinematic genre—*film noir* or the Gidget series. Grayson was a decent partner in intellectual combat foreplay, although he seemed more earnest in his quoting of William S. Burroughs than did she; it was like he was channeling God and she was just trying him on for size. At any rate, he had most of the right stuff, and after he emitted a particularly right-on citation from *Wired* magazine by Sandy Stone, the oracular transsexual prophet of techno-culture, she turned to me and said, "I keep him around because he's cutting edge." The Third Male tittered, perhaps hoping he'd ascend to the throne if Grayson ever got cut from his edge.

On the third day I attended the panel at which Vanessa was to present her recent thoughts on "Beyond Baudrillard: What Is Next in the Culture of Post-Simulation?" She wore painted-on black studded jeans, a black turtleneck sweater from The Gap, á la Sharon Stone's courageous Academy Awards fashion statement, an embossed black-on-black Japanese silk scarf tossed loosely around her neck, and six-inch black leather platform boots that made her look tall, which she wasn't. In fact, the only thing not some shade of black touching her body, other than her earrings, was that white stripe in her hair. She looked every bit the Pomo Princess she was. But whereas everybody else doing postmodern criticism seemed "bored and hyper," miming the culture they described, Vanessa's frame had just enough slack in it to suggest a resigned calm in the face of the undeniably fatal failure of the American imagination.

Vanessa's paper was an oxymoronic marvel. She began with the dramatic manifesto from Donna Haraway that "I'd rather be a cyborg than a goddess." After a pause to reveal the studded earlobe just long enough to let the audience ponder which one they thought she was, she systematically deconstructed this by-now canonical statement, her thesis having something to do with how the cloning that produced "Dolly" is a watershed moment that renders both Baudrillardian simulation and Harawayian cyborgization obsolete, thrusting us into a new regime in which the "ecstasy of communication" is mirrored back to us on the ubiquitous Media Screen, no longer as simple, run-of-the-mill pornography but as brute apocryphal bestiality. Neither a cyborg nor a goddess could thus reconstitute Aristotelian *eudaimonia*, or living well, within such a culture because the clash between technological progression and feral regression has produced a stasis in which there is no viable site left for either women or machines to occupy with whatever semblances of authenticity they may once have thought—however pathetically—they had.

When she finished, Grayson, the Vamp Goth, the Pet, and the Third Male attempted to boost the applause to an ovation, but realized just in time the unseemliness of such exuberance at an academic event, and sat down. Much of the audience remained inert, paralyzed either by Vanessa's numinosity or fears of their own obsolescence. But perhaps it was the reference to the classics that got "Professor Shakespeare" steamed enough to attempt a rebuttal. How dare she cavalierly throw in references to the father of Western culture in the same breath that she pronounced it Dead on Arrival, all within such a thin, cult stud, pomo-schmomo mish-mash of half-baked French apocalypticists and fag-hag feminists whose project was the destruction of the legitimate canon in higher education? He spoke from his seat without waiting for the moderator to recognize him: "What makes you think we have even reached the point of Baudrillardian simulation, much less moved beyond it? Couldn't we all agree that he attributes an absurd degree of power to the media to reconfigure our existence?"

"Baudrillard was an essential stage in plotting the trajectory of the decline of literate culture," Vanessa replied, unshaken, "but he has been rendered extinct by the same simulations he has so eloquently named."

"You are an educated lady," he said, and I couldn't tell for certain if he knew how profoundly that word would irritate her. "Surely you don't mean to suggest that the over-publicized results of a ridiculous moment in the history of science have done away that easily with the entire tradition of Western culture?"

"I am not inclined to weep over the demise of Western culture, given its radical phallocentric dispossession of anyone other than white heterosexuals with dicks," Vanessa replied dismissively.

Gasps from the audience. All heads toward Professor Shakespeare.

"Perhaps you should be," he retorted, pausing for effect, "since you have obviously grown one."

The crowd laughed hysterically, but as Vanessa's face seemed to begin glowing with the inner light of eminent intellectual ambush, things got real quiet. I suspect she had encountered this sort of "if-she's-gorgeous-and-smart-*and*-she-knows-stuff-I-don't-know-she-must-be-a-man-in-a-girl-suit" routine before. I thought I could see her entertain and reject the decision to sink to his level of genital defamation. Instead, she simply moved up a few chakras to reply steadily, "And perhaps *you* should be interested in recent advances in simulation, since it is obvious to me that you have the Scarecrow Complex."

"I must apologize," replied Professor Shakespeare. "I've been reading the Bard lately, not one of your Continental darlings. Do explain for those of us who still have respect for great literature what the 'Scarecrow Complex' is."

"It's from *The Wizard of Oz*—that brilliantly prescient techni-color precursor of the postmodern condition. Surely you saw it if indeed you were ever young?" It was this irreconcilable blend of trash culture cool, lit-crit savvy, and lite but lethal scorn that gave Vanessa her special brand of terror. The Professor just stared, not sure what he should do.

"Here's a hint," she teased, and Vanessa began to hum, imitating Ray Bolger's stiff, but endearing movements.

Professor Shakespeare still didn't get it, so Vanessa motioned to the crowd in a "sing along with me" manner.

If I only had a brain! several of the less timid sang the words with her.

The room erupted in laughter. Professor Shakespeare's face turned to stone. The moderator, in a transparently desperate attempt to reestablish normalcy, nearly begged the audience for further questions. She reminded everyone that they still had fifteen minutes left. Was it just me, or had Vanessa's hair risen and writhed—just for a split-second—as she demolished the professor's standing among his students and his peers? It was probably just me.

I attended this convention again the next year. Vanessa was once again holding forth, her captivating radiance undiminished. As she trailed her ducklings from one party to the next, I remarked to myself that "some things never change." Moving up close for a better look, though, I did notice a few differences. The Vamp Goth had cleaned up well, the Pet had been replaced by a Bon Jovi clone, and Grayson, I found out later, had mysteriously dropped out of the doctoral program. But who was that fair-haired, slight young man who was lighting her cigarette? Yes, I thought so, and soon I knew for sure. With noticeably more confidence in his bearing and in his repartee, I saw now it was The Third Male.

SILENCING THE SIREN

There are plenty of men who would like to have "broken" Vanessa, as if she were a filly that would become a danger to mankind—at least that portion corralled within the Ivory Tower—if allowed to go wild. I still overhear comments about her in convention lobbies, bars, and suite parties—academia's equivalents to the men's locker room. They are less jocular than those about Lisa, more like what I imagine they will be about Melody if she stays in academe and perfects her game. Most of these remarks center around how her scholarship is "faddish," how she doesn't really understand the theorists whose names she drops, and—only occasionally—how one of them bested her in scholarly disputation, preferably in front of an audience. For the most part, though, these men cling to their ships' staff, knowing the fatal allure of her voice.

Having since gotten to know Vanessa a little, I have seen how hard she works. She is a genuine scholar, who reads voraciously and writes prolifically. She is not shallow—indeed, her depth of knowledge rivals that of the most influential scholars in several fields. She takes a "trendy" turn, it seems to me, more because she *can* rather than because she has to. She plays with the latest intellectual fads like she plays with men when she senses their fear. But she is also capable of genuine empathy, and of helping younger scholars to make their mark.

Often there are knowing looks and winks about Vanessa's beauty, although these are more belittling than appreciative—attributing seductiveness to *her* and disowning their own desires. Except, of course, when a fantasy of domination erupts ("What that woman needs is to be beaten at her own pretentious game"). Polly Young-Eisendrath notes that a man often experiences a woman's beauty as a humiliating trick: "'She knows she's looking really good' and . . . she wants to 'use that and flaunt it.'" He is trapped in a double-bind pervasive in male-dominated societies since the ancient Greeks—namely, that he can't trust a beautiful woman, but if he does not want to dominate her sexually he won't be trusted by other men.[15] In fact, he'll be taken for gay. If this is true, then heterosexual men must entertain such fantasies of intellectual/sexual rape or they cannot bond with each other.

Beautiful women in academia are frequently assumed to be

Pandoras.[16] You probably know Pandora as the empty-headed but seductive curse of mankind whose curiosity led her to open her box full of evils, leaving only hope shut tightly inside. Like many of the myths we have been considering, this one is a patriarchal desecration. Robert Graves calls Hesiod's tale, the one with which we are familiar, "an anti-feminist fable," for Pandora originally meant "all-giving" and was the Earth-goddess Rhea.[17] Pandora's vessel was not a "box" but a honey-vase or Cornucopia, an ancient womb symbol of death and rebirth. Her vase, or earthen jar, became Pandora's Box only late in the medieval period, when Erasmus mistakenly translated *pithos*, or vase, as *pyxis*, or box.[18]

In academia, beautiful women who are assumed to be "trivial" and "empty-headed," like Hesiod's Pandora, are not particular threats. They can simply be dismissed, literally or figuratively. But a woman who breaks the Pandora mold by being *both* beautiful and smart must be ostracized or intellectually beaten because she becomes a Siren, and such a woman is infinitely more dangerous than a Pandora. This is, I believe, what many men want to do with Vanessa, although their wish remains unfulfilled because she seems just too smart to be "broken." It was also men's fantasies about Catherine. This time, they won.

~

I got to know Catherine when we were both graduate students at the same university. Catherine immediately stood out from the other PhD candidates not only because of her formidable IQ and previous training with important theorists at European universities but also because of her age (44) and class (upper). A mother of four, Catherine came from New England's "landed gentry," her family having both political connections and money; it always seemed to me she should have known the Kennedy's, although I don't believe she did. Her husband was a prominent cardiologist, and she was on the boards of several charitable and community foundations. They both circulated with a Hollywood crowd. She was quite lovely in an assured and aristocratic way. Her salon-styled haircut was always perfect, even when playing in a faculty/grad student softball game (which surprised me). She shopped in Milan and Paris for her couture, and I don't believe she'd ever been inside a Wal-Mart.

Catherine could take charge of a classroom even when it was not her own. When she talked, people listened. She once arranged for the governor to address a disciplinary event, and of course she introduced him. She could, and did, enter into the ritual of jokes, storytelling, and witticisms that typically put men at center stage in informal academic gatherings. I marveled at her ability to wrest the spotlight even from highly skilled and famous men. It was hard for faculty members to keep straight that Catherine was not one of them. That is no doubt how she got appointed to things like faculty search committees rather than the student government's lecture series committee. Professors seemed, at least at first, to learn as much from her as she did from them. Her beauty and worldliness created an aura that made her almost untouchable, as if none of them—or us—could quite measure up.

A few months into her PhD program, Catherine began an affair with a well-known scholar from another department on campus. Catherine didn't seem particularly concerned that people knew. When his writings were debated in seminars, she would often "correct" an interpretation offered by the professor or another student by saying the scholar in question had told her personally what his meaning was. The two didn't bother to arrive and leave separately at faculty functions. It was as easy to tell these two were "together" as it was with Vanessa and Grayson, although the scholar tried hard not to fawn.

One of Catherine's professors told me the story of her independent study with him on "interpersonal communication." After a few weeks of dutifully reading his assignments, she told him "I have an assignment for you." She wanted to take him to a party for Truman Capote, who was just returning from a long lecture tour on college campuses. "*You'll* find out something about interpersonal communication there," she teased, as if what she had learned from him was "academic," and now he was going to get on-the-job training. The evening of the soiree she picked him up near his office in her bronze Mercedes convertible—how she was allowed to drive and park it on our strictly controlled urban campus, he never found out. As they arrived at Capote's house in Beverly Hills, she said to her teacher "Watch carefully. This is what I do."

Catherine circulated among Hollywood's luminaries and rascals with the ease of breeding Jay Gatsby never had. "Robert Blake, John Candy—this is Professor David Smith from USC. David is teaching me about interpersonal communication in informal social settings," she said, her voice implying ever so slightly the irony that she was in charge here. "David, you remember Robert in Truman's *In Cold Blood*, don't you? And John is this fabulous comedian you're going to be hearing a lot more from soon."

"She would introduce me to a pocket of people, say something interesting about each one, drop all our names about five times so I wouldn't forget, and then disappear to let us get to know each other," the professor explained. "Then she'd come back for me and do it again with another pocket until I knew everyone there. It was like I was a tray of hors d'oeuvres she was passing around to her friends."

"Robert Blake—you mean Baretta?" I queried. "What was he like?"

"He just glared at me as if I were not from Planet Hollywood," the professor remembered. "He had a . . . how shall we put it, a 'manly' odor."

During the evening, the professor spoke with Alice Cooper, in full make-up; Joanna Carson, a very nice ex-wife of Johnny; and Eileen Brennan, "reclusive, but smart." He got to hug Truman Capote, who "felt like a sweaty bowl of Jell-O," and who was tired from his trip, but gracious, and to listen to Alan Carr hold forth for hours with brilliant, biting humor about making movies. Meanwhile, Catherine circulated deftly, flirting with the men just enough to get them to reveal something interesting enough to put in her independent study paper, but not so they'd consider it an invitation. She had already conquered Hollywood and seemed more interested, the professor thought, in the academic game.

"Did you enter into the repartee?" I asked the professor.

"No. I couldn't compete with whatever Carr was on. But Catherine could. As everybody else got drunk and sloppy, she just got more focused. I've never forgotten that. I thought I was pretty good at party skills, but I wasn't even in her league." As Catherine dropped the professor off at his home, she touched his knee ever so briefly and said, "So, David. Now do you see how it's done?"

Within just a few more months, Catherine had begun another affair, this time with an even more famous scholar from another part of the country who she met at a conference. Given that she seemed even more eager to plant "news leaks" about this one, her first scholar/lover looked hurt and confused. However, he did not drop her nor she him; rather, he seemed more determined than ever to escort her to social functions and disciplinary events, as if she were an elegant prize, and he was holding his own with her more-celebrated paramour.

By the time Catherine began her third affair—this time with one of the pillars of a different discipline from another university—the first scholar/lover finally got mad and began an informal defamation league. I heard him call her a "star-fucker," and imply one of those stars was "Governor Moonbeam." Catherine didn't hear this, but it did get back to her, as such things will. She apparently decided to exclude him from her favors, although not (in a rare but egregious error) from her comprehensive exam committee. Catherine's standing within her interdisciplinary milieu appeared to turn a corner, as the rumor about her amorous adventures lost the flavor of distant veneration, and other men figured she wasn't untouchable after all.

Professor Smith sat on Catherine's orals, although he was not her chair. Catherine's scorned lover had combed her written answers for flaws, and apparently found some. When she was out of the room at the beginning so the interrogators could talk about her, he pronounced her answers "facile, but lacking in depth." When she was called back in, he posed the first question. It was, according to Professor Smith, who wasn't exactly gender-sensitive, "a nut-cruncher." Catherine began to answer with her usual unruffled aplomb, but as the scorned lover followed up with cross-examination, "she cratered." This created an opening for her other examiners, one female and the others male, who seemed to enjoy it that Catherine was finally getting her come-uppance. Her own star tarnished now, according to the professor, her teachers were finally able to retaliate against her for making them feel inferior to her in ways they couldn't quite articulate.

During the course of the two hours, Catherine tried several times to recover, but she eventually went virtually mute. "It wasn't pretty," Professor Smith said. "She just sat there twisting her hair. She was fighting back tears—which proved she was a 'chick' after all. That's a cardinal sin in academia."

"Yes, I know," I replied, thinking of Tom Hanks, and of Shandra crying when her professor said she wasn't confrontational enough for academia.

Catherine's committee dictated that she rewrite her exams and take another orals during the next semester. Professor Smith, who still valued Catherine's talents, both academic and interpersonal, tried to revive her interest in finishing her PhD.

"What happened to her after that?" I asked.

"She never took the exams or wrote her dissertation," he answered, "and she avoided my notes and phone calls. I think her academic spirit was broken. I heard she went back to her charitable foundations and began work on a political campaign."

Just as the Siren is alluring to men, *being* one holds some allure for women. At least the Siren is not a passive recipient of Pygmalion's designs on her development; she may have real power of her own—to charm, to distract, to disarm. But I have termed the Siren's call to women a "fatal attraction," for playing this card does not always turn out well. There are not that many Vanessa's in the academic world, who can hang on to their intellectual prowess despite men's desires to bend them. Even if they do exercise such power, they must be ever watchful of attack, for men may want to dominate them and women are often jealous of them. The price for such hegemony might well be isolation from others, both women and men. And those who are not as skilled as Vanessa, as we have seen, may lose more than they gain from their abilities to enchant.

Odysseus and his men successfully navigated the waters through Siren Land, resisting the sweet song that promised them foreknowledge of all future happenings on earth. "Thus the ship sailed by in safety, and the Sirens committed suicide for vexation."[19] After many more trials, Odysseus eventually reached Ithaca.

CHAPTER 7

VEILED WOMAN

> Neither [wives] of [seignors] nor [widows] nor [Assyrian women] who go out on the street may have their heads uncovered. The daughters of a seignoir . . . whether it is a shawl or a robe or [a mantle], must veil themselves . . . when they go out on the street alone, they must veil themselves. A concubine who goes out on the street with her mistress must veil herself. A sacred prostitute whom a man married must veil herself on the street, but one whom a man did not marry must have her head uncovered on the street; she must not veil herself. A harlot must not veil herself: her head must be uncovered. . . .
>
> Middle Assyrian Law ʃ40,
> 15th–11th century B.C.

Mrs. Wilson had a clever means of crowd control in her first-grade homeroom. She told each of us to find a magazine picture that looked like us, paste it to a piece of cardboard, and cut around the reinforced figure. We deposited our little self-images on the chalk tray, standing at attention against the blackboard in a motley row of paper soldiers. When any one of us was "bad," Mrs. Wilson turned our picture around so that it couldn't be seen. Whereas this happened routinely to the other children, once was enough for me. My offense was talking to the girl at the next desk. Thoroughly disgraced with one quick movement of Mrs. Wilson's hand, I vowed then and there never to speak out of turn again. I would be perfect. The teachers would reward me. I would not lose my face. After that, I was always picked first for being the stillest kid in the great teacher's ruse called "the quiet game."

Like a bud to the blossom, this first-grade episode contained the rest of my academic career as if it were compressed between the pages of a forgotten book. Eventually I learned to cloak my exuberance so as to be acceptable in school. But first I was allowed to fully flower. For most of elementary school, my peers and I were uninhibitedly "colorful."

Mrs. Todd's third-grade classroom was, in fact, a riot of color—so different from my current office's white concrete blocks, upon which I have foolishly wasted many a picture hanger. Every week our artwork adorned the walls until no vacant space prevailed. I'm not sure why it's the paper Pilgrims at Thanksgiving that remain in my memory bank, but there they are. We drew flowers and birds on our spelling papers with 64-count boxes of Crayolas, and an arithmetic paper with no tulips (by the girls) or monsters (by the boys) was rare. Here I learned that play and imagination—even decoration—were good things, and that they could accompany academic learning *on the same page.*

By junior high, all this excess was pretty much squelched, or at least moved out of the classroom and into "extracurricular activities." By graduate school it was downright eradicated. I clearly recall the definitive moment. Having been a speech major as an undergraduate, I had learned that you get the audience's attention before you hit them with your three main points. In Monroe's "Motivated Sequence," a standard textbook recipe for making a good speech, this is called the attention step, and it requires your snappiest material (a joke, a quote, a hypothetical example), something that makes them want to hear the rest. So when I wrote my first research paper in a seminar in persuasion, I imagined the professor as my audience and devoted my best efforts to the first paragraph. He liked my research well enough, but the essay came back with the entire first paragraph crossed out in heavy red ink, and these words written boldly in the margin:

JANICE: IN GRADUATE SCHOOL, WE DO *NOT* DO ATTENTION STEPS!

I can now publish refereed journal articles with the best of them. There are exciting exceptions, but these meat-and-potatoes basics of academic scholarship are what I read in the middle of the night when my insomnia kicks in, because I've heard that you can put yourself to sleep by doing something "mildly obnoxious." The trick is to avoid an activity that is too pleasant, which will reward your overworked brain for not sleeping (like eating chocolate) as well as one that is too odious, which will make you stew about not wanting to do it (like paying bills). If you choose the middle ground of something only slightly boring, your resistant unconscious decides that sleep is a good deal after all.

Perhaps you are thinking, with St. Paul, that of course "when I became a [wo]man I put away childish things"—maybe even that it is a cliché to lament the inevitable exchange of childhood's fancy for adult reason. But this loss of colorfulness is relevant to the burial of the feminine below the academy, which links "playful," "spontaneous," "childish," "decorative," "embodied," "sexual," and "trivial" to "feminine." We have already seen how the male-identified Brainchild avoids the Mother in order to be accepted. Female-identified women fare worse: Pandora is deemed an empty-headed curse, and the Siren is ostracized or destroyed. Thus, most women who wish to be successful in academia learn early to hide or to disguise their femininity. The more they associate their truest selves with things feminine, the more they must go "under the veil" to get along.

The veil has long been a prop of feminine roles. One would be hard-pressed to think of a man wearing one, but many feminine images come to mind: the bridal veil, the nun's veil, the female mourner's veil, the femme fatale's dark veil, the Saudi Arabian *abaya*, the Afghani *burqa*. For the most part, however, the veil is a male invention. This chapter is about the ways a metaphoric veil is imposed upon academic women, and how they disappear behind it, losing voice and sight. They may also choose it themselves for purposes of disguise and seduction. As you may have come to expect, we'll take a look at how the veil originated—first in history, and later as it plays out in mythology.

IMPOSING THE VEIL

In *The Creation of Patriarchy*, Gerda Lerner finds the origins of veiling in the neo-Babylonian period during the reign of Hammurabi (1792–1750 B.C.). A law dictated the death penalty for a certain class of temple priestesses, or cultic sexual servants, who entered or ran an "ale house," or brothel. This law implies that the commercial prostitution flourishing around the temple may have encouraged a moral laxity among the temple servants: priestesses keeping temple donations for themselves, and priests using slave women as commercial prostitutes in order to enrich the temple. In addition, women of the propertied class were increasingly regulated sexually, and the virginity of their daughters became a financial asset to the family. Commercial prostitution, then, became more of a "social necessity" for meeting the needs of men. "What remained problematic was how to distinguish clearly and permanently between respectable and non-respectable women."[1]

Middle Assyrian Law ∫40, which opens this chapter, is probably representative of regulations in other Mesopotamian societies. The practice it dictates, marking the respectable woman as one who wears the veil and the non-respectable one as going without, has been ubiquitous and lasted for many millennia into the present. It is based clearly on women's sexual activities. "Domestic women, sexually serving one man and under his protection, are here designated as 'respectable' by being veiled," writes Lerner, and "women not under one man's protection and sexual control are designated as 'public women,' hence unveiled." The punishment for a woman breaking the law or for a man failing to report an infraction was severe.[2]

Since September 11, 2001, media coverage has made the Western world increasingly aware that similar practices and punishments are still in effect in some parts of the world. For viewers of *Inside Afghanistan: Behind the Veil,* an undercover documentary about the Taliban shown on CNN, it is impossible to forget the filmed footage of a woman who cannot be seen beneath her heavy veil being dragged to the center of a Kabul football stadium and shot to death, to the cheers of the crowd. Saira Sha, the British reporter who wore an Afghan veil and used a hidden camera to film life among the Taliban for this documentary, reported that the *burqa* was so thick it was difficult to breathe, and if she tripped and exposed her ankle she could be arrested. She found women risking arrest in underground beauty parlors where they lacquered their nails and painted their faces, defiantly preserving their femininity even underneath their robes, and risking their lives to hold schools for girls.[3] Many of us in the West rejoiced with these women when we saw the press photographs of them burning their *burqas* in jubilant celebration at the ousting of the Taliban.

I do not mean to suggest that the metaphorical veils worn by some women in Western academies can in any way be compared in severity to those worn by women under oppressive political regimes. Once she knows she is "wearing" one, a Western woman may remove it without fear of violence. But the historical origins of veiling in sexual ownership are, I think, still relevant. A woman who is bound in a "dark marriage" to the academy as a masculine institution is likely to "veil" her femininity, whether merely playful and decorative, or more overtly embodied and sexual. She remains respectable by hiding that which is threatening to the patriarchal order. The woman who is more detached displays herself freely without the disguise of a veil. Although she may or may not be sexually available to men, the woman who reveals her femininity is not wedded unaware to a "husband" she cannot see. She is, then, a "public woman" who may be heard and seen outside the confines of a "private" arrangement.

In some senses, the veil is imposed on everyone within the academy, in that traces of the feminine have long been embattled in scholarly language and thought. With a background in rhetoric, I am familiar with one source of the trouble. In ancient Greece and Rome rhetoric was oral persuasion, which later expanded into written composition and eventually mediated communication. The early theorists of rhetoric—Plato and Aristotle in Greece and, later, Cicero in Rome—wanted to extract the art of communicating from the oral tradition of Homer and the poets, which in their view insufficiently distinguished between abstract thought and storytelling allure. Enchanted by the beautiful speech of the bards (or we might say, "charmed" by the sweet song of the Sirens), a crowd could not think clearly or act reasonably.[4] For Plato, both rhetoric and poetics, arts that imitated appearances in the world, and which were themselves imitations of the unchanging Ideas in the mind of God, were ethically suspect, being "twice removed from the Truth."[5]

In the *Rhetoric*, a book which was to set the course for the study and practice of speech for two-and-a-half millennia, Aristotle reclaimed rhetoric from the unethical, but separated argument from style, and logic from emotion, seeing linguistic figures and emotional appeals as important for persuasive purposes but clearly secondary to rational thought. Thus was born a tendency to view metaphor and appealing language as ornamentation, a sort of decorative dress covering the foundational body of reason—necessary because audiences are not persuaded by logical thinking alone—but not really fundamental.[6]

Through a searching historical index of the influence of Aristotle on the theory of rhetoric, Jane Sutton argues that rhetorical "figuration" gets imagined henceforth as an untamed "horse," a wild and feminine beast that must be corralled within the pen of a more masculine philosophy. That which is free and in flux must be yoked to that which is pure and unchanging.[7] Is it any wonder, then, that we find this passage within the section on "Linguistic Devices" in the American Psychological Association style manual that is widely used today by scholars in many disciplines?

> Devices that attract attention to words, sounds, or other embellishments instead of to ideas are inappropriate in scientific writing. Avoid heavy alliteration, rhyming, poetic expressions, and clichés. Use metaphors sparingly; although they can help simplify complicated ideas, metaphors can be distracting. . . . Use figurative expressions with restraint and colorful expressions with care; these expressions can sound strained or forced.[8]

When my professor outlawed the "attention step" in my paper on persuasion, he was just doing his job within the academy, excising the "colorful expressions" that didn't fit the scholarly mold.

When I say that a veil is imposed on us all at the university, then, I mean, not the ornamental "covering" of "feminine" language and style, but exactly the opposite. It is the masculine-decreed cloak that contains the trivial or wild "feminine" in women and men within acceptable boundaries so that thought may remain unsullied. For a woman married in the dark to an academic groom, this is, then, a *bridal veil* that marks her for "one man" and makes her respectable.

DONNING THE VEIL

I have implied that I learned to "take the veil" progressively in school—that it pretty well checked my grade-school freedom by the time I got to graduate school, although I sometimes let it slip to the side. As a good Brainchild, I wanted so badly to be respected among the people who "count" in my field—most of whom are men—that I labored long and hard to express my thoughts about such things as myths and movies in arduously constructed arguments I thought my detractors could not penetrate. My essays were girdled by pages of heavily cited theoretical substructure before I even got to the film I was interpreting. An essay I wrote on *E.T. the Extra-terrestrial* began with one of my momentous argumentative foundations.[9] Although I winced, I also had to laugh at a line in a review written by one of those men I tried to impress, who was also a good friend who wanted me to succeed: "Repeat after me," he wrote. *"It's only a movie!"* Still, I continued to thicken my veil of language and thought until even *I* was hard pressed to penetrate it when re-reading my own articles years later.

The desire to gain respectability by meeting the standards of patriarchal language and custom is also very strong among women with whom I talked. In one sense, we can say that women don the veil voluntarily in order to hide their too-feminine aspects. But the standards we try to meet are so synonymous with academia that we seldom identify them as masculine—they are just "the way things are" in academia if we want to succeed. It would be misleading to say that hiding behind the veil is completely willed; sometimes we are not really aware that is what we are doing.

Sophia, however, was unusually aware of the standards for writing and speaking in academia. They also troubled her, as she wanted as much as I did to meet them, yet she knew this would require compromising her own voice, which she considered more feminine than those of most successful academicians. Sophia had just been promoted to professor. She was a riveting teacher in an out-of-the-way college. With an eccentric and somewhat outrageous sense of humor, she wasn't everybody's cup of tea, but she could turn a terminally bored student into an evangelistic major and a skeptical colleague into a crusading advocate for her financially besieged department. She had developed a fascinating line of research in a characteristically off-to-the-side but important subject. She passionately promoted feminist issues, and thought carefully about women's place in the academy. I had, in fact, known her for a long time, and although she did not use the metaphor, her struggles with the veil continue to shape my thoughts about it as much as anyone.

Sophia was on a rare visit to my part of the country, and was able to come to my home for several hours of engrossing talks.

"What do you love about academia?" I asked her, as she dug into a half-gallon of chocolate mint ice cream she had liberated from my freezer. I could never figure out how she did this and stayed so slim; it must have been the triathlon races in which she still competed.

"Talking ideas," she said, with no hesitation. "That's the most exciting thing in the world. My dad was an engineer, and my mom stayed home and cooked. I thought, wow, my dad's life is so interesting and my mom's is so boring. So I became fascinated with that world, and I loved that freedom—ideas, people, places to go, just a big draw. My mother didn't like it at all. She expected me to watch soap operas with her, but I'd just go up to my room and study. At some level my mother's proud of me, but she sees my life as a repudiation of her, and in some ways it is."

"Is there any loss there, or is it good riddance?" I asked, picturing Sophia doing a hilarious rap to her feminism-innocent mom on how soap operas rot your brain.

"I don't regret it, but there is a loss in terms of time spent to develop a home. I'm interested in it, but I don't have time. I connect with creating things— gardening, growing herbs . . ."

"What are the worst parts of academia for you?"

She thought about this a bit longer than usual. "I do want to get published by a big university press. But it's so hard. You have to give up a lot. Sometimes I have a lot of doubts whether I can do it—whether I have the skills. What makes it so rough is that you have to fit in a certain mold, the way you're supposed to write."

"What do you mean?" I asked, although I had an idea of what bothered her.

"I find that very painful because I can't be true to myself," Sophia answered. "The journal form is very depressing at times. All the people you have to cite. Books require that too, at least in the introduction. You have to satisfy an editor and reviewers. What attracted me to the academic life is that it's so freethinking and intellectual, but really it's all about continuing what someone else said, tagging on and into a continuing conversation."

There being nothing left in the ice cream carton, Sophia put down her spoon and assumed something like the lotus position.

"The academic mode of writing isn't very metaphorical, like I am. It's kind of a tunnel—not layers opening up, like a rose. I'm not so sure that I'll stay in this mode. I don't know if I can keep living my life this way."

"What bothers you so much about this 'academic mode'?" I probed.

"You have to set up a space to show they're inadequate," she said, "but many times what you have to do is contrived in order to make your entry into the battle. It seems unfair to me. I think the classic case is when Aristotle opens up his books by criticizing what came before. I mean, why not a dialogue?"

"But it's still important to you to get this book done, and with a prestigious press. Why?"

"I'm not sure I want to know," Sophia smiled self-mockingly. "But I think part of it is, that's what men do, and also a part of it is about if you want your position to be legitimate, you have to have that kind of foundation. Or, is it about being one of the boys? I don't know."

We traded memories of failed attempts at being "one of the boys." After listening to my earnest explanation of why myth was so crucial for understanding the state of American values, a colleague of mine once patted me on the head. It reminded me of that time-honored dismissal: "You're so cute when you're mad!"

"I have so much anger at that," Sophia commiserated. "Pretty much that's what people like Jeff [a well-known theorist in her field] would do. 'Go do your quaint thing, Sophie. Go do your trivialities.'"

"Do you usually lash out or retreat?" I wanted to know, realizing that I'd never seen her angrily confront an inquisitor, despite her fiery energy.

"Retreat. I've been trying to get in touch with where my rage comes from. How come I'm so damn pissed at Aristotle?"

"Well, maybe if you decide you like Aristotle, you'd have to go after the real boys that are out there now."

"The real motherfuckers!" she cried.

"That isn't very metaphorical of you."

"Yeah, it is," she replied, and we laughed so hard we had to get two Coronas before we could go on.

~

Like many others, Sophia was torn between wearing the veil of masculinized tradition and trying to remove it. Mostly, she tried to make it fit her and was frustrated that it didn't. And she was angry with those she held responsible. Maggie, one of our Maiden Lovers who eventually shed her maidenhood to become a well-regarded scholar, was similarly rankled at the journals of her field, in which she had racked up "more rejections than I can number," for their criticism, not of her essays' content, but their "colorful journalistic style."

"What do you think that means," I queried. "Colorful?"

"Well I would say 'accessible,'" Maggie countered. "'With relative lack of jargon.' 'Clear.'"

"So you mean you worked at being accessible and then you got knocked for it?"

"Yeah. And it really pisses me off! The *meanness* of the reviews, the need for a reviewer to inflate himself—if you'll forgive the image—by beating down someone else and forgetting that there's a real human being behind this. They've written this, and they care about it. And I think that is part of the patriarchal learning patterns, the patriarchal knowledge structure—'we are the priests of the temple' and . . . . "

"We gotta keep that fire going," I continued.

"We've got to keep the *heathens* out! And we've got to make sure that we are the ones that make the decisions."

I asked Maggie if she adapted her writing to fit the style that she considered intentionally exclusive. She said that she does some adaptation, but "to some extent I say to hell with the journals, I'll write a book. Because, quite frankly, my university press wants me to be accessible. I select topics in part because I want people to see the world around them in new ways. I want to open doors, and bring people and ideas together." We laughed ruefully at how naive that heartfelt statement of her scholarly mission would sound to a board of editors. Maggie was seriously considering not writing for academia at all any more, but for *American Heritage* or *The Smithsonian*, which, she thought, would appreciate her more narrative and "educational" style.

~

Some women who opted completely out of this linguistic veil or who did not think they wore it successfully were still haunted by it. Earlier I introduced you to Laura, who struggled with the roles of Maiden Lover, Muse, and Mistress before attaining a second PhD and leaving academia for another profession. Although she had published a successful textbook, she did not consider herself an academic writer. Toward the end of our conversations I wanted to know if she had any regrets about that, and her answers helped me understand the attraction of the veil for many.

"Yes," she said. "I wanted to show that I could do it—it's my perfectionist thing. It's hard to know that I'm bright when there's nothing to show for it. I know I'm bright, but it doesn't show. Writing is still the proof of it for me."

"But you were such a great teacher," I pointed out. "And now you're at the top of your field. Is this so strong that it still affects you after you've been out of the system for so long?"

"I think it's because in the academic world writing is what really counts. It's how you get tenure. It's how you get all of the rewards. I can't find the right words for why it's so hard, but it's something to do with shaping your own individual voice—it's like, 'I know this, I claim it, the way I say it is important, I figured it out, this is my idea.'" Laura paused for a minute. "But that's not female-gendered."

"You have to enter the male world to do that," I suggested.

"Right. For somebody like me, and for so many women who are—I'm not stereotypically feminine, but I'm feminine—it's counter to gender."

"What kind of writing is counter to the feminine gender?" I asked.

"Academic writing," Laura declared. "It seems to me that writing that has to do with the personal experience, or something like that, could be deeply feminine."

"Yeah, because it's getting deeply into the life of the person."

"Yes, it's relational. Or oral histories—you know, like Claire Douglas' writings," she reminded me. "That's intensely feminine, yet very scholarly."

"That's true—she really brought it together. There are ways to bring the genders together . . . "

". . . as a writer," Laura finished my sentence. "Her first husband was J.D. Salinger, you know. I'd like that kind of research—where you're finding things out rather than trying to prove things. Research in high school and college meant going to the library and figuring out what there was to learn."

"You didn't have to prove anybody wrong!"

"I loved that," Laura reminisced. "I mean I didn't love all of the last-minute stuff, but it was intriguing—it was like a mystery. It was like archaeology, uncovering layers." I was struck by the similarity of Laura's metaphor to Sophia's—who wanted to let her writing unfold in layers like a rose. Although Sophia tried to meet them and Laura felt guilty that she hadn't, both women disliked the linear demands of scholarly argument—the veil that would mark them as "a respectable woman" within academia.

SHAPE SHIFTING

Along with many other women, both Laura and Sophia were anxious about the inability of their feminine selves to occupy the "masculine space" of academia. Most women I know have only scorn for Freud's notion of penis envy. They don't want to be men, yet they do worry about how their feminine looks or presentational style will affect their success. Many have a vague dis-ease with their bodies and their voices in such a masculine space, like girls who wandered into an Elks Club by mistake. Sophia and I discussed some women we know who have become "like a man" in order to negotiate this space—dressing and speaking to minimize their feminine features, so that their veils became more like armor. We agreed that they are taken more seriously than more "feminine" women, but that they are still not "part of the club."

In 1987 I had a dream I called "Trading Bodies," and although it has a magical quality to it that is far from realistic, its symbols are telling.

> I talk to Megan Carter at school, and I suggest that we trade bodies for awhile. She's not sure this will work, but I think we can. We go into a sort of trance; I slip into her body and she slips into mine. We stay this way for about a week. I perform various tasks at school, including going to a faculty meeting and operating a computer, in her body. I do these things quite well, and get a lot done. I comment on her hair—that it's grown a lot since she cut it recently. Finally, I decide that it's time to get back in our own bodies, and we go back into the trance again and into ourselves.

Megan Carter was a colleague in another department whom I considered both congenial and quite "masculine." She had short-cropped hair and always wore pants and button-down shirts. When she appeared once at a social event in a dress, everyone was shocked. She was matter-of-fact, competent, and practical, showing little emotion or relational finesse. I got along well with her, although she was in most ways my opposite. Her hair grew when she was "me," or when she took on a more feminine persona, and I got more accomplished when I took on her more masculine one. I think the dream is a psychic experiment in getting through my work week in a more masculine disguise—a kind of ultimate veil, in a fantasy sense. It would be easier to operate, the dream suggests, if people couldn't see me as I am.

Sophia seemed haunted by the same fantasy: that things would be easier if she were a man, but she did not want to give up her self. This is still another double-bind that many academic women face: succeed by becoming more masculine while you lose your femininity, or express your femininity and don't succeed. It was not just an issue of scholarship for Sophia, she felt it at a biological level.

"One of the things that scared me about graduate school is that I didn't want to become a man," Sophia told me. "I wanted to be a woman, but at the same time if you're a woman you get dismissed. When I was in graduate school the feminist movement was strong. There were these elemental questions. Can you wear makeup? What kinds of clothes do you wear? I watched this good friend of mine leave graduate school because she wanted to have children, but in academia there's not that kind of space."

"Did you want to have children?" I asked, thinking what an inspired choice of a parent Sophia would be.

"Not in grad school, but now I'm considering it, whereas before I would *never* have considered it. You're haunted—bugged—by these things. These are the things that are sitting on your shoulder. You're not a man."

"Which boils down to you're not good enough?" I asked a more leading question than I should have, remembering the number of women who had expressed this sentiment.

"It's sort of like you don't have any business being here, rather than you're not good enough," Sophia discerned. "Because some of the women are really, really bright, they do better work than, whatever . . . but there's always this sense that your 'business' is elsewhere. You just don't *look* right. I wonder what people would think of my work if they didn't know I was a woman."

Of course, none of us *can* shift our shape into that of a man, at least without benefit of surgery, so we can't know for sure. But several women speculated on what it would mean if they suddenly appeared as a man—in the "ultimate veil."

"GRAB YOUR PARTNER. . ."

Whereas I have never seen a woman actually take the step of becoming a man in order to be respected, many struggle with the notion of partnering their ideas with a man's. This partnership may also be sexual, as we have seen, but sometimes it is simply practical, as described to me by Frances, the 70-year-old president of a university, who was seasoned by her experience in many positions, from assistant professor on up, in various regions of the country.

A friend of mine who serves under her as a dean escorted me into Frances' tenth-floor office. It is one of the few times I can ever remember being so high up in a university—metaphorically or literally—and the only time I ever met a female president. Frances motioned me over to her couch and sat across from me, immediately asking questions about my mythological approach, suggesting materials I should read, and asking me for a reading list. She was enthusiastic and inquisitive, seeming to forget her busy schedule for the time she had devoted to me, and getting caught up in recounting her life in school.

Frances radiated a friendly confidence. Another high-level administrator working for Frances told me "She didn't fit my mold of what a university president was supposed to be. She's not very stately, not very elegant, she's kind of this frumpy lady—you know, her hair's messed up, and her slip's showing. She doesn't have any of the trappings. But she was very disarming. When she came in two years ago, she was just such a breath of fresh air—she didn't have any of that pomposity. She'd just say 'Well, what are we going to do about that?' She was very approachable, very open, really wanted to hear other people's ideas." Everyone else I talked with who worked with Frances confirmed my impression that she was respected and forthright, both on her own campus and in her state-wide university system. Surely this woman, of all those who conversed with me, would not have had any difficulties being taken seriously.

Frances told me several stories, remarking that she realized the problems of being a woman much more after going into administration. She began with an episode that happened at a previous university.

"One day I was talking to my boss and I said, 'You know, I'm beginning to think we ought to drop the graduate records exams for the doctoral programs, and he said—he was always interested in ideas, and I thought I'd be able to bring it up to him—he said, 'That's an interesting idea.' Then a couple of days later he said, 'You know, I have an interesting idea, what would you think if we dropped the GREs?' He had literally, totally forgotten that it came from me and it was not his idea!"

"This has happened to me and to other women I know so often I even named it. I call it the Reduplication Strategy," I said.

"Yeah, it happens a *lot*," Frances indicated.

"So you mean it happens even at your level?"

"Yes, I even have trouble getting called on in my group—the presidents of the university system. It's become sort of a joke," Frances replied.

"Do you have to be especially assertive to get your ideas across?" I asked.

"Well, you have to be careful about that, because if you push too obviously, it becomes a weapon that can be used against you," Frances answered. "I'm not interested in the personal stuff because—obviously, I would love the recognition, but sometimes I have an issue I really need to get attention on. And I feel that I can't do that by myself, by just pounding, pounding, pounding. I have to find other ways. I have to find partners."

"A male partner?" I asked. "If you find a male partner do you just let him present your ideas?"

"Well, by that time it becomes ours, so . . . who cares? It's all a game. I play the game. I say to myself, why are you doing this, is it for personal aggrandizement? Sure, I wouldn't mind—in many instances I wouldn't mind a bit—but I remind myself, what am I doing this for?" She also frequently partnered with a male directly below her in rank. "We make a great team," she said, indicating that people pay more attention to her ideas when she presents them with him.

Even this highly regarded woman, obviously at the top of her "game," considered it advantageous to don the veil of a male partner from time to time, burying her need for personal recognition in order to get her job done.

Sophia refused to form such a public partnership with a man, though there were several in her field she considered close intellectual colleagues.

"I think that I have purposely avoided co-authoring with Nick, as much as I admire him," she said when I asked her why she always wrote by herself. "I've worked on my separate identity. It's not the same with Nick and Angelo," she pondered, referring to good friends who often write together. "When a woman gets next to a man, her identity gets collapsed into his."

I thought back to the early years of my own writing partnership with Tom, when people in the audience at conventions would frequently refer to our co-authored publications as "Tom's work," directing their questions to him. We have been publishing together now for a quarter-century, trading off first authorship, and I still see citations of work in which I was the senior author printed in reference lists with his name first.

VEILS OF SEPARATION

I asked Sophia if she ever considered partnering with a woman. She thought back to a stint she had as a visiting professor at a prestigious university with a large department in her field. I wasn't sure why she was talking about this instead of answering my question, but I went with it anyway.

"It was very exciting," she remembered. "On the other hand, it was lonely. I have to work really hard to develop relationships with women outside of academia, because it's such a different world, and so many other women have children. The idea of two women sitting around talking about theory is really a hard concept. But at the same time it's hard connecting with men. So, it's like, where am I?"

"Has that feeling changed over time?" I wondered. It had been several years since she had worked at the other university.

"No, in some ways it's intensified because I find it hard to develop relationships with academic women. The men have this kind of network, but the women are not organized, they don't have that kind of unity, or community."

"Why not?" I asked, taking her at her word.

"I think it's because women don't have the time. They still have to do housekeeping. . . . You can go down to the bar and see tables of men—the Big Guns, as they call themselves, having a drink, but you don't see tables of women," Sophia said. "Or if you consider, for example, my relationship with Tina [a prominent scholar with whom Sophia has much in common intellectually], she doesn't work at the relationship. I think academic women need each other, but we have a hard time."

Certainly not all women with whom I spoke felt this way about other women in academia, but many did. As one woman put it, "I have virtually no female friends in academia. I meet as much as I can with women on the outside who can be supportive and give me perspective on what I am going through."

Lerner considers how the practice of veiling has impacted not only women's position in relation to men but also their relation to each other. Men take their place in the class hierarchy based on their occupations or their father's social status. Women's class distinctions, from MAL ∫40 forward, are based on their relationship or absence of it to a man who protects them and regulates their sexual activities. The distinction between "respectable women," who are protected by men, and "disreputable women," who are out on the street and free to sell their services, has been the basic class division for women. "Historically, it [veiling] has impeded cross-class alliances among women and obstructed the formation of feminist consciousness."[10]

Certainly, the feminist movements in the West and beyond have worked hard to change this lack of consciousness. But it is worth noting the extent to which men in academia still depend on "their father's social status"—that is, the prestige of their mentors. Do women, lacking such status based on female mentors, and depending instead on male mentors who protect them or on the masculine institution to which they show fealty, sacrifice hierarchy for "respectability"? And does this veil of "respectability" (as opposed to "respect") inhibit their relationships with each other? For to cross hierarchical lines that provide male protection might be to lose that protection in exchange for affiliation with women—and for some, perhaps the freedom that transgression allows is not worth the disrepute it might imply.

LOSING ONE'S TONGUE AND EYES

The consequences of wearing the patriarchal veil can cut deep—not only into a woman's relationships with other women but also into her sense of self. I introduced "The Handless Maiden" in the Brainchild chapter, and it continues to be relevant here. This fairytale symbolizes the cutting off of self in a curious and graphic way. If you remember, the maiden lost her hands when the Devil demanded that her father cut them off because her tears were washing them clean, preventing him from taking her away. As we left her, the benevolent king she married fashioned silver hands for her until her own could grow back.

But the Devil kept at her, not satisfied with the sacrifice of only her hands. The king went off to wage war in a foreign land, as husbands in such tales often do, leaving his bride to the care of his mother. The young queen gave birth to a healthy babe and the king's mother sent a messenger to tell him the good news. The Devil was, of course, lurking in the forest, and through an exchange of distorted messages, told the mother that the king ordered her to kill his bride and her child, and to "keep the tongue and eyes of the queen to prove she has been killed." The old mother refused to obey, killing a doe and hiding away its tongue and eyes instead. Then she helped the young queen bind her babe to her breast, veiled her, and bade her flee for her life. Thus commenced another period of wandering and descent before the king and queen were finally reunited and had many more children.[11]

As Clarissa Estes observes, the Devil here "symbolizes anything that corrupts understanding of the deep feminine processes."[12] Surely, to don a veil unconsciously or compulsively decreed by a patriarchal system is to hide one's deepest feminine being from others, and often from oneself. But why does this predator demand specifically her *tongue and eyes* as proof she is dead? "Here we already have a maiden without worldly grasp, without hands, for the Devil ordered these cut off," writes Estes. "Now he demands further amputations. He wants her now also without true speaking and without true sight as well."[13]

This mutilation motif seems both horrific and archaic to modern women, particularly those with a developed feminist consciousness. But the talk and dreams of women who have "taken the veil" of academe—and most of those I spoke with would call themselves feminists—refer often to the loss of voice and the failure of sight. Usually, they are interrelated; a woman loses one along with the other. Let us see how women imagine these things, before we turn to the next motif in the fairytale, in which the maiden veils herself to wander again.

Sophia, as should be clear by now, was distressed that the "male space" of academia left little room for her and other women to express their femininity. Yet she kept trying to wear the veil, to make it fit. As our conversation went on, some poignant images emerged that illustrated how this bind affected her sight and voice.

"What are some of the characteristics that define a male space?" I continued. "Do you feel excluded from that?"

"Very. Very excluded from that." Sophia's voice was now more sad than mad. "Not long ago I was on a panel with Nick, and he told Jeff, 'I have this student and he should study with you.' This student is at *my university*, but the men don't think of saying 'You ought to study with *her*.'"

Sophia shared a feeling many women had—that unless they did something outrageous or threatening—became a "non-respectable woman," for example—they were often invisible within academia. The motif of losing one's eyes, seen not only in "The Handless Maiden" but also in many other myths (Oedipus comes to mind), most directly refers to one's own loss of "vision" or consciousness. But this loss can itself be induced by a feeling that the woman is invisible—that *others* cannot see her for who she is. If she internalizes her own erasure from the professional screen, or comes to see herself as others do, then her sight is indeed impaired. She cannot see the jewel in her soul, and comes to devalue herself.

Claire Douglas subtitled her account of Christiana Morgan "The Veiled Woman in Jung's Circle." As this suggests, Morgan was shrouded from sight through her "sexual ownership" by Harry Murray and others. Although she fought valiantly against it, her bridal veil ultimately kept her from being the "public woman" she would have been without it. She could not be seen in the same way that Jung or Murray could be and, as we discovered, her positive view of herself did not survive.

~

Frances had a very good sense of herself, it seemed to me and to others. Still, even as the president of her university, she felt this same sense of not being seen. I asked her if she thought her ideas were taken seriously when she was able to get them heard.

"Sometimes," she said, "but very often not," and she gave me several examples. When I again expressed incredulity that she would not be taken seriously even in such a high position, she said "Let me give you another example.

"When I was the chancellor at another university, I was the only woman on a council dealing with economic development who attended the meetings. I was the only woman in this very large conference room except for a staff director (an attorney) who was taking minutes. I was sitting on one side and she was sitting on the other. They had a speaker there who was not a member of the council. He got up and addressed the group and said, 'Now, gentlemen . . . ' We were invisible, we were *invisible!* Since she was a staff person, he probably figured I was, too. He didn't know who I was."

Laura related what she called a "disappearing act" that occurred when she moved to a new job in the same department with a man she would later marry.

"The faculty knew that Scott and I would probably be together when I was hired here," she told me. "But that thing-that-happens-with-women happened. About three to four years later I had been promoted and we were interviewing someone. We were at a restaurant, and John (the chairperson) started telling the story of my coming there, and he told how they worked it out so that I could get a job in the town where Scott lived. What actually happened is that 103 people applied for my job. I was clearly their top choice—nobody wanted anybody else. John forgot and revised history as though they worked it out to do something nice for Scott, when I was ranked before they knew anything about us.

"I confronted him about it the next day," Laura reminisced. "I regret that I lost it. I started crying. I tried to get him to understand what he'd done and how I felt. And he didn't get it. I know I really exposed my self to a person who didn't understand. He wasn't trying to be cruel, he just didn't understand. I regret that I did that. But it hurt."

"Did anybody else pick up on it?" I asked.

"No one. I needed a career that had nothing to do with men. That's why I got the second PhD. I needed a career of my own."

Laura did not don the academic veil completely, as she did not become the academic writer she thinks she should have been. Still, she internalized others' perceptions of her own effacement, in which she lost both her voice and her visibility.

"I have an intricate variety of dreams in which I'm trying to say something and people have their backs turned to me, or they're seated where they can't see me or I'm talking but I can't be heard. I'm in a room and I seem to be invisible. There is just a variety of disappearing acts."

~

Sophia's dream rather astonishingly recapitulates both Laura's and the Handless Maiden's dismemberment. I asked her: "How do you feel when you're at conventions, at formal and informal groups, and people start talking about ideas—at a bar or in a hotel room, or after a panel? Do you feel that you can enter in?"

"The men will go off and talk, and once in awhile they'll include me," Sophia said. "But . . . I had this dream. I had heard a paper presented which asserted that, in the Hippocratic corpus, there are a lot of stories about women getting sick because they can't speak. They lost their voices. In my dream I'm sitting in a convention meeting room and on my lap is my tongue—it's just lying there. In Ovid's *Metamorphosis*, there's a story about a woman who gets her tongue cut out, and it lies there on the floor and is just whimpering. It's an ugly image, isn't it?"

It is distressing, I agreed. But Sophia's image is also tender, for she is holding her tongue in her lap, cradling it like a child. It made me think again of Ada in *The Piano*, who had refused to speak since she was six, perhaps in reaction to untold injuries, but also as a response to the patriarchal system that let her travel to a foreign country and be married to a man she had never met. She kept her voice alive, however, in the music she played on her beloved piano. Sophia may have been treating her voice like the newborn babe that the old mother bound to the maiden's breast to keep it safe for her final descent.

"What is it that personally feels so bad to you that you'd feel like your tongue is cut out?" I asked gently.

"The lack of response. It's almost a feeling that you're tolerated, you're 'put up with.' But they're not interested in what you have to say. It's the same thing, for example, with Maud Gonne and William Butler Yeats. If you talk about her, people want to know about Yeats. Can you see her without Yeats? Or Simone de Beauvoir and Sartre. I think *The Second Sex* is far more interesting than his works. I think probably men admire Simone de Beauvoir, *but it doesn't impact what they do.*"

~

The laments of Sophia, Frances, and Laura about their invisibility and loss of voice are echoed by scholarship showing that the increased participation of women in public life does not necessarily equate with increased influence. In her forthcoming book *Women in the House of Speech,* Jane Sutton uses the veil as a symbol of this contradiction. She tells the story of Lt. Col. Martha McSally, the highest-ranking female fighter pilot in the United States Air Force as of January 2002, who is required to wear a Muslim-style *abaya* when at the military base in Saudi Arabia. Her male counterparts do not have to wear the garb of Muslim men, and the wives of American dignitaries do not have to wear the head-to-toe robes. Her heavy veil does not exclude her from speaking—she is included in decision-making discussions and is invested with a position of power. But the *abaya* worn over the military uniform signifying her authority excludes her from being *seen* as a high-ranking communicator, Sutton argues. "In effect, it covers her speaking in a lack of authority. . . ."[14]

The veil over McSally's uniform epitomizes women's situation in academia, as well as elsewhere. Women are in many ways more active in public life than ever before. For example, in 1870 fewer than 1% of students enrolled in college were women, while in 1999 the number had risen sharply to 52%. But this is not the whole story, as Sutton points out:

> Repeatedly, women can be observed speaking and acting in a variety of public spaces and, at the same time, women cannot be observed as such for they are not seen in textbooks, are reduced to a couple of sentences in a history, are mistaken for a house page in Congress, forced to cover their authority with an *abaya*, or simply absent as "Heads" from 495 of 500 tables of decision makers in the top businesses in the United States.[15]

This indicates the "tenacity of a pattern," Sutton argues, "in which women are repeatedly there in the space of the public and yet they are not there, as it were."[16] No wonder that many see themselves as having lost their tongue and eyes.

CHOOSING THE VEIL

Returning once more to "The Handless Maiden," we find that the king's mother binds the babe to the young bride's breast and veils her before sending her out to wander in the forest. The mother, an

Old Wise Woman common in myth, is not acting in accord with the patriarchy here; on the contrary, she kills a doe rather than her daughter. This veil does not seem to be the same as the one we have been describing. It is not worn for respectability, but *chosen* for the maiden's journey, rather like the novitiate chooses her veil when she enters the convent.

The sacrifice of the doe by the old mother, who knows the cycles of life and death, harkens back to older Goddess religions, Estes explains. It was an ancient rite meant to release the deer's energy, which was bounding but gentle. The veiling is likewise part of the Goddess tradition; it is what a Goddess wears when traveling on sacred pilgrimage, when she does not want to be recognized or diverted from her intention. Many Greek sculptures and reliefs show the initiate of the Eleusinian mysteries being veiled and awaiting the next step. Estes concludes that the Goddess voluntarily dons the veil when she is wandering or in descent. It is the difference between *hiding* and *disguising*. "This symbol is about keeping private, keeping to oneself, not giving one's mysterious nature away. It is about preserving the *eros* and *mysterium* of the wild nature."[17]

The bride has just given birth. In the Grimm brothers' version of this fairy tale, Estes points out, the child is a boy and is called Sorrowful. But in the Goddess religions, this spiritual child of the woman's marriage with the underworld king (we could consider him the *animus*—or the "man with heart") is called Joy. It represents new ideas, or a new view of life. "Sometimes we have difficulty keeping our new life energy in the transformative pot long enough for something to accrue to us. We must keep it to ourselves without giving it all away to whomever asks, or to whichever stealthy inspiration suddenly happens upon us, telling us it would be good to tip the pot and empty our finest soulfulness out into the mouths of others or onto the ground."[18]

The purpose of the veil as a disguise, then, is to inspire others with awe at this mysterious woman in the visage of a Goddess—to strike them with reverence so that they leave her alone. The woman needs to be away from total immersion in the cares of everyday life for awhile, to be untouchable. As Linda Leonard puts it, "The veil, in preserving the inner mysteries, allows the sacred time and space needed for the soul's wedding."[19] And Estes asserts: "No one would dare to raise her veil without her permission."[20] In C. S. Lewis' novelization of the "Eros and Psyche" myth that I will employ in the last part of this book, Psyche's sister Orual suddenly becomes queen when her father, the king, dies. She is not beautiful like Psyche, but she has a strong sense of her self and her authority. From then on, she is never seen without her veil, and she becomes a Mysterious Woman who wields considerable power in her kingdom.[21]

I encountered several women who appeared to be in descent, choosing a veil of disguise to protect something new in their lives. In each case, the woman wanted to keep secret a fresh idea, or something new that she was doing, to protect it from harm, like the Handless Maiden securing her child to her breast to keep it from forest predators.

Abby, the director of a research center who found academic research to be so "penetrative," was just back from a year's sabbatical. As she was serving her one-year payback, she was thinking of leaving her job. I asked her what she would do, and she replied that she didn't know for sure, but she harbored the desire "to do something feminine and spiritual for others"—she didn't know exactly what. She had been trying some creative writing, maybe she could turn that into a vocation. Whatever "this thing" was that she had to do, she did not feel she could do it in academe. An energetic and assertive "little fireplug," as I heard another faculty member call her, she assumed an uncharacteristically timid demeanor when she told me about her not-yet-fully-hatched plan.

"I'm embarrassed to tell someone like you about this."

"Why?" I asked, startled, not thinking of myself as in any way threatening. But I remembered I had felt exactly the same way when I was writing my screenplay. I did not want to talk about it within my academic circles.

"Because you seem so goal-directed," Abby declared.

Perhaps the other veils we wear—the patriarchal ones that have made us "respectable"—do indeed separate us from each other, even when we have decided to exchange the ones that hide us for the ones that disguise our secrets.

In the Mistress chapter I spoke only briefly about Christine, the friend I meet Same-Time-Next-Year at the same convention to discuss our joys and travails in the academic world. The last time we met she was wondering whether she could now stay in this vocation that had lured her out of another successful career. She was especially troubled by the attitude toward teaching that she saw herself developing under the pressure for tenure.

"I'm scared in every moment I devote to teaching because it takes away from my publication," she disclosed. I assured her that many of us feel that way much of the time, even though it may have been teaching that drew us into this profession in the first place.

"Yes, but I said that in a committee meeting with my colleagues!" she revealed. Now 52, Christine may have been just too mature to monitor her voice as carefully as she had seen others do.

When Christine told me she was going up for tenure next year, I asked her if she thought she had enough publications to make it.

"I think I have some good work behind me. I have a good chance," she replied thoughtfully. "I have to tell you what I'm really excited about, though. I am working secretly on a degree in spiritual direction. I have a person I've been working with. She is a very ill woman who is in the process of dying. This is one of the most meaningful things I have ever done. It is a gift."

Christine shared with me some of the readings she has been doing for her own spiritual journey and in order to help the dying woman. I wrote down the references, hoping I could get to them soon.

"Can you put these activities on your *vita* under Service?" I asked, more ironically than seriously.

"No," she said with quiet certitude. "I wouldn't do that. I don't want this defiled."

~

I met Bernadette serendipitously when she came to the home of another woman I was interviewing. She already had six years' training as a mind/body therapist, but she was getting her PhD so she would be considered "legitimate" and so she could do research in body movement and emotions. But, as she heard about my project, her profound ambivalence about her academic experience emerged. She said that she had been noticing lately what she calls "negative space" in academia—that which doesn't get thought about or said.

Perhaps because she was interested in studying mother-child interaction, she found it especially perplexing that "the whole hierarchy of academia is built on negative thinking. Academics aren't curious. Children are. They have this whole sense of 'Oh, that's interesting, I wonder what about that might be true?' They're open to the whole world of experience. But the whole mode in academia is one of attack. It's Oedipal—boys attacking their fathers."

Bernadette was more baffled than angry; I think she had gone back for her doctorate sincerely hoping to find answers to her many questions. But she had reason to be confused. She had worked for six months with a woman in a coma, touching, communicating with her, "getting data." She had been trying to write up her studies with this patient and others.

"I *know* there's interaction going on between us," she declared. "I know it. But my professors say I can't do this study because 'there's no consciousness there.' They say there will be no memory if she comes out of it."

She was obviously frustrated. Referring back to the academic "Oedipal thing," she mused: "They're motivated by the unconscious, but they don't think it exists. How ironic!"

Bernadette wanted to write her dissertation on how mothers and babies move and explore together in an "interactive field." She planned to watch them play. "My advisors want me to strap the babies in a car seat. I told them if I'm studying movement, I need to watch them *move!*" she cried. "But they said this is too complicated. There is no paradigm for it, so I can't study it."

Bernadette said she had almost dropped out of the doctoral program because of "the work of doing the translation. It's like a foreign language to me. They don't work to understand me, and I work constantly to translate their language into mine. They say they're doing research on emotion, but I don't recognize any emotion at all in what they're doing!"

"I guess you get really tired of that," I offered.

"People like me don't stay in academia," Bernadette said. "We don't fit."

Bernadette tried to find a niche by starting a collaborative research group with other female graduate students. "It was going really well. We had a female advisor who was very encouraging. But she went on sabbatical and a new female professor and a male professor came into the group as 'directors.' We all started to talk to each other in that citation language. Eventually I said to the group, 'You guys realize this is getting ruined?' and they agreed with me."

"So did you bust up the group?" I queried.

"No, we're still meeting. But we don't tell the professors about it. We're doing it out of sight."

"Putting a veil over something increases its action or feeling. . . . To be behind the veil increases one's mystical insight," writes Estes.[22] Karen, Christine, Bernadette and I all spoke with great feeling of our "extracurricular activities," treating them like precious but vulnerable mysteries. We each had a "newborn babe" strapped to our breasts while we wandered in search of something different from what we had known in academia. Whether creative writing, spiritual work, or innovative research, we all kept it secret, veiling ourselves in the Goddess' disguise so we could keep this child safe while it grew.

THE VEIL OF MYSTERY

There is a paradox inherent in wearing a veil. It does hide and disguise, as I have been exploring. But anyone who watches the groom lift the bride's veil at the moment of the kiss, or a dancer discarding one item of clothing at a time, knows the ecstasy of slow revelation. Salome's Dance of the Seven Veils seduced Herod into promising her anything she desired. (Unfortunately, she wanted the head of John the Baptist!) "Ironically," Estes observes, "though the veil has been used to hide one's beauty from the concupiscence of others, it is also femme fatale equipment. . . . In feminine psychology, the veil is a symbol for women's ability to take on whatever presence or essence they wish."[23] And, using the veil symbol again for women's speech, Sutton writes: "The articulate woman though can use her appearance, the striptease of a woman as she begins to divest herself of gloves, scarf, and hat, to train what the audience [sees and hears]."[24]

Ever since I learned from the first grade forward to turn my Self from view to cover over my exuberant Crayola colors so that I would be a "respectable woman" in school—I think I have secretly wanted others to see through this veil. My favorite arts-and-crafts project for many years in elementary school was one you may also have done: you draw an abstract design of interlocking swirls on a piece of construction paper and color each piece of it, using every shade in the box. Then you color over the entire thing with a black crayon, making sure to completely hide the entire picture in layers of heavy black. This part was kind of hard. I usually broke or used up several black crayons doing this and, being something of a perfectionist, it took the better part of a day. It was worth it, though, because the fun part was to take a sharp object such as a key or a toothpick, and to draw a picture by scratching through the black to let the rainbow hues come through in the shape of a flower, a bird, a mountainous landscape. It didn't really look good enough to hang, but my mother let me put it on the refrigerator anyway.

Much of my writing and speaking career in academia has been like those scratchings, or like a verbal striptease. Protected by coats of argument and citation, I have hidden my love of myth and passion for deep knowing of the self, hoping a few can see me as I see myself in those truest moments when I cast off the bridal veil of my dark marriage to academe. Covered in layers of black, I have let a flower petal show through here, a lacquered red fingernail and a bare ankle there. I have wanted to be both a "respectable" and a "free" woman.

This book is my coming-out from behind the black.

CHAPTER 8

AMAZON

Sometimes you have to stand and fight.

Xena, Warrior Princess

The Encyclopedia of Amazons: Women Warriors from Antiquity to the Modern Era defines *Amazon* as:

> a woman who is a duelist or soldier, by design or circumstances, whether chivalrous or cruel, and who engages others in direct combat, preferably with some semblance of skill and honorability. . . . an Amazon is best exemplified by *the* Amazons of Greek mythology.[1]

Although I have long known about Amazons, even counting myself a fan of popular culture icons such as *Alien*'s Ripley and TV's Xena, this has been the hardest chapter for me to start. I have read and read about them—their fascinating trajectory from pre-Greek to modern, their debated status as historical vs. mythological, their psychological and sociological significance in Western culture. But I have had trouble getting words about them onto this page.

Perhaps this is because, of all the types in this book, I am the least like them. Arriving right on time, I was still so tiny at birth that my sister says they put me under "grow lights" in the hospital, which evidently didn't work since I was always the smallest girl in my class, making up for my lack of stature each year by winning the spelling bee. It is true that Jo was my favorite of the *Little Women,* and I could beat anyone at the standing broad jump and the 50-yard dash. But I threw a ball "like a girl," and showed no taste at all for contact sports. I was continually chosen last for basketball teams and first to "come over" in Red Rover. To this day I dodge verbal combat, showing some honorability in collaborative discussion, but no skill whatsoever at argumentative warfare. Among family and friends, I am the peacemaker. No one ever called me an Amazon.

Yet maybe my image of the Amazon relies too much upon brawn and not enough upon brains. Many classical writers saw the Amazons as worshipers of the Great Mother in her various forms, particularly the warlike Artemis of Ephesus, who can be traced to the Phyrigian Cybele and the Cretan Rhea, honored at Rhodes, Pontus, Galatia, North Africa, and elsewhere.[2] The Amazons have been associated with the orgiastic aspect of the Great Mother practices that Greek patriarchal religion later tried to replace.[3] Yet they had no children, and Batya Weinbaum depicts them as daytime counterparts to the Furies of the *Oresteia* for, like them, they shunned marriage and sexual intercourse with men. Most important, they operated as one force, not as individual heroines.[4]

Certainly I have striven for intellectual power, compulsively enacting the "Sarah Conner syndrome" to accomplish my academic work, soldiering on long after my inner Kyle Reese lay limp and bloody at my feet. Possibly I am more Amazonian than my undersized self-image has allowed. And, knowing quite a few academic Amazons by this broader definition, I have admired their intellectual prowess, quoted from their works, and honored their willingness—when the situation calls for it—to stand and fight.

Still, mine is an homage from afar. I have not, at least until recently, befriended these female warriors. I have not formed the emotional bonds that would take me beyond revering them to actually knowing them. I now suspect this is because, although they seem on the surface quite similar, the Brainchild proclaims with Athena that "I am always for the male with all my heart, and strongly on my father's side."[5] The Amazon, as Abby Wettan Kleinbaum puts it, "can leave her mark on the shape of events because she is free to act without having to depend on men."[6] Even more than that, she fights them, and according to legend, she "devalued men by eliminating them from all ruling positions. . . . Men were not needed in the society because the Amazons took over all the male functions."[7] I have kept myself distinct from these "man-haters" because I have wanted men—and "feminine" women—to like me.

More than any of the types I have discussed thus far, the Amazon stands as an archetype separate from men. Yet I have placed her in the middle section of the book as a "fatal attraction," for though her very name evokes strength, courage, and independence, she has, like the Siren and the Veiled Woman, also been co-opted to suit men's needs. As Jessica Amanda Salmonson reflects, "The archetype of the Amazon has always been with us and appeals as easily to the dreams as to the dislikes of women, and to the desires as well as the fears of men." An ambiguous figure, "the Amazon thrives in a shadowy area that neither serves nor entirely destroys the patriarchal order," and so feminists are divided for and against her.[8] How did these glorious and fearsome figures, riding their steeds in full battle gear over the landscape of myth and marble, become the tragic Penthesilea, whom Achilles killed, only to rape her corpse in grief? Or the Barbie-figured Wonder Woman, doing superheroic deeds in her stars-and-stripes maillot for the hormonal gaze of adolescent boys? Or the virile and beautiful Xena, known as much for her chain-mail sex appeal as for her single-combat triumphs? The Amazon is not one single type, but many, and in order to understand her variety within academia, we must get a glimpse of her long and colorful history.

FROM COLLECTIVE FORCE TO INDIVIDUAL ANIMA

The image of the Amazon has evolved dialectically since Homer, says Weinbaum, as "each epoch has invested the chameleon-like symbol with its own particular spirit of place and time."[9] Some scholars see the Amazon entirely as "a dream that men created, an image of a superlative female that men constructed to flatter themselves."[10] But Weinbaum argues that the Amazons underwent a metamorphosis from a "primary form" as a collective horde of fighting women—as found in pre-Homeric myth and Homeric poetry—into a "secondary form," in which they appeared as "individuated *anima* figures" serving psychological and cultural purposes for men. This change marks the transition from oral, collectively performed women's laments, to literature written by individual men. Homer's poetry—drawing from and still part of the oral tradition—depicted the Amazons as a feared band of androgynous warriors who strove against men and took their own initiative in battle.[11] As men withdrew in private to write their own points of view, fictional Amazons were increasingly subordinated into helping out in the affairs of men, and ceased to defend their own territory and avenge their captured women leaders. Like other mythological figures, the Amazon's history plays out the dramatic confrontation between earth-based, female-centered culture and that of the newly emerging patriarchal Greek city-states.[12]

Weinbaum expands Esther Harding's psychological treatment of Jung's *anima* to explain how the Amazons as a primary collective force became fragmented into the secondary individualized portraits that have proved much hardier in written literature.[13] Critical of Jung's essentialist slant on the *anima*, Harding sees it as a collective picture of woman as she has been depicted through the centuries in relation to man. Harding finds an underlying wholeness in woman before patriarchy splits her into pieces. Elsewhere, Harding uses the figure of Virgin in its original sense of "one-in-herself" to represent this autonomous and whole woman, so different from today's "virgin" as chaste and not-yet-despoiled.[14] But as a woman, fictional or "real," becomes *anima* for a man, receiving the projections of his unconscious feminine soul, this part is split off and divorced from other aspects of her. This atomization can thus represent not only psychological warfare between the sexes but also within a woman. The man conquers or carries off only that part of her that serves his soul needs. And, in that segmented function as the man's *anima*, she engages in war with the other parts of her self that he does not recognize.

Stories of the Amazon represent this internal warfare with the capture of the Amazon queen (her annexation as the man's *anima*), who then fights her female comrades (the other parts of herself). Often her former partners attempt to rescue her, but just as often she kills them off. In this motif, the Amazon's history reflects what Meredith Powers calls the more general "bitter social competition that would later be so common to female characters as literature came to revolve around a central male experience."[15]

Like the Siren, the Amazon is an enticing *anima* target for men who wish to enhance their own heroic egos. The Amazon has a supernatural quality, as does her contemporary counterpart Wonder Woman, says Kleinbaum, and this makes her a splendid opponent, for a man who does not ordinarily think of doing violence against a woman can fantasize freely about killing an Amazon:

> The conquest of an Amazon is an act of transcendence, a rejection of the ordinary, of death, of mediocrity—and a reach for immortality. If the Amazon excels in military prowess, then the skill of the hero who defeats her is even more extraordinary. If she is beautiful and pledged to virginity, then the sexual power of the hero who wins her heart and her bed is without measure. . . . To win an Amazon, either through arms or through love or, even better, through both, is to be certified as a hero.[16]

Indeed, by the secondary phase, Amazons were depicted as beautiful and vulnerable.[17] Page duBois demonstrates that Greek vase painting of the fifth century increasingly depicted Amazons as erotic objects, "seductive perhaps because they were indeed outside the institution of marriage."[18]

Several Greek myths tell of encounters between Amazon queens and Grecian warriors, "with the apparent intent of glorifying bittersweet male victories over brave, noble, beautiful, but squashed females."[19] Hippolyte, whose name means "of the stampeding horse," and who is a model for Wonder Woman, was Queen of the Amazons. Heracles' ninth labor was to deliver her war girdle, a gift of her father Ares, to the War-priestess Admete. In one version, she was impressed by Heracles and gave it to him willingly, but her Amazon army, fearing he would abduct her, attacked. When her horse threw her, he offered her mercy, but she would rather die than give in, and so he bashed in her head with his war club. In another version, she survived but was later won by Theseus, and gave birth to their son, Hippolytus. Determined to win back their queen, the Amazons fought Theseus and the Athenians. Some say Hippolyte fought against the Amazons and on the side of the Greeks. Others say that the Greeks killed her along with her women.[20]

In post-Homeric stories of the Trojan War, Penthesilia, called the "last queen of the Amazons" and whose name means "compelling men to mourn," came to the aid of Troy. Ignoring the warning of

Hector's widow Andromache about Achilles' great war prowess, Penthesilea dashed into battle, only to be speared by Achilles through the right breast, then impaled atop her horse as she lay dying. But as Achilles gloated over his kill and reached down to liberate her of her glowing armor, he was seized by the very essence of womanly beauty and fell in love. Grief-stricken, he killed several of his own soldiers who had gouged out her eyes and chided his emotionalism.[21]

When Penthesilea is reduced only to the man's *anima*, claims Weinbaum, she dies, "as male projection eclipses her real self." To be all things to all men kills her.[22]Although she continually reemerges, the Amazon then retreats mostly underground, under water, or onto an island, where she joins her similarly vanquished sisters. In Celtic myths, for example, the enchanting Amazon queen has the power to withhold growth, but she and her women are more like charming nymphs than fearsome warriors.[23]

In the influential late medieval/early Renaissance romance, *Sergas de Esplandian*, one of the first mass-produced books in Europe after the invention of the printing press, Garcia Rodriguez de Montalvo initially represents the Amazons as they had been in Greek oral literature. By the end of this massive twenty-four-volume work, men have brought the Queen of the Amazons into their "natural order"—removed from their beasts and protected by men. A male sage is empowered by animals and nature—as the women once were. The Queen of the Amazons has married and handed her kingdom over to a man, although the men let their wives fight with them occasionally on their colonial campaigns. All of the main characters of the Old World are enchanted by a sorceress named Urganda the Unknown (obviously a model for Disney's Ursula the Sea Witch in *The Little Mermaid*), and frozen beneath the sea. The women's lost power does return, but in the shape of a dystopian island where "unnatural" women lead men into an unknown but exciting future. From then on, feminist reclaimers of the myth often recreate the theme of an island of women constructing a utopian civilization at one with nature. Even Wonder Woman hails from the legendary island of Amazons.[24]

Despite her abduction as men's soul-mate, however, the Amazon has proven a remarkably resilient character:

> Parts of her will rebel—even if uselessly—against this sudden death of her being. This is Penthesilia's experience. This myth of

> the Amazon portrays, then, in comparative symbology, the conflict and warring parts within the woman. The loss of an Amazon queen and the pursuing battle portray the woman's own battle for her lost soul."[25]

Men cannot ultimately reduce the Amazon queen, or any woman, Weinbaum concludes, to live only for men.

Especially since the resurgence of feminism in the 1960s (although certainly in notable cases before then), academia has formed a vivid backdrop for the Amazon to play out her many roles—from relatively free warrior, to strong woman taken over as man's *anima*, to hardened cohort fighting alongside men against her sisters. A few of these women avoid the company of men, although most do not. They may be lesbian or heterosexual. Most also play roles in addition to Amazon at times, such as those I described earlier. What they have in common is that, when they do wield intellectual power, often in service of a cause, they are "skilled in battle" and thus forces to be reckoned with.

FREE WARRIOR

Most academic feminists, myself included, have read the books of Judith, a present-day Amazonian, who is skilled in intellectual battle and who has not surrendered to men's *anima* needs. But I learned about Judith's more personal side serendipitously when I interviewed her former student, Anna.

Thirty years after studying with Judith, Anna welcomed me into her rather dingy office, not at all fitting to her status as ex-chair of a large arts and sciences department and current post as a high-level campus administrator. Pretty, engaging, and somewhat petite, Anna, who didn't emerge in my mind as an Amazon herself until much later, reminds me once more that these fighters come in all shapes and sizes.

"When I was an undergraduate my mentor was Judith," she said, causing me unconsciously to turn up the volume on my tape recorder. "She would never call herself anyone's mentor, she didn't like the word because it comes from a male myth. She believed in this sort of spiritual journey that everyone takes. What was nice is that it was the period of campus activism when I was involved in the anti-war movement, and that was kind of interesting because it was a Jesuit campus—so it was this conflict between the Catholicism with which I had been raised and people talking about the immorality of this war."

As Anna explained it, Judith's classes initiated a kind of spiritual journey for her—of sorting through the beliefs of her upbringing and coming to new forms of consciousness. Because Judith was as steeped in Catholicism as she was, and yet had left it all behind, Anna was able to challenge her own Catholic family in which protest against the war was immoral. "My parents would defend the kids who went to war, and it took me awhile to be able to say in a sophisticated way that I wasn't blaming the kids who were going."

Anna also learned from Judith about the Goddess' three forms—Maiden, Mother, Crone—and how powerful she had once been. "The word 'trivia' comes from the Triple Goddess," Anna enthused, "so she's always looking at how female mythology has been diminished."

"Right," I interjected, excited at how the subject of this interview was coinciding with that of my book. I decided to take this ball on my mythic territory and run with it. "Was she your first real hero intellectually?" I asked.

"You know, she's kind of outstanding. Not just in terms of who she was to the world. She was a woman who herself came out of a working-class Catholic background. She could recite the whole Catholic mass in Latin. She had two PhD's and a masters' in a different field, and she took her doctoral exams in two languages. She was not only this radical Lesbian feminist—but I could also see my grandmother and my mother in her. Of course, my grandmother's words before I went to college were 'Stay away from that Judith.' But I could see the similarities."

I wanted to know whether this impressive intellect paid personal attention to her student. The aloof intellectual—what one woman called "the Lone Ranger mentality"—is almost a cliché in academia.

"Oh yes, she did. But of course, she was constantly questioning the groundwork on which we stand, and the concepts we use and whether they're patriarchal and all that. A few of us worked on her books with her—I worked on one of them." When I returned home, I ordered that book (from amazon.com, of course!), and sure enough, there was Anna, prominently cited in Judith's acknowledgements.

"In the late sixties Judith had to fight to get tenure and she had published a famous book," Anna remembered, "and they didn't want to give her tenure at her college. That was in *Newsweek*—she was a wonder at getting attention. She had a habit of excluding men from her classroom."

Anna recalled that, even though Judith liked to say that academia is "male academic bullshit," and she often railed against the conventional rituals of academic initiation, or hoop-jumping, she often made a point of failing them with great flair.

"She would never encourage any of us to be a part of academia. Her first book in particular had some useful strategies for living in the patriarchy. But when I'd say 'Judith, I want to go do this masters' program,' she'd roll her eyes and say 'What do you want to do *that* for?' She'd still write me a letter though. She was this separatist, but she helped me. I don't think her talent was for helping people to make it in the world. She wasn't practical, she was an intellectual. She had extraordinary intellectual gifts but not many practical gifts."

"What do you remember the most about her?" I wondered, and Anna summed up her experience: "That the first time I sat in her class I was just dumbfounded. She was incredibly brilliant. But she was also a mother figure to me."

My impression of Judith, corroborated by her writings and her student, was of a cerebral Amazon who guided her arrows with sure aim, not against individuals, but against the patriarchy. Forced into early retirement by one of her infamous refusals to conform to academic norms, she remains to this day undeterred from her mission, and is widely known as indispensable to the establishment of feminist history and theory in the United States.

Nurtured by Judith, Anna also characterized the free warrior Amazon spirit, becoming the practical "helper" that Judith wasn't. Another mentoring experience toughened her for the battles she would later fight through more legitimate channels. In that sense, Anna played Martin Luther King to Judith's Malcolm X; they both fought institutional oppression, but in radically different ways. Anna obviously felt blessed by the strong female influences in her college experiences, but I asked her whether anything in those experiences had been difficult.

"Yes, unfortunately, but it was the advisor for my dissertation. I wrote my dissertation on Virginia Woolf."

"Virginia Woolf sure is a magnet for strong feminists," I said, remembering another Amazonian woman I had interviewed who also chose her as her dissertation topic. Anna acknowledged the extent to which she identified with Woolf.

"Well, when it came time for me to apply for positions, my advisor wrote this incredibly bizarre letter of recommendation, describing me almost in fictional terms. I hadn't finished my dissertation, and I was writing a chapter that was, well, it wasn't really lesbian criticism, but she had to know I was a lesbian. I had no personal relationship with this woman, and I thought she was a really good feminist scholar and she would help me do feminist criticism. I was by that time in my thirties, and I knew I had to just make somebody be my mentor. She compared me in her letter to a nineteenth-century 'spinster out to change the world.' My other two advisors, who were women, thought she'd gone off the deep end. Basically, they thought it was homophobic. But the curious thing is, they weren't going to talk to her about it. So I went in and said 'Please change this letter,' which she did."

"Was that hard to do?" I asked.

"Yes, that was hard. She said, 'Oh, I was just trying to make it stand out,'" Anna laughed ruefully. "My confronting her was probably illegal, but I just wasn't going to let that happen. It was clear to me that it was her problem, not my problem. I would rather not have gone through that, but it did teach me how homophobia can affect you. You just have to watch it."

In her professional career, Anna displayed a pattern that I found prevalent among academic Amazons: they transformed their "otherness" into the ripened passion that fueled their battles, typically for equality and a voice for the disenfranchised. Henrietta, an African American dean, considered herself a protector of young non-white assistant professors, her "children." Toni, a Puerto Rican administrator who did a U-turn in a path that might have ended in a university presidency, considered her goal in life to be "social service"—in particular, she wanted to enact policies "to make sure every K–12 student in the state has a good teacher. That really inspires me. All the studies show there is nothing that predicts a child's success better than if they have a good teacher. I want to increase the pathways available to people." Elaine, a white woman in an inter-racial marriage, worked tirelessly to recruit racial minorities at all levels of her university system, and to transform the curriculum to reflect more diversity. Cara, an Asian Indian physicist who had no female teachers and only one fellow female student in five years of graduate school, fought energetically to improve the situation for women in her almost exclusively male department.

Anna, too, considered herself "social service–oriented." Even when I asked what had been the "Aha!" insights of her career, probably expecting some grand intellectual epiphany, she turned toward the distress of others.

"I guess, being chair of the department," she reflected. "It was very painful, but I learned a lot. I found it extremely painful to have so many part-time lecturers. We are so under-funded. I had a woman who had breast cancer, and other people with serious physical problems who weren't getting health insurance. We were serving 2,000 students, scheduling 80 sections per quarter—we were as large as some schools. It was an uphill battle, but I fought to get benefits for those lecturers. And I served as chair because I cared about the students."

"You have impressive scholarly credentials. Would you like to work at a Research I university?" I wondered, looking around her cramped office.

"I would choose a state university over a private institution," Anna said decisively. "I find lots of satisfaction teaching on this campus, which is so diverse. I go walking around campus and just realize the diversity when I'm depressed. It makes me feel better to know that [they] have the opportunity to go to a campus like this. I wish it had more money, but it does do a great service. This is where I belong."

I thought about my own years of yearning to be in a topflight research university, of telling myself that the reason it didn't happen was that I was married to a professor in my own field. And I pondered whether I could be as fulfilled as Anna, fighting as a warrior servant to better the lives of others.

Many an Amazon was fostered by the political ferment of the sixties counterculture—a fertile ground for rooting the sort of commitment that often became their life's work.

I met Patricia for cokes in the student union on her campus. A 57-year-old vice chancellor with a staff of twenty-five, and a pillar of her community serving on many national boards for countless volunteer causes, she was generous to devote two hours to me in the middle of her workday. Her impressive height, trim suit, and perfectly tied silk scarf befitted her high office and made me wish I hadn't worn my tie-dye dress and sandals, but her clothes could not conceal the mirthful warmth of her demeanor. Aware of the demands on her schedule, I initiated the interview after a minimum of chitchat, with the same question I usually asked: "How did you get into academia?"

"I married at 16 and my husband died before I finished undergraduate school, during my junior year," Patricia began. "I started college when my daughter was 8 months old. I remarried my senior year. He wanted to enter the Peace Corps, but he was kicked out because he had 'too much sympathy for the underdog.'" It was the end of the McCarthy era, and her husband was a peacenik. The two of them got arrested once for not taking cover during an air raid drill.

"He was a Marxist historian, and way 'out there' politically," she continued. "He ended up getting fired from various places he taught—at a historically black school in the South, and at a poor Appalachian college. I became the stable breadwinner, and he was all over the place, doing his thing. We managed to stay married for about twelve years," Patricia marveled. She got pregnant with her second child while earning her masters', which she completed in a year and a summer, and got tenure before she finished her PhD, while she was taking classes, teaching, and caring for her two children.

Patricia and her husband were vocally involved in civil rights and anti–Vietnam War protests. Several people in her department got fired for it. "The department was sexist, they fired the men, not the women," she laughed. "We called ourselves the 'Mothertruckers.' It was an exciting time. We marched against the war and did teach-ins. When my babysitter found out, she wouldn't take care of those little commie pinko babies any more. We had to find new childcare. It *was* a great time to be in school!"

"Have you been juggling that much ever since?" I asked.

"Well, I was, in effect, a single parent. I got involved in the women's movement in the sixties and started teaching women's studies. I probably taught the first women's studies course at my university. It was really interesting and exciting—we were designing new courses, and we developed some model affirmative action plans. My husband got a job in another part of this state, and I interviewed here and got the job. I loved the landscape, but my ignorance about the state was complete. I'd heard about a famous far-right politician, but didn't really know anything. I think I'd been here less than a year when my husband decided he was having a mid-life crisis and ran off with an undergraduate."

"Did you tell him he was living a cliché?" I asked.

"Probably. But there was a very vibrant women's community here—it was an exciting place to be. I was the university's first high-level woman administrator."

"So was it a Good Ol' Boys Club?"

"Oh yeah, yeah," Patricia answered without bitterness. "I was already a pretty militant feminist and made no bones about it. I don't know if they quite knew what they were getting. I wasn't militant in ways that would embarrass them particularly, but I would certainly speak up about the generic 'he' and many other issues. It was coming out of my Yankee mouth too. I had to learn the Southern way. I do love that—it's softer. In the Northeast there was a tendency to go head-to-head a lot faster and also a fear—no, suspicion—of casual friendliness."

Patricia was the only woman in higher administration at her university for many years. I asked her whether that had been isolating for her.

"Well, I was pretty used to making my own way. But it wasn't isolating, because there was a real feminist community here. Women and women's groups have been a sustaining force for me. I was in a consciousness-raising group when I first moved here—we met once a week for five years. We still get together for a feminist vegetarian Thanksgiving."

Thinking of Patricia as downright heroic, I asked her if she identified with any particular heroine of myth or literature. She answered with how she thought she was seen by others. "I'm sure some of them thought of me as an Amazon, with affirmative action, etc." While she acknowledged that she was Amazonian in some ways—that she was a fighter for causes—she added, as if to dissociate herself at least somewhat from that label: "But I also think it's important to value some of the things we see as stereotypically feminine. I like the values of cooperation and collaboration. I *can* confront, but my predilection is to see if we can work out a solution. I like mediation, and I'm involved in an all-female mediation group."

I was reminded of the way the early Amazons used to ride *together* as a collective fighting force, so different from the individualized heroines and tragic Amazon queens of later myth. But like other contemporary Amazons, Patricia seemed to have absorbed the notion that to be "Amazonian" means to be "individualistic."

Patricia was obviously a warrior—for many causes, including feminism. But, unlike Judith, she did not feel oppressed. "I don't feel put upon or oppressed, or like I've been denied things because I'm a woman," she emphasized. "Now sometimes I get a little annoyed at people in the current generation who don't understand what women's liberation did for them." Rather, Patricia's activism seemed to grow not only from her political era but also from her matter-of-fact habit of making her own way despite the absence of male partners, and with the considerable help of other women.

~

Younger than Anna and Patricia, Jenny's Amazonianism was forged not by the counterculture, but by, as she put it, "the school of hard knocks." She had grown up in poverty as "a bit of a deviant." "Academia was not in my family," she explained. She met the father of her child at 14 and dropped out of the ninth grade, supporting herself and her daughter in many low-wage jobs. She got known around town as lead guitarist for her band, "Jenny and the Juveniles." Encouraged by her grandmother and sister, she earned her GED when her daughter was 6. She enrolled at the university in her hometown, eleven years later received her PhD from a major university, and had been an assistant professor at her undergraduate institution for four years. Now she was *teaching* a course on deviance. She felt that she had arrived home again, but as a grownup. She recounted in detail how she had gotten to this point.

"I honestly didn't even have a clue what I was in for—just enrolling in college was a really, really awesome experience," Jenny recalled. "I didn't know how to study, I didn't know how to manage my time, I didn't have any of those skills. I had no confidence in myself as a student. So all that baggage, I dragged with me into college. The belief in myself that I could really accomplish something didn't come until later."

"Did your mentors help you with that?" I asked.

Jenny was grateful for many of her teachers and fellow students who encouraged her, particularly as an undergraduate. But graduate school was a different story. "I'm sure you know, graduate school is an insidious place," she said. "There's so much wasted energy—talk about deference! That's where you really have to play the game, and it's all symbolic, it's all about cultural capital. For me, it was a really painful experience in important ways, but also good."

With ironic sweetness and a big laugh that continually beat back what could be righteous rage, Jenny recalled her relationship with her advisor, for whom she had chosen that particular school. "Victor was the biggie there. I was a hillbilly from the backwoods, and it was hard for him. As he explained it to me, he wasn't sure if he could work with someone like myself because of our class differences. His father was a philosopher—he grew up on the Upper East Side in Manhattan, and his father hobnobbed with the literati. We just came from different worlds."

"Was he empathic about the class differences, or was it more like, you don't measure up?"

"He kept trying to push me off on other advisors," Jenny recounted. "I will never forget the hard conversation we had. I said, 'I feel like the Ugly Duckling here, and I know I didn't come in with high scores, but man, give me a break, I'm a hard worker!' And he was absolutely blindsided by that—he had no idea that had been my perception. And after that we developed a pretty good working relationship, and his explanation to me of why I would probably go on to do OK was that people of my class have a strong work ethic."

"Nice of him to give you that," I said.

"But I'd have to work harder than my colleagues—he just had

to warn me that I would have trouble, because I got a slow start. I hadn't read the right people. 'You need to know Derrida, not Daisy Mae,' he'd say."

"How'd you feel when he said that?" I asked, horrified.

"I felt incredibly insulted, but I also felt that he might be partly right. Honest to goodness, I think he loves me and was looking out for me in his own way, bless his heart. And my response was 'I'm so grateful that you can see beyond my raising—you are a very generous person.'"

Her laughter was completely infectious. "Did he get it that that was tongue-in-cheek?" I asked.

"Oh God, no, he didn't get it, he took it as a compliment! I had a lot of tearful nights in graduate school—I mean really traumatic times. There were seventeen in my graduate class and only three of us finished. It was a really tough program. It had a lot of what I call symbolic violence," Jenny remembered.

"You mean weeding out?"

"Yeah, and not necessarily academic, some of it was personalities. There was no indication whatsoever that anybody wanted me there. With my GRE scores so low, I had to prove myself. For years I guarded that information about the GED. I'm a bit of a chameleon, and a survivor, years and years of working in service sector jobs, and I learned a long time ago how to abstract from the situation I was in and use it in the new situation. That's how I got by. Put that in your report. Prerequisite for graduate school: Waiting Tables 101."

Jenny saw both her poverty and her graduate school trials as transformative rather than inhibiting. "You know, poverty has its own time clock and its own socially constructed reality, and none of that says PhD," she reflected. "But I'm *tough* today because of that. I know how to advocate for myself. Graduate school was like going through boot camp, and I learned that if you don't fight for yourself, nobody will. In fact, if they smell blood . . . I know that sounds like a battlefield mentality, but you just have to learn to stand your ground and fight."

Jenny did indeed learn to fight for herself. She won the grudging respect of her advisor. When she asked him for advice about leaving her current job for another college, "He kind of fell back into, well, you're lucky to have what you've got—you know, in Outer Slobovia." But he was astonished to learn that she had published thirteen articles at this early point in her career. She had also written a book on the non-profit agency that had helped fund her undergraduate education. She was absolutely giddy about what had just transpired that week: a famous female celebrity with political leanings had written the foreword. At this news, Victor had said, "'Hell, we got people here coming for tenure with half of that! So go wherever you want to go! Or stay in the swamp!"

What I found most remarkable about Jenny's Amazonianism was that, although she was proud of her accomplishments, there was so little of the notion of personal heroism in her tales. Rather, she had moved immediately to glorify as well as volunteer for the agency that helped her. She wanted her research to effect social change. And when I asked her what she loved about academia, it was evident that she cherished the opportunity to transform it for the better:

> What I love about it is that I never have an excuse not to learn something new every day. I love the ability to write, because I've never had the opportunity in my entire life. I love working with students. When I see a student develop an imagination, I feel excited! I feel solidarity with them, I feel that maybe we can change the world after all. I have a social agenda, which is to make people more tolerant of diversity. And I don't give a shit what they say about research and objectivity, I'm here because I believe we live in an intolerant world, and there are concepts that we share with our students that will make them more tolerant. That's my method—unapologetic!

Upon hearing this speech, I, too, wanted to stand and fight. Jenny's enthusiasm was so persuasive.

Of all the mythic roles I have thus far ascribed to academic women, the Amazon comes closest to what we call "heroic." Still, none of these women stressed their own brilliance or fame, and they tended to frame their successes in terms of what they still wanted to do for others—typically, underprivileged groups of people. These women warriors were just as likely to "fight" collaboratively as combatively, they often valued the more "feminine" style of communicating—i.e., ameliorating and nurturing rather than penetrating and conquering—and they did not see this style as hindering their own effectiveness. All of them saw their battles as unwinnable if not waged in solidarity with others, usually other women.

When Jenny described her graduate program as having a "battlefield mentality," for example, I told her of the difficulties many of our masters' students had when going on for their PhD's. I described our program as relatively nurturing, and wondered whether this is a good thing. "When they go out they have a much more kick-in-the-butt kind of experience," I said. "You know, the tough question is, what does preparing them for that mean, does that mean *we* have to be like that?"

"I don't think we do," she said thoughtfully. "I couldn't look at myself in the mirror if I was like that. And the other thing is, if they have this humane experience to compare, then maybe if they wind up at a doctoral program, maybe they won't be one of those arrogant people. Maybe there would be enough anticipatory socialization that they won't."

Jenny and the others I call Amazonian seem to fit the pattern of heroism that Powers ascribes to the pre-patriarchal goddess—that is, less concerned than later generations with heroic individualism—perhaps even precluding the period of separation from the tribe delineated by Joseph Campbell in *The Hero with a Thousand Faces*. According to his well-known monomyth, the hero must experience a period of isolated struggle, a "road of trials" culminating in both personal wisdom and a boon for society. In contrast, the archetypal goddess was more like Demeter, concerned with the mother-child dyad and the life of the tribe. The story of Demeter and Persephone, Powers suggests, "is a story of interdependence, of feminine networking, of a building up of strength through connection toward the ultimate achievement of a goal."[26]

We often think of Amazons as violent and bloodthirsty—as "masculine" women with little patience for their more "feminine" sisters—and some of what I will now describe does approach this image. But I believe these qualities define women who belong to the masculine academic world more than do those who "ride with the women." And it is the latter that best carry on the tradition of the free Amazon seen in the earliest myths.

THE CAPTURED AMAZON

We have seen how the myth of the Amazon evolves as she is appropriated to serve men's *anima* needs for a strong feminine figure to fight, bed, and conquer. Academia gives rise to some "Amazon queens" who have surrendered to their captors, fighting with them against their female peers, or against any appearance of "feminine" qualities that would undermine their position in the palace of intellectual power. Like the Mother Monster's challenge to Ripley in *Aliens*, the appearance of overtly feminine characteristics threatens women's ascendancy to equal status, and provides an opportune target for heroic individualism. Such capitulation is understandable. As I have hoped to make clear, women and all things marked "feminine" are under-rewarded at the university. Certainly, women must prove their intellectual and argumentative prowess within a fraternity that has been dubious of those skills. Whereas academic feminism has made it taboo to publicly discriminate against *women*, however, such feminism has not enhanced the communicative styles and values traditionally associated with the *feminine*. Thus, an ironic situation has emerged in which women fight, not against other women, but against their perceived characteristics. Even some feminists, it would seem, fall prey to the "prime male directive" that most boys learn at an early age and never leave behind: *Don't be female*.[27]

When I interviewed recently for a position as director of a women's studies program, I learned from a friend at that university that some of the women dismissed me as a serious candidate because of my long blonde hair. Instantaneously, I was transported back to grade school—too small, too soft, too "girly" to compete in the more rambunctious games. Several women with whom I talked commented on the isolation from other women that they felt in the university. Sophia, whom we met earlier as a Veiled Woman, was particularly hurt by the reproof of a female colleague who I would consider Amazonian. Many suffered criticisms from other women about their inability or unwillingness to compete on the battlegrounds of penetrating thought. As one woman put it, "I feel shunned by [the top women of her field] because I have no taste for blood when it comes to academic contention over this or that theoretical presumption.

I will defend my statements, but I don't like going after those of other people."

As followers of Artemis, the Amazons were hunter-warriors, "wild women" who were more at home in nature than in culture.[28] There were many different Artemises, hailing from various cultures, but the Amazons have been linked with the more war-like version from Ephesus.[29] Artemis was the Lady of the Wild Things, huntress as well as goddess of childbirth, protector of young animals and virgin women, presiding over death and birth as inevitable aspects of the cycle of nature. She was one manifestation of the Great Goddess, a figure who encompassed but transcended the human, who represented the drive toward life, who was both infernal and regenerative.[30] She was inherently plural, able to appear as Maiden, Mother, or Crone, and ever-generative, giving birth not only to others but also to herself in various forms.[31] Artemis and the early Amazons were *of* nature, but not *over* it. They could kill, but they did not, at least until they were conquered, hunt their own kind.

The powers of the Great Goddess, of whom Artemis is one form, were so mysterious and threatening to the male-dominated tribes succeeding her "that a large part of the energy of Western man has gone into the process of reducing and disarming her."[32] Much of this book is, of course, about that process, but we can view a snapshot of it in relation to Artemis, the Amazons, and academia in the story of the twins, Artemis and Apollo—the girl having her roots in goddess cultures and the boy a Greek invention. As the embodiment of constant re-creation, so the story goes, Artemis rose just moments after her own birth to help her mother Leto give birth to Apollo.[33] In fact, Apollo can be considered a masculine version of Artemis herself, who was demoted from a sun to a moon goddess as the beautiful Apollo took over the throne at Delphi by conquering the snake Python, the son of the earth goddess Gaia.[34]

Perhaps taking a clue from his sister, Apollo becomes the god of archery. But unlike Artemis, he is also the god of intellectual clarity, of scientific measurement, and of sculpture.[35] Sculpture observes and attempts to still and "capture" the human and animal body with the artist's studied gaze.[36] In Apollo, an academic god if there ever was one, *rational knowledge* is thus associated with the hunt and with rendering the warm body inert by visual examination.[37] In Plato's dialogues Socrates quests after the truth, in philosopher Martha Nussbaum's words, like "a hunter, out to immobilize the beauty of his object . . . ."[38] Gregory Max Vogt compares scientific theory to the hunt, to artistic discovery, and to sexual penetration. In all of these, he says, the man attempts to understand what is mysterious, although he inevitably falls short.[39] And what was most enigmatic at the point of patriarchal depreciation of the Goddess myths was, of course, the Goddess herself. In mythic terms, the mysterious forest, scene of the hunt—called the "virgin forest" when impenetrable and before it is laid bare—is a widespread image of femininity. Thus sexual penetration is "the normal impulse to discover the way to the inside."[40]

At the dawn of Western civilization, then, the hunt is associated with masculinity and the rational investigation and sexual penetration of a feminine prey. It is no wonder that in Euro-American mythology, the hunter's prey is also symbolized as the feminine object of the male's desire—whether that object is a "feminine" animal such as a deer or bear, the pure and "virgin" land before it is despoiled,[41] a "feminized" and mysterious racial Other such as the Native Americans, or a literal woman as the target of a sexual chase or rape.[42]

Academicians are obviously more likely to hunt after knowledge than an animal or human prey. But putting all this together, I would suggest that we have a strong tendency to sexualize the quest for knowledge, such that the *knower* is coded masculine and the *known* is feminine. Although Joseph Campbell is elsewhere extremely helpful in understanding the takeover of the Goddess by invading patriarchal cultures, this duality has infected even his explication of the heroic monomyth. In Campbell's formulation, the hero is presumed the male *knower*, and what must be *known* is the woman, the Queen Goddess of the World.[43]

As you might well imagine, no one with whom I talked saw herself as violent against or voyeuristic of the feminine in any way. But in academia, where the pen is mightier than the sword, war is often waged against femininity in a linguistic attitude that seeps through even pro-Other and specifically feminist discourse. When a woman, however unwittingly, fights by the side of the institutional man, it is as if her veil of respectability hardens into a shield or, since we are "talking Amazon" here, into an arrow aimed at the soft heart of her kin. At this point, the primary difference between the conquered Amazon and the Brainchild is her venue (the Amazon's is nature and the Brainchild's is the city) and her mission (the Amazon's is war and the hunt, and the Brainchild's is craft and diplomacy).[44] And whereas the Amazon's stance is offensive, the Brainchild's is defensive.

This "hunt" is visible, I think, in some of the methods used to conduct academic inquiry, and, like the hunter's reverence for the weapon he carries, in our love for those methods themselves. Both the humanist and the scientist—through analytical critique and scientific investigation—often employ these techniques like a hunter employs his weapon to bring down the prey. Theory and jargon erect an intellectual edifice that guards against getting "taken in" by a beguiling object of inquiry, a sort of academic siren song that could succeed in destroying the knower.

Many of us academicians write and talk in what Catherine MacKinnon calls "highly coded conversations," in "ways that no one understands."[45] Indeed, the parodies of deconstructive and postmodern language style that have appeared in print and become a staple of Internet humor demonstrate how detached the "look" often is from the looked-at. Especially those critics who have an egalitarian agenda are industrious and unfailing in the dissembling of deceit, more interested in truth than beauty (unless to unmask the latter), more realistic than romantic, and more sober than playful. This is serious business, this dissembling of the cultural masquerade that hegemonic culture constantly parades before us.

Once I casually perused a handful of published critiques in my library, and turned up these, admittedly selective but recurring, verbs indicating what critics—both women and men—intend to do to their textual object of inquiry:

> examine, investigate, scrutinize, grasp, refute, deconstruct, contest, investigate, combat, interrogate, decode, disclose, unmask, unveil, demystify, uncover, lay bare, open up, reveal, pin down, fasten onto, penetrate, probe, attack, dismantle, destroy.

There are notable exceptions, but rarely do critics, not to mention scientists, represent themselves as open, appreciative, or receptive to revelation by their objects of inquiry—for that would be to fall captive to their spell. Unlike the goddess huntress, who *was* nature, this academic hunter must *control* her.

Here is an example of what I am talking about. It is especially apropos because it is from Laura Mulvey, a remarkably influential feminist critic whose theory of the "cinematic male gaze" attempts to deconstruct how the masculine "look" dominates the female within Hollywood films through the kind of voyeurism I have been discussing. She wants to challenge the cinema of the past for its courting of masculine pleasure at the expense of the feminine, and so she intentionally declares war:

> Psychoanalytic theory is thus appropriated here as a political *weapon*, demonstrating the way the unconscious of patriarchal society has structured film form.[46] [emphasis mine]

And here is how that weapon shall be deployed:

> It is said that analyzing pleasure, or beauty, *destroys it*. That is the intention of this article. The satisfaction and reinforcement of the ego that represent the high point of film history hitherto must be *attacked*.[47] [emphasis mine]

Turning her own linguistic gaze upon the very gaze she would demolish, she herself becomes a remarkably similar sadistic voyeur.

This is what I mean when I suggest that an Amazon—even an exceedingly well-meaning one—can turn against her kin. Having unwittingly joined the patriarchy by adopting its values and its language, she lances the mysterious heart of the feminine with her words.

UNDERGROUND AMAZON

The captured Amazon queen is not always a willing combatant against her sisters. She is often forcibly isolated from the upperworld action. Many an Amazon fighter has felt so severed from the academic hierarchy that she has left or wanted to leave it altogether. No wonder Abby, who found research to be so "penetrative," was planning to leave the academy after she finished paying back her sabbatical. I have heard the epithets hurled at unrepentant Amazonian types: "strident," "overly opinionated," "humorless," "angry feminist," "bitch," "bull dyke." *How many feminists does it take to change a light bulb? One, and that's not funny!* So the joke goes. Women face still again a double-bind whereby "femininity" brings disrespect, and toughness—the very mark of success for a man—spells ostracism for a woman.

In Montalvo's epic as well as in other myths, the Amazon is ultimately forced to live underground, under water, or on an island, where her threat is controlled, if her mystery remains. If she has been sexualized, as so often happens, she is, as a fish-woman or island nymph, almost indistinguishable from the Siren. Some of the women we met in the Siren chapter were also Amazonian—especially the brilliant Vanessa—and whereas she had not let herself be excluded from the conversation, she did evoke fantasies of domination from her male colleagues. And, the more she practiced her intellectual prowess, the more isolated she became from men and from other women.

Sooner or later, the Underworld seems to claim each and every one of our mythic female characters. There are reasons, as we have seen, why the Goddess in all her revelations has been relegated to this shadowy realm, and there are reasons, as we shall see, that she needs to visit there periodically. But there are no good reasons why she must stay. Now it is time to consider how she might emerge into the light.

PART THREE

ONE-IN-HERSELF

We have been looking at some of the ways women struggle to define themselves separately from men. The mythological Siren, the Veiled Woman, and the Amazon take us partway to independence. The Siren has a powerful allure, the Veiled Woman can use her covering to protect a nascent potential, and the Amazon fights with women against other warriors, often men. But each has her downside. The Siren's power is linked only to her sexuality and can evoke domination from men. The Veiled Woman must separate herself into two figures—the one in bondage, who is "respectable," and the free woman, who is a "whore." And the Amazon has often been a target for men who boost their heroism by conquering or bedding her.

But we do not have to leave it at that. The ancient Goddess was sometimes called "Virgin." But this word meant something completely different from today's reference to a chaste or pre-sexual woman. The Virgin in her original sense was a woman who was autonomous, whole, and free. Whether sexually experienced, promiscuous, or abstinent, she was "one-in-herself"—not dependent on any man to define her. The word applied to a woman who belonged only to herself.[1]

I have chosen the myth of "Eros and Psyche" as a model of a woman coming to terms with herself. As a story of a relationship, and ultimately a marriage, it is particularly relevant to academic women, who I have claimed are often bound in a "dark marriage" to an academic man or to academia itself. This is Psyche's predicament, and yet she frees herself from the darkness while also growing her relationship to Eros. Thus, this story is an unusual model of how a woman can be one-in-herself without finally separating from men. It is a complex myth, and so we will consider it in three chapters—her marriage, her labors, and her child.

CHAPTER 9

PSYCHE'S MARRIAGE

In the same body she hated the beast and loved the husband.

Lucius Apuleius, *Amor and Psyche*

Near the beginning of this book I recounted the treasonous way my body commented on my PhD commencement ceremony. In many ways I envy the more deliberate anti-rituals designed by Juliana and Jenny to celebrate their doctoral accomplishments. Certainly, they exhibited a good deal more flair. Juliana burned her dissertation in a jubilant bonfire attended by her husband and friends. Jenny burned hers on a camping trip, divvying up the chapters among her husband and her friends. There *was* a difference between their acts. Juliana meant her flaming sacrifice to stick. Although she was highly regarded as a promising social scientist, she refused to graduate, to this day remains an ABD (all but dissertation), and is flourishing as a brilliant novelist. Jenny, whom you met in the last chapter as an Amazon, burned hers in effigy. "I had a backup, I assure you!" she said. Jenny is now happily ensconced as an assistant professor, enjoying her research and her teaching.

All along, I have been exploring how collegiate women can be bound within a dark marriage, whether the groom be a literal man, the institution of academia, or her own inner *animus*. Juliana represents a path suggested by Abby and followed by more than a few: *Get a divorce!* Her deepest creativity flowered after her conflagration, as if fertilized by its ashes. Jenny decided to stay married to academe, so to speak, but to liberate herself from her "fear-based subservience" to an advisor who considered her achievements to be won despite her low class, which he believed she could never thoroughly transcend. She threw the acknowledgements to her dissertation—which of course included a thank-you to him—into the flames herself. She called her campfire "my rite of passage," indicating it marked the end of a long period of quavering self-esteem and frequent tears, like the Handless Maiden washing clean her mutilated arms. The inner demon that spoke often of her inferiority seemed after that to skulk back into the black forest outside her circle of protection.

The form of these women's rites of passage is as significant as it is amusing. Simultaneously destructive and creative, fire has long stood for enlightenment—a banishing of the clouds of unknowing that keep humans unconscious of their bondage. Prometheus' theft of fire from Olympus is often noted as the mythic act that set humanity against the gods by plotting the course for science and technology to free us forever from the obscurity of ignorance. Along with Apollo the Shining One, Prometheus is the Greek patron saint of academia. And, as we shall see, the light of fire is crucial to the liberation of women from their vows to an academic god, so often solemnized in the dark.

Prometheus' deeds and those of these women were passionate acts of defiance in the service of liberation. Yet they also differed markedly. Prometheus' exploit was noble but rash, as his name (Prometheus = foresight) ironically implies; the women's were planned and invitational. Prometheus stole from the heavens, while the women's thefts were connected to the earth. Prometheus' was a heroic conquest that produced an individuated martyr; the women's were communal rites supported by their "tribes." Prometheus stole knowledge from the gods; the women incinerated knowledge they themselves had produced.

In their quest for a Self that is not defined by the patriarchy, academic women must light the lamps that enable them to see where they have been and where they might go. But I believe they typically achieve this in ways that are opposite to those employed by men. To me, the myth of "Eros and Psyche" (an image of which graces the cover of this book) not only expresses these differences, but enlightens the path for many women, who are more likely than men to seek freedom *within* relationship—whether that be a relationship with a specific man or men, with academia itself, or with the voice of the *animus* inside. As Joyce Fletcher points out, the central tenet of feminist relational theory "is that growth is not so much a process of separating and individuating oneself from others, but something that occurs in a context of relational connection with and to other people.[1] Ruth, a 54-year-old successful chairperson, said, for example, that she does not commit to controversial issues "unless they're *really* important—because they risk relationships." Yet Ruth was respected by her large department, by the university faculty as a whole, within which she held high office, and by administrators who were her superiors.

For some, Psyche's redefining of her marriage to an unknown god may be a destination of sorts, although the journey of one's avocation never really comes to an end. Others may see it as an intermediate step—the clarifying and maturing of important relationships before she strikes out on her own. Whichever may be true for you, Psyche's quest does elucidate the stories of many women with whom I spoke.

The most complete written version of this tale comes from the *Metamorphoses* or *The Golden Ass* by Apuleius, written in the second century A.D. Like all the Greek or Latin myths I have considered, this one can be read with patriarchal overtones, leading some scholars to dismiss it as yet another debilitating transmutation of earlier Goddess myths. Meredith Powers, for example, sees it as telling "of a wife who learns to contain her curiosity and become deferential."[2] Instead of finding the divinity within herself, Psyche finds it within her husband, "as the male became the single absolute repository of divinity allowable in Western thought."[3]

Yet Powers seems to ignore several relevant factors that associate this myth with the very Goddess religions she is trying to recover. According to Powers, the archetypal feminine divinity is committed to *eros* rather than *logos*.[4] Psyche, of course, is quite literally *married* to Eros. She does not passively await redemption from without, but actively creates it herself—although, assuredly, with help from other creatures.[5] One of these helpers is Eros, but he is not the one who lays down the conditions of her redemption—his mother Aphrodite does. Psyche also travels down under the earth to meet another abysmal goddess, Persephone, Queen of the Underworld. Such movement is more common to female than to male patterns of heroism, suggesting the descent of the Sumerian Inanna to meet her dark sister Ereshkigal and of Persephone herself. Psyche mourns a lost love, as Demeter did her daughter Persephone when Hades abducted her. Above all, this is a myth of individuation through *relationship*, a model which many, including Powers, see as based in pre-patriarchal Goddess religions that placed more emphasis on the unity of the tribe than on the glory of the individual.[6]

Indeed, Erich Neumann finds parallels in "Eros and Psyche" to the Eleusinian mysteries of Isis, which were central to the Goddess religions and much older than Apuleius, who describes in *The Golden Ass* his own initiation into these mysteries. And the myths and mysteries of the chthonic Aphrodite, who propels the action here, are not Greek but from the Middle Eastern domain of the Great Mother.[7] Apuleius certainly added his own sexist touches, as we have seen that men-running-alone-with-their-pens are prone to do, and we should be on the lookout for these. Yet the core of the story is still valuable for contemporary women.

Here I will tell the first part of the tale—of Psyche's predicament and her critical decision to enlighten herself with regard to her husband. In the next chapter I will pick up the story with the tasks Psyche must perform in order to find out who she is.

Eros and Psyche[8]

A king had three beautiful daughters. The youngest, Psyche, was so beautiful that people said she was the new Aphrodite, and they began to worship her rather than the ancient Goddess. None deigned to court Psyche, however, for her loveliness rendered them speechless. The king asked Apollo's oracle to send Psyche a husband, but the oracle pronounced a horrible decree, which could be traced back to the enraged Aphrodite: Psyche should be dressed for her funeral and taken to a high mountain crag, where she would be married to a dreadful monster of Death.

Aphrodite had sent her son Eros to shoot Psyche with one of his arrows and enflame her with love for the vilest of beasts. Instead, he fell in love with her himself and determined to wed her secretly. At his bequest, the West Wind lifted her from the mountaintop into the Valley of Paradise. Inside a jeweled palace, her god-husband visited her only at night, promising her everything she desired as long as she did not look upon his face. If she broke that promise, he would leave her and their child would be born mortal.

But Psyche's two sisters, having been married to old men without the riches that Psyche inherited, became jealous beyond endurance. Because Psyche had never actually seen her husband, they convinced her that he was a serpent, and bade her place a lamp and a knife near the bed. Upon lighting the lamp, she would see that he was a beast, and she was to sever his head from his body while he slept.

Making the preparations her sisters suggested, Psyche gained the courage one night to light the lamp. She beheld not a monster, but the very god of love, the most beautiful on all Olympus. Trying to plunge the knife into her own heart with grief at her own foolish disloyalty, she dropped it, accidentally pricked herself on one of Eros' arrows, and fell in love with Love, just as a drop of hot oil awoke him.

Winged Eros took flight and, perching in a tree, admonished poor Psyche that he would punish her sisters and leave her forever. Psyche clung to her fleeing husband in despair, until she was borne out of Paradise and fell to the earth, her energy spent. Eros flew back home to his mother to nurse his wound and endure fierce recriminations under her lock and key.

APHRODITE AND PSYCHE

This myth begins with a motif that ought to raise our feminist shackles. The demeaning beauty contest among women—such as the Judgment of Paris in the *Cypria*—became a ubiquitous patriarchal innovation that set goddess figures, originally aspects of the single goddess or the trinity, against each other with petty in-fighting.[9] Certainly, this kind of competition endures today in popular culture, such as television's insidious *The Bachelor* and its spin-offs, in which women become foes for the favors of a man. *Don't hate me because I'm beautiful,* the impossibly gorgeous TV celebrity taunts other women in order to sell hair color. Even in academia, in which beauty is not openly prized, such rivalries can divide women. We saw, for example, how my honors professor arranged a contest of intellectual prowess between my friend and me for his erotic affections. We also saw how Kate's and her best friend's dissertation advisors set up a "horse race" between the two young Mistresses, who were both looking for jobs in the same field.

Yet, despite this trivial overlay, the conflict between Aphrodite and Psyche runs deep. Erich Neumann, in fact, sees it as the central motif of the story. It is the struggle between the once all-powerful Great Mother—said to be older than Time—[10] and the "second Aphrodite," "the newly begotten and newly born," and thus it heralds a "radical transformation in man's relation to Aphrodite."[11] You may remember our young pot-smoking, ocean-surfing, wet-haired, debate-winning Maiden Lover Maggie, whom I likened to Botticelli's "The Birth of Venus," ethereally floating to shore on a seashell. In fact, Aphrodite's oceanic residence is the maternal unconscious. Born when Uranus' severed phallus fell into the sea, she also represents the union of the anonymous powers of Above and Below, and of masculine and feminine. From her viewpoint, the masculine and the feminine are not that distinct in humans and in animals; she is the un-individuated principle of sexuality and fertility, and beauty is primarily for initiating that process. She is as ruthless as she is irresistible. She is the Great Mother, intent on punishing Psyche for the hubris of upstaging her, as in the constellations of Greek tragedy. Her son's arrows are her weapons.[12]

Psyche, on the other hand, is earthly and human, having been born when a dewdrop fell on the land.[13] Thus she represents the newer evolutionary principle of conscious individuality. "Over the material-psychic love principle of Aphrodite as goddess of the mutual attraction between opposites rises Psyche's love principle, which with this attraction connects knowledge, the growth of consciousness, and psychic development."[14]

As we can also see at a glance, the title of this myth unites love (Eros) with knowledge, awareness, and psychic development (Psyche). Throughout this book, I have honored those ancient goddesses long buried under the towering structures of patriarchy, including the ivory one of academe. Not the least of these is Aphrodite, whose magical powers spark the fires of many a romance within academia's walls. As the principle of universal, otherworldly sexual love, Aphrodite's presence fuels countless pairings, fruitful or otherwise. Yet, if a contemporary woman, most centrally an academic one, remains under Aphrodite's spell, she does so at her own peril. For Aphrodite is not in the least concerned with knowledge or her own development—she simply *is*. Once, the students in my graduate seminar paid me the premature but supreme compliment of a bright red t-shirt with the phrase I KNOW WHAT I KNOW printed in white on the front. I jogged in it for decades, until I finally had to relegate it to my heap of threadbare dust cloths. To survive within academe, a woman not only needs to be knowledgeable but also to know what she knows. Because at least part of her is likely to be about relationships, she needs to get past the lush, raw power of attraction to her dark mate and see who she is in relation to him.

MARRIED TO DEATH

The funeral procession of Psyche in preparation for her dreadful wedding is a vestige of the ancient ritual of the marriage of death, or the "death of the maiden." From the matriarchal point of view, every marriage is the "rape of Kore"—the Virgin aspect of the Triple Goddess—who is carried off by the hostile male.[15] But even though she is afraid, Psyche seems to accept her fate, perhaps from an inner knowing that it is necessary.[16] As with "The Handless Maiden," who was also given away to a monster by her father, it is this separation from parental containment, harsh though it may be, that will force her to evolve into a mature woman. Hades abducted Persephone, you might recall, while she was picking flowers—of which the most attractive was the *narcissus*, a symbol of her unreflective containment in the parental circle. Though it also seemed harsh, Juliana and Jenny seemed to know that they must incinerate their foremost intellectual accomplishments in order to bring death to their academic maidenhood and evolve into mature women.

Psyche actually admonishes her parents to put away their

weeping in the kind of naively prescient antithesis only possible in youth:

> Lead me on and set me on the crag that fate has appointed. I hasten to meet that blest union, I hasten to behold the noble husband that awaits me. Why do I put off and shun his coming? Was he not born to destroy all the world?[17]

Following the torch-lit funeral march to the top of the crag, she then trembles and weeps before she is carried away on the breath of the West Wind.

Psyche expects to be seized by a vile beast, but she is instead lifted off the mountain by a soft breeze. As we have seen, the Maiden Lover is often "carried away" by her intoxication for a man she idealizes as an Underground Genius. Laura described her relationship with her advisor Al as a "romantic haze"; Maggie spoke of living "on the edge" when her debate coach Rick fell for her; Carrie recounted being "swept off her feet" by Greg when she interviewed for a job on his campus. I rode the waves of countercultural rapture when my honors professor pursued me. I have also felt captivated by my many Critical Fathers within, who pin my soul to standards of perfection that "disarm" me. Many women speak of their early academic experiences, whether fair or ill, in these terms of being overwhelmed and out of control.

Neumann calls Psyche a "feminine Prometheus" because both disobey the gods in order to attain knowledge.[18] It may help to look again at their differences. In an act both foolhardy and heroic, Prometheus seizes fire from Olympus and gives it to humankind so that they may have light. Psyche's development, on the other hand, "does not occur in a Promethean-masculine opposition to the divine, but in a divine, erotic seizure of love, which shows her to be even more deeply rooted in the center of the divine Aphrodite."[19] In Greek, *Psyche* means "feminine soul."[20] As this myth would have it, the feminine soul's first initiation into knowledge happens by *being seized* rather than *seizing*, and in relationship to the god, rather than in defiance of him. It is as though she must allow her ravishment, not knowing how it will turn out, in order to put an end to her narcissistic attachment to maidenhood. Perhaps this is why so many women, considerably after the fact of their early initiatory experiences, spoke with reverence for what they had learned from their "seizures." Serving as Pygmalion's Maiden Lover, for many, was paradoxically the beginning of the end of their blissful maidenhood—in this case, their youthful obliviousness to academic realities.

Prometheus acts first and suffers later. Psyche suffers first and acts later. My husband Tom, is an excellent Promethean. Not only is he rooted in the masculine experience, but on the Meyers-Briggs test of psychological types he is also an intuitive-thinker, possessed of what David Keirsey and Marilyn Bates call a "Promethean temperament."[21] In scholarship he demands to know, and, in teaching, he demands that his students know. He is often motivated by bettering the condition of those below him, and he will readily "seize knowledge from the gods" in order to do so; for example, he will find out a secret from an administrative "god" and share it with his students without thinking of the consequences to himself. He tends to know what he thinks and wants ahead of time (Pro + metheus = "foresight"), and if it turns out that he is mistaken, he will suffer the penalty later. It is Tom's nature to "think deviously," as in the time Prometheus tricked Zeus into choosing an inferior sacrifice by covering the unappetizing bones in fat.[22] Like the trickster that Prometheus is, Tom seems willing to "suffer the fool" to prove a point—*his* point! So what if he is compelled to go back and undo his certitude in order to appease the gods of scholarly citation or pedagogical correctness? Tom wants fire, and he will get it at any cost.[23]

More of the feminine earth than Tom's fiery Titan, I am like Psyche. Now that I understand my process of knowing, I refer to it as "composting," expecting something green will sprout from the muck. When I am decomposing, though, I do not have this sort of hope. It is as if I am blind, like Audrey Hepburn in *Wait Until Dark,* and must simply accept my fate. The process is this: any significant knowledge that comes to me, whether about myself, my relationships, or my work (actually, it's usually all of these together), occurs after a period of darkness in which I descend into Hades, suffering the agonies of the damned, and fall into a death-like resignation or sleep. Often I lose faith that I will find my way above ground. Inevitably, however, if I submit to such a seizure by the "monster of death," I will, after what seems like an eternity, find myself in a clearing, and not one of my own making. As with Psyche, "the tempest passes from my soul," and I can rest for awhile until the next one arrives.

My way of knowing and Tom's are equally valuable to the academy. Zeus' mind is the static mind of a patriarchal institution, if not those within it. It is, as Carl Kerényi puts it, "precisely like a mirror that takes in everything without distortion and reflects it. It contains a motionless image of all being, of all deeds good and bad with their consequences, hence it is free from all will or desire to change anything."[24] More than any other god, Prometheus reminds us of Hermes, "whose deception springs from a creative art, which enriches the divinity of the world with playful magic."[25] Prometheus thus ushers in the "deviation" which changes Being to Becoming, and he does it through *contest*. Just so, Tom upsets the apple cart of dry academic structure. Although academia is not pleased when it is tricked, it does honor Prometheus' way, for his is fundamental to "the advancement of knowledge," often cited as the raison d'être of higher education. My way of knowing, like Psyche's, is also capable of bringing up water from a dry well. But, as should be evident by now, it is not as valued within academia. And that is one reason we need to look further into this myth.

THE IVORY PALACE

Psyche expects to meet her beast, but instead is carried to a luminous palace. Here is Apuleius' luxuriant depiction:

> The tempest had passed from her soul. She beheld a grove of huge and lofty trees, she beheld a transparent fountain of glassy water. In the very heart of the grove beside the gliding stream there stood a palace, built by no human hands but by the cunning of a god. You will perceive, as soon as I have taken you within, that it is the pleasant and luxurious dwelling of some deity that I present to your gaze. For the fretted roof on high was curiously carved of sandalwood and ivory, and the columns that upheld it were of gold.[26]

It is hard to ignore that this palace is made of *ivory*, as if the myth were anticipating our use of it. As I read Apuleius' portrait, I looked back at my own retrospective on arriving at UCLA for my first full-time academic job, as if I had been deposited there miraculously by some unforeseen fair wind. Here is my description from the "Alma Mater" chapter:

> Walking one perfect day from Royce Hall to the student union across expansive lawns connecting the archetypally collegiate buildings, I felt I was in one of those Hudson River Valley paintings where the beneficence of God shines down through the clouds, surrounding the tiny human figure with an otherworldly column of light. "This is it," I thought, "I've arrived."

Certainly not every woman relates to her collegiate or career academic experience as the Valley of Paradise. But some of the phrases we retain to speak of academia do attest to its numinous attraction for many: "Ivory Tower," "Ivy League," "ivy-covered walls," "college town on the hill," and "hail to you, my alma mater." Whereas you might think these images are reserved for freshmen co-eds and alumni returning for homecoming, I found they also had a tenacious hold on women who entered or re-entered academia in mid-life. Over tacos in a remote mountain town I spoke with Beth, a 54-year-old divorced mother of two daughters who both have PhD's. She had recently ended her twenty-five-year marriage to a successful man and gone back to school for her own doctorate. She was looking for the perfect college teaching job, and had traveled widely to determine where that might be. It should be a "classic college town," not too large and not too small, in the mountains or on the coast, with beautiful surroundings, cultural offerings in the arts, and a liberal approach to political issues. "I entered academia to seek liberation," she explained. "I cannot settle for just any campus with a job opening."

Of course, the brilliance of Eros' ivory palace prolongs Psyche's acceptance of the untenable situation to come. C. S. Lewis underlines the illusory nature of the palace in *Till We Have Faces* by having only Psyche be able to see it. Her sister Orual tries hard to catch a glimpse of it, but cannot. Those academic Maiden Lovers who are infatuated with their Pygmalions dwell longer in the mirage than those who avoid such couplings. And so do Brainchildren such as I, who carry the Fathers' banner and "speak for the male with all their hearts." The Ivory Tower's luster goes far to maintain the perfectionist ideal that keeps many of us in thrall to its demands.

As is true of most aspects of this myth, however, the ivory

palace has its more beneficent uses. While prolonging her innocence, it also becomes the crucible that protects Psyche within its comforting environs until she becomes strong enough to question her secret lover—and perhaps until she is strong enough to do without the dwelling, if it must come to that. In addition to "female soul," "Psyche" means "moth" or "butterfly," and Psyche is sometimes shown in art as such because the early Greeks believed that human souls could occupy flying insects while passing from one life to the next.[27] For those women intoxicated with a male lover—whether in the flesh, in the tower, or in their dreams—the ivory palace can serve as a cocoon that shelters her until, true to her nature, she develops the wings to break out and fly toward the inevitable light.

AN ECSTASY OF DARKNESS

As a stranger in the palace, Psyche is soon soothed by "disembodied voices" and the secret visitations of her lover. Even before it happens, Eros seems to know that Psyche's sisters will cause trouble because he implores her early on to ignore their lamentations; he anticipates any sign that will ruin her ignorant bliss. She assents to his demands, but weeps when he is away. He upbraids her when he hears her crying, and she replies:

> Sooner would I die a hundred deaths than be robbed of your sweet love. For whoever you are, I love you and adore you passionately. I love you as I love life itself. Compared with you [Eros]' own self would be as nothing.[28]

"Yet this ecstasy in which she murmurs 'Husband, sweet as honey' and 'Psyche's life and love' is an ecstasy of darkness," writes Neumann. She may not look upon his face or know who he is. "It is the ever-recurring 'Never question me,' the order not to enter the 'closed room,' whose infringement is to encompass Psyche's ruin."[29] It is like Bluebeard's injunction that his young wife never enter the forbidden room containing the skeletons of his former wives,[30] and Zeus' refusal to let any of his mortal conquests see him as he is, on pain of death.

Psyche's "closed room" is not the same as the chest of drawers in which I created my own sacred circle, the basement cubicles in which women sang in my "Lost in the Halls of Science" dream, the Handless Maiden's protective circle of chalk, or many other women's ways of protecting their tender new projects. Psyche assents to it because she doesn't know any better, and it is imposed from without, not chosen from within. In academic terms, if Eros can be viewed as an outer man or—true to the fact that he only visits her at night—as her inner *animus*—then Psyche's night chamber constitutes all the prohibitions against women's seeing imposed by men and the masculine institution, as well as the "disembodied voices" inside her head. Sometimes there is ecstasy within this secret chamber; when there is pain, it seems to me, the woman is waking up.

I asked many of the women I interviewed, "What are you not supposed to see within academia?" My intent was to evoke those aspects for which they expected punishment if, like Psyche, they were caught looking. Many of their answers reflect things that are now well known, due to feminism's rigorous exposure of such gender inequalities: Women are not supposed to notice that a Good Ol' Boys' Club still excludes even women at upper ranks or having superior qualifications from the true fraternity inside the Tower. They are not supposed to comment on women's lower pay or the diminishing number of women as the ranks get higher. They are not supposed to complain that men have traditionally had wives to support their tenure and promotion process by tending the home fires, while women do not have such support systems. And they are not supposed to see that an entrenched informal system favors men mentoring men over women mentoring women, or even the pattern discussed in this book, men mentoring women.

You are likely to recognize these prohibitions, as well as what punishments they may elicit: namely, that speaking them aloud risks further ostracism from the club. But the framework of myth exposes some additional forms of deep knowing about men and the academy that women are not supposed to see. Although scholarship increasingly addresses these prohibitions, few women know how to articulate them clearly, due to the extreme effort that patriarchy has expended in keeping them hidden over the millennia. However, many of the stories the women told me comment indirectly on these signs of the closed room.

The fundamental prohibition of the academic closed room is against looking at how deeply the Goddess, in her ancient as well as her more-evolved forms, is buried under the Ivory Tower. Although they have often been mortal enemies, as in the battle between faith and science on issues such as creationism vs. evolution, the academy and the church are partners in the exile, rape, and murder of the divine feminine. As a result, traditionally feminine ways of knowing do not typically inform life at the university.

In his bestselling novel *The Da Vinci Code*, Dan Brown dabbles in truth, not fiction, when he writes of the Goddess' interment:

> The Catholic Inquisition published the book that arguably could be called the most blood-soaked publication in human history. *Malleus Maleficarum*—or *The Witches' Hammer*—indoctrinated the world to "the dangers of freethinking women" and instructed the clergy how to locate, torture, and destroy them. Those deemed "witches" by the Church included all female scholars, priestesses, gypsies, mystics, nature lovers, herb gatherers, and any women "suspiciously attuned to the natural world." Midwives also were killed for their heretical practice of using medical knowledge to ease the pain of childbirth—a suffering, the Church claimed, that was God's rightful punishment for Eve's partaking of the Apple of Knowledge, thus giving birth to the idea of Original Sin. During three hundred years of witch hunts, the Church burned at the stake an astounding five *million* women.[31]

Perhaps you fastened onto the phrase "female scholars" in this quote. I certainly did. I also found it chilling that they are lumped with "priestesses, gypsies, mystics, nature lovers, [and] herb gatherers," for all these female roles describe ways of knowing that are foreign to academia. We do not usually think of this history of witch hunting when we refer to the Holocaust, but surely it qualifies.

Were the Goddess ascendant, many of academe's most sacred rituals and requirements could not hold sway; they would be sundered by her wrath or—what might prove more devastating to their pretension—by her laughter. For anyone "suspiciously attuned to the natural world" would have to question publish-or-perish standards that demand she be always *up* and never *down*, as if she were totally untethered from the Earth, whose rhythms are cyclical. All creative processes mimic those of the Earth, alternating periods of stasis when everything green disappears below to decompose before it emerges in the spring with a promise of fecundity. Yet at "research" universities, young professors must hit the ground running, preferably with several publications already in hand, increasing the pace over the few short years before they go "up" for tenure. No "down time" is allowed, for they must prove themselves immediately productive.[32]

The academy does retain some vestiges of a ritual that honors the work of the creative soul. I am speaking of the "sabbatical," which stems from American universities' connective origins with Judeo-Christianity. Granted in seven-year intervals (if one is exceedingly fortunate), the academic sabbatical is based on the Biblical adoption of the holy number "seven" as the day God rested from his creative labors, and also the commandment from Leviticus to rest in the seventh year. According to Plutarch, Judaism adapted the "sabbath" from the festival of Dionysus at Delphi. Dionysus is, of course, the god of the vine who was cut into pieces by the orgiastic maenads each year, only to be reborn in the spring.

The origins of this rite are certainly with the Goddess. To the ancient Babylonians, *sappatu* meant "the time for quieting the heart," and *shavat* in Hebrew means cessation of work, a time to let the fields lie fallow and remain unplanted. But the academic sabbatical has somehow transformed into a time to get *more* work done, not less. We have completely reversed the meaning of "sabbatical" and forgotten that even an academic "field," much less a person, must be watered to stay alive.[33]

Many of the women we have already met lamented their lack of time to tend to the soil—literally or figuratively. Sophia had a fondness for "growing things" and regretted that she could not find time to have children or to concentrate on her home; perhaps that is why, one year, she planted a thousand daffodils around her house. Claire liked to spend time with her sister's and her neighbor's children, and enjoyed "creating things—gardening, growing herbs and flowers." Shandra and her husband wanted to have a child, but she regretted that she did not have time. Laura wanted to write something more "feminine" than what she considered "academic," but exited academia instead. Christine loved her mystical spiritual studies, but hid them from her department. Monica, a young professor trying to earn tenure in a creative field, said "I love my job, but I hate working in the university." When I asked what she meant, she said there was never enough time to nurture her students' artistry, much less her own—she was too caught in the "daily grind" of teaching several courses a semester, serving on numerous committees, and being pressured to out-publish another assistant professor hired when she was.

All these women knew they were not to talk about such things in public, for that would risk losing it all. For all its detriments, academia still promised considerable riches. A bodiless voice spoke to Psyche when she tentatively explored the wondrous palace. "'Why, lady,' it said, 'are you overwhelmed at the sight of so great wealth? All is yours.'"[34]

The Goddess' repression ushered in a concurrent prohibition against seeing what happened to male power within the university, and that is the movement of its seat upward from phallus to brain. We have noted Zeus' handy trick of swallowing Metis in order to give birth to Athena through his head. In this story, Powers points out, "Hesiod begins the permanent association of phallic and cerebral," a juxtapositioning which became quite popular as a justification for the male-dominated hierarchy.[35] Powers argues that this process of cognitive reorganization reached its zenith in fifth-century Athenian tragedy, which led culture toward *logos*, the masculine, analytic way of knowing associated with Olympian religion, and away from *eros*, which was "feminine, connective, but also mysterious, threatening, and deemed repellent. With the emerging of *logos* as a dominant idea, the genital aspects of male sexuality were downplayed in favor of loftier phrenic activities."[36]

In this rather spectacular feat of parthenogenesis—reproduction without concourse between opposite sexes—the birthing function within those realms that privilege *logos* not only was co-opted by patriarchy but also shifted *upward* from the genitals to the head. Nativity "suspiciously attuned to the natural world," like herb-gathering or midwifery, became suspect. Contemporary colloquialisms preserve the connection, as when we call fellatio "giving head," restrooms "the head," and the forcing of any process "bringing things to a head." In academia, the erect phallus is often the hidden blueprint to assess the "birth" of an idea or argument, as when we say, "I thought that *up* myself," "He *erected* an impenetrable theoretical structure," "She was not thinking *straight*," or "He is a straight shooter." It also looms behind many standard academic practices, as when we say, "The scientists wrote *up* their report," "We sent the proposal *up* for consideration, "I worked hard and long on that project," and "We measured their productivity by a *yardstick* of success."[37]

This link between phallic and phrenic is more than linguistically cute. As implied by the metaphorical "yardstick," which evokes images of discipline as well as a standard by which one might measure a penis, the phallic/cerebral nexus is associated with domination. This came home to me serendipitously one night when I was out for dinner with several friends. Edie, a young second-year assistant professor whose field considered her headed toward superstardom, began to tell our group about her recent experience at a small conference of researchers in her area. She spoke of being "repeatedly attacked and cornered" by a well-known older male professor. Although he did not physically strike her, he would position himself physically so that she could not free herself from the walls where she was "pinned in" without causing a scene.

Thus positioned, he came on to her sexually while belittling a paper she had just presented. The arguments in her research had countered his well-established theories on a social science problem that had, perhaps not coincidentally, to do with the contributions of the sexes to culture. Edie felt scared and disoriented during the conference, and began to avoid any functions where this man was likely to be—which at a small gathering meant that she was cut out of the intellectual conversation. "I didn't realize it at the time," she related, "but my colleagues helped me to realize I had been sexually harassed. Actually, I felt as if I'd been raped."

"Did you tell anyone there about what you saw happening to you?" I asked.

"Oh no," Edie said. "I didn't want to get a reputation as a troublemaker. I figured it was best to just avoid him from then on." I wondered if she would even continue her line of research after this event.

Of course, one reason it is difficult to see this conjoining of the lingum with the logos is the Pygmalion/Maiden Lover scenario that seems so prevalent in the university. Although the men and women in these relationships were hardly of equal power, many of the women were caught up, like Psyche, in a blissful liaison. The combination of intellect and sex is intoxicating for women as well as men, as both Maggie and Laura implied when they called it "heady." Many of these pairings ended beneficently. But when the women progressed into Muse, and especially into Mistress, the dominating quality of the head/phallus ligament usually became apparent. Here, if not before, the women began to see much more clearly, to enter that closed room and question the ecstasy of their darkness.

LIGHTING THE LAMP

Psyche's sisters are kin to the evil stepsisters in many fairy tales; they are jealous of her wealth and alleged young husband. In setting her on a path they believe will bring her ruin, they bring it on themselves instead—both are dropped from the high mountain crag by the very West Wind that saved Psyche. Like Aphrodite, the sisters represent the offended matriarchal Goddess principle—especially that which has become enslaved to patriarchy, as they are married to old men who use them as servants. Yet as Psyche's dark side or shadow, they also represent what her unconscious already knows—that she must end her somnolent bliss before she can mature. She is going to have to cleave her rapturous union with the one she cannot see. Thus, the sisters actually set Psyche on the path of enlightenment, as does even Aphrodite, who sets up Psyche's entire journey. Or, we might say that the older Goddess, even in her debased form, has wisdom needed by the new.[38]

The sisters' instructions are very specific. Psyche is to hide a knife and light an oil lamp:

> Let the light teach you how best to perform your glorious deed, then raise your right hand, put forth all your strength, and with the two-edged blade hew through the joint that knits the head and neck of the deadly serpent.[39]

If the locus of masculine power has shifted upward from lower body to head, then these two parts must be separated if Psyche is going to know what she is dealing with. To cut off the man's head with a knife, says Neumann, is "an ancient symbol of castration sublimated to the spiritual sphere."[40]

When Psyche makes her decision, she is "left alone—and yet she was not at all alone, for the fierce furies that vexed her soul were ever with her." She is racked with "[i]mpatience, indecision, daring and terror, diffidence and anger . . . and, worst of all, in the same body she hated the beast and loved the husband."[41] Now that she admits that her husband might be the monster of death to whom she was betrothed, she is torn by suspicion that nags at her rapture. The "beast" is he who ended her narcissistic envelopment in childhood and carried her off into the dark paradise of marriage that is her "husband."[42] Which is the one who comes to her at night, monster or lover?

Psyche must find out, and so she draws her dagger and lights her lamp. Like the moth to the flame, a part of her dies, for she loses both her innocence and her love. She can never go back to either as it was—either her ecstasy of darkness or a love that is separated into beast and husband, lower and upper. She manifests the loss, not by performing the prescribed operation—she does not separate Eros' head from his body because she sees that she has been mistaken—but by trying to kill herself. As Neumann says, "She is no longer merely captivating and captivated. . . . In this love situation of womanhood growing conscious through encounter, knowledge and suffering and sacrifice are identical."[43] As we have seen, Juliana's and Jenny's rite of passage into greater awareness was to move from their suffering to sacrifice their own dissertations.

Psyche's suicide is aborted when she drops the knife. Instead, she pricks herself on one of Eros' arrows, falling more deeply (and more consciously) in love—this time, with the very god of love himself. But when she sees him for who he is, he leaves her—that is, the two separate. One way to look at this is that she sees her *animus* for what it is—not the whole of her, but only a part. "The *animus* seems so potent and godlike, and her conscious ego self so worthless and helpless by comparison."[44] When she faces this aspect of herself, it loses its divine power over her. She will now have to decide what or who she loves; it will not be imposed on her by an outside force. "Psyche and Eros now confront one another as equals. But confrontation implies separateness."[45] The Almighty Father/Lover, for example, so potent a force in the life of the Brainchild, now becomes less, rather than more, god-like to her. She can make her own choices about what is important to her.

But what does it mean that "Psyche fell in love with Love"?[46] If we see Eros as a person, perhaps it means merely that she recognizes her husband for what he is—a separate being. Johnson writes "When one truly shows the light upon another person, he finds a god or a goddess."[47] The paradox of this scene is that, in dividing from her lover, Psyche creates the possibility for unity within herself. Up to this point, she has been projecting the "beast" and the "husband" outward upon Eros. Now that they are separate, she will have to deal with the two creatures inside. If it is she who has allowed herself to be carried off by the monster of death and to accept a princely lover that she cannot see, then *she* is the beast and the husband! Moreover, it is only she who has the power to change her condition, not anyone else. In fact, in the remainder of the myth Psyche shows herself to be stronger than Eros. Her inner Eros "is in truth a higher and invisible form of the Eros who lies sleeping before her," writes Neumann. "This greater, invisible Eros within Psyche must necessarily come into conflict with his small visible incarnation who is revealed by the light of her lamp and burned by the drop of oil."[48]

For the academic Psyche, lighting the lamp simply means that she recognizes her "mate"—whether outer man, inner man, or masculine institution—for what he is. For all of the women who told me their stories, this moment of recognition diminished his power over her, even if she remained in love or her love for him grew. For, when she could look him in the face as a detached being, she could also look more closely at herself.

~

Beth, our mother of two daughters with doctorates who got her own PhD later in life, got a heavy draught of realism when she could not find the perfect teaching job in the perfect college town. What was even more sobering, she realized that starting on a tenure track in her mid-fifties was not going to work. Universities did not want to "invest" in a woman who would be sixty by the time she got tenure. She had also not realized that academia was "so incredibly patriarchal," and divulged that she had needed to see it as emancipatory because her marriage was not. "I entered academia to seek liberation," she said. "Now I have to be liberated from *it*." Still, she did not bail on her chosen profession; she loved her field, and she wanted to teach. Instead of giving up, as Psyche did at first, she changed goals. She did find a job in a wonderful college town, but she no longer even wanted to enter the tenure track. She decided she could practice what she loved without it, and still have time for involvement with the arts and her family. In fact, she was already on a "track" that she found quite satisfying when she had her epiphany, and she was able to let go of any illusions of grandeur attached to an unseen academic god.

Many of the smitten Maiden Lovers ended up leaving their Pygmalions when they lit their lamps, whether or not they stayed with academe. Despite her advisor's trying to prevent her from leaving by telling prospective employers she "wasn't ready," Laura got a good job elsewhere. She realized it was a power-balancing move. "I thought, 'Yeah, you can have all this power, and I'll just leave.' Of course, I had to maintain enough civility to get my dissertation accepted and done." Many years after leaving graduate school, Kate got "past being angry" at Ted and steadfastly ignored his attempts to hook her emotions.

Amy eventually jettisoned her plans to leave graduate school because of Mr. Rogers, and friends convinced her she "had to get him completely out of her hair." She realized that she was not responsible for his depression, and that she did not owe his departmental benefactors (Burl Ives and Orson Welles) any attempt to placate his feelings. She gave all of Mr. Rogers' materials back, quit doing research with him, told him point blank that she could not interact with him any more, and dropped him from her committee. "But it made me feel like an idiot that it took me so long to put it all together," she lamented. She probably did not know that many women were slow to light the lamp; most of them did not want to spoil the relationship, even if it had turned more damaging than beneficial.

Maggie, who retained her good feelings about Joel and owed her emergence as a scholar to him, concluded our talks by reflecting, "I remember sort of outgrowing him at some point. My knowledge became more sophisticated than his, ultimately. I wanted him to get more involved in research—he was such a smart person—but he wasn't going there." Although Joel did not try to prevent Maggie from leaving, he still writes notes to her telling her he loves and misses her. She thinks he has "never bounced back completely," clinging to memories of the past rather than moving ahead with his life.

Maggie felt bad about leaving Joel, harboring at least a twinge of responsibility for his sadness. This pattern was common among grown-up Maiden Lovers, who more often than not "dropped the knife" even when they saw their "husbands" in the light. Psyche's envelopment in Eros' dark paradise is a variation on the hero's engulfment in what Joseph Campbell calls "the belly of the whale,"[49] though in the heroine's myth, such containment is often overlaid with pleasure rather than disgust. The gingerbread house disguises the witch from Hansel and Gretel, for example. The male hero typically lights a fire and *cuts* his way out of the belly of the monster. He dismembers his captor in order to gain his knowledge. "In its feminine variant," Neumann observes, "this need of knowing remains bound up with the greater need of loving. Even where the heroine Psyche is compelled to wound, she preserves her bond with her lover, whom she never ceases to conciliate and transform."[50] In fact, the fuel for the lamp is oil, which comes from the plant world, and is associated with the feminine. Psyche comes to know by kindling the fire of passion, not by rending her container.[51] I am reminded of Elizabeth's search for an "alchemical" relationship—of a quest for knowledge fired by love, like that of Abelard and Heloise.

Sarah, a brilliant associate professor in her forties, spoke of the infatuation with older men she thought many young women felt when they were graduate students. This is always commingled with a quest for knowledge, she said. Echoing so many others, she spoke of this magical mix as intoxicating. "I don't really feel dependent on any of those male elders any more," she reflected, "although I certainly did at first." Her relationship with her advisor had been one of those passionate intellectual liaisons that she eventually broke off after realizing the need for a separate identity. But when she began getting the recognition he had wanted her to have as an important scholar, he turned from being a "proud father" who introduced her to people to shunning her completely for two years.

"When I was getting attention and he wasn't," she said, "it was hard to even shake hands with him. I think it was really hard on him." Although she refused to tamp down her own work to protect his ego, it worried her greatly, and she kept seeking an "opening" for a healing talk. Eventually they had one, and he admitted that it was the first time that one of his graduate students moved so quickly into what he viewed as a competitive relationship with him. She seemed curious that he would view their relationship as competitive, as if he could not reconcile that with their earlier closeness. Now they are good friends again, and she is relieved.

Repeatedly, academic Psyches took responsibility for mending their broken relationships. Even if they had been hurt, they generally did not want their lovers to be. Like her mythical counterpart, they accepted the light and dropped the knife.

EROS FLIES AWAY

Awakened by the hot oil of Psyche's lamp, Eros leaps from his couch and flies away without a word, with Psyche clinging to his leg until she tires and falls to earth. Eros perches in a cypress, tree of the Great Mother,[52] and admonishes himself for disobeying his mother and Psyche for disobeying him. He pronounces judgment on her sisters, and says to Psyche "You I will only punish thus—by flying from you."[53] Eros, it seems, is something of a Mama's Boy. As Apuleius put it when Aphrodite set him the task of inflicting Psyche with love for a beast, she "with parted lips kissed her son long and fervently."[54] As the son-lover figure of the matriarchal Goddess, Eros is a *puer aeternus*, or "eternal boy," who, like Peter Pan or "The Little Prince," tries through flight to keep his distance from the mother earth who would envelop him, yet rarely resists her call back to unenlightened, womb-encircled Paradise.[55]

As a typical Greek god, Eros has heretofore desired and done as he pleases, remaining un-illumined, leaving the suffering to the mortals. In one of my favorite passages, Apuleius writes that Eros is:

> that wicked boy, scorner of law and order, who, armed with arrows and torch aflame, speeds through others' homes by night, saps the ties of wedlock, and all unpunished commits hideous crime and uses all his power for ill.[56]

Yet Psyche has wounded him—a necessary step in his own enlightenment.[57] Although in an outer sense he now goes limp, safe but locked up with Mother, and Psyche takes an active role in her own liberation, and his, we could also say that he flies back into the inner world of Psyche and sends her help when she is in trouble.[58]

When any one of what we could call our "triple-headed god"—a man, woman's *animus*, or academia—is allowed to play a god, he just goes on wounding others, allowing them to suffer while he leaves the scene. Because in academia the woman is so often in the role of Goddess—whether Aphrodite, Galatea, Muse, or Psyche—it is up to her not only to evolve herself but also to grow *him* up as well. As we have just seen, many former Maiden Lovers did not make a clean break from their Pygmalions; they wanted the relationship to change but last, and often they wanted him to realize his potential. We will return to this theme shortly.

~

As the moth, Psyche has been burned by her own flame, and again she tries to die. As far as her sight extends, she watches Eros' flight. "When the beat of his wings had borne him far, and the depth of air had snatched him from her sight, she flung herself headlong from the brink of a river that flowed hard by."[59] But the "kindly stream" would not take her, and laid her unhurt upon its banks. It is said that the moth transports the feminine soul from one life to the next. And Psyche is not yet finished with her incarnations.

For now, Psyche's task is herself.

CHAPTER 10

PSYCHE'S LABORS

> I needed to . . . get back to a place where there were no standard forms any longer, a time and space before school began.
>
> Jane Tompkins, *A Life in School*

As we left Psyche, she was lying on the ground watching Eros, with whom she was now hopelessly in love, fly away from her forever. This is how the story continues:

> Bereft, Psyche threw herself in the river, but the god Pan encouraged her to pray to Aphrodite instead. Condemning Psyche with a blistering attack, Eros' mother set the wandering Psyche four tasks as a condition for her expiation. First, she must sort a gigantic pile of seeds before nightfall, or she would die. Psyche was distraught and sat stupefied before her tasks, but the ants sorted the seeds for her, and she escaped death.
>
> Her second task was to cross a river and gather some golden fleece from the deadly rams that lived there. She collapsed again and entertained thoughts of casting herself down a cliff and into the river below, but a green reed near the river told her not to go until dusk, for the rams were maddened by the heat of the blazing sun. Thus, going at dusk when they had spent their fury, Psyche was able easily to gather some of the wool from the bushes that the rams passed.

Thwarted by Psyche's success, Aphrodite laid out Psyche's third task: to fill a crystal jar with water from the river Styx. Because the banks were guarded by monsters who would kill anyone who came near, Psyche wanted again to drown herself in the river. But an eagle of Zeus procured the water for her, and Psyche returned the filled crystal jar to Aphrodite.

Then Psyche received her fourth and most difficult test. She was to descend into Hades to get a cask of Persephone's beauty ointment. She climbed a high tower, thinking to throw herself from it, but the tower counseled her to take two coins in her mouth and two pieces of bread in her hands. A lame donkey driver would ask her to pick up sticks, but she must refuse him, pay the ferryman at the river Styx with a coin, ignore a dying man as he reached out of the water for help, refuse to aid some old weaving women, toss one of the pieces of bread to the three-headed dog, Cerberus, who guarded the entrance to Hell, and enter while the heads were quarreling. Furthermore, she must avoid all but the simplest food while in the underworld, and repeat the entire process on her way back.

Psyche successfully navigated her way to Persephone, retrieved her ointment, and started to return. Suddenly, however, she was overcome by curiosity. Would not this gift of divine beauty win back the love of her husband? But as she opened the cask, a Stygian sleep came over her and she fell to the ground as if dead.

Meanwhile, Eros had recovered from his wounds and, slipping from his confining bedchamber, flew to Psyche's side. He wiped the sleep from her, put it back in the container, and bade her return to Aphrodite. For his part, Eros appealed to his father Zeus to intercede on their behalf. Determining that Eros' passions should now be nipped by wedlock, Zeus gave Psyche a drink of ambrosia that made her immortal, and even Aphrodite blessed their wedding.

Near the beginning of the 1995 movie *Apollo 13*, astronaut Jim Lovell and his wife Barbara survey the damages from a champagne party that just finally died out in the wee hours. Barbara says, wearily, "I can't deal with cleaning up. Let's sell the house." As we pick up Psyche's story, she must feel this and much more, for her plucky disobedience has made a big mess. Lacking the Lovells' humor, though, she "tormented her soul with lamentation."[1] Things are going to get much worse before they get better, too, for Aphrodite is now in a colossal rage. Psyche wanders "in restless agitation," looking for her husband. Instead, Aphrodite finds her, has her whipped and beaten, tears her clothes and dishevels her hair, buffets her about the head, and sets her four seemingly insurmountable tasks. If these don't kill her, her mother-in-law will.

As a professor, I experience Psyche's torments regularly. Since I have been living with this myth for some time now, I have come to distinguish between my "little Psyche moments" and "Psyche's deaths." The little ones occur quite often, as the daily demands of academia, which don't ever go away, even on weekends or during the famed professorial perk of a "free summer," separate me from what I love about my job—namely, the creative aspects of teaching and writing. Sometimes these remind me that there *is* crying in academia, even if I'm over it soon and on to the next task. It is the big ones—such as the mid-life descent in which my love for academia seemed gone for good—that feel like death, whether Psyche's intended suicides or her mandated descent into Hades. Eros has flown out of sight, and all seems lost.

I am convinced that I'm not the only academic woman to undergo such Psychic episodes. As I said before, however, something usually comes of them, especially the bigger ones. Psyche's tears, her wandering, and her descent into the land of Death are like the Handless Maiden's. "Her tears are a germination of that which preserves her," writes Clarissa Estes of the Maiden, "that which purifies the wound she had received."[2] In myth and fairy tales, tears do three works: they call the spirits to one's side, they ward off predators, and they heal the injuries of poor human bargains.[3] Psyche's parents give her away to Death just as the Handless Maiden's father gave her to the Devil, and Psyche also received the "poor human bargain" of bliss in exchange for ignorance. However, it is really *Psyche* who inflicts the injury on herself by lighting the lamp. The labors assigned to her are not just Aphrodite's revenge, but the means to transcend, through struggle and affliction, the separation she accomplished. When the Handless Maiden wanders for three years without a husband, as Psyche does for a long time without Eros, it is incubation. "The work of these three years is to strengthen oneself as much as one can, to use all one's psychic resources for oneself, to become as conscious as possible."[4] As Robert Pirsig writes in *Zen and the Art of Motorcycle Maintenance*, "The real cycle you're working on is a cycle called 'yourself'."[5]

Though Eros goes back home to nurse his wounds, he is not altogether absent from Psyche's life. If we take this as primarily Psyche's story, he has gone inside and, as her *animus,* is helping her in the forms of the ant, the reed, the eagle, and the tower. He is also doing his own incubating and is being strengthened by Psyche, matured out of his boyish tricksterism by her suffering and love. She labors, he cooperates. At first, Eros and Psyche are fused and in the dark. Her decision to light the lamp brings tension from the inevitable conflict between opposites. And finally, Psyche's individual, not unconscious, love for him brings them together.[6]

Psyche's first three tasks deal primarily with her relationship to masculinity. While Eros helps her, these tasks are also his manifestations as the dragon-monster. For, on the deepest level, Psyche has not completely recognized him for himself, and thus he reveals his true form to her only gradually. The fourth task deals with Psyche's relation to the feminine, particularly to the Great Mother realm of Aphrodite.[7] To mature fully, Psyche must not only know her mate but also relate to him differently than does the ancient Goddess.

The myth presents Psyche's tasks as a progression, whereby she gains potency from each to go on to the next. It would be ideal if it worked that way for us, but in reality, it usually doesn't. We are likely to face more than one or all of them at once, which can only magnify the intuition of defeat.[8] In showing how some academic women have faced Psyche's tasks, I will depict them in order. For, though they are intricately related, each has something important to teach us about our dark marriages to the man inside, the men out there, and to academia as "the man" writ large.

SORTING THE SEEDS

The pile of unsorted seeds confronting Psyche is pretty easy to interpret if we note the archaic expression, "the seeded womb"; in fact, in a throwback to older times, we still speak of a man "sowing his seed" when he has sex with a woman. In sexual intercourse, a woman's body "chooses" among the millions of seeds a man gives her as the rudimentary act of sorting.[9] Because Aphrodite's pile of seeds is a huge jumble, they can be seen as primitive masculine promiscuity, and Psyche's task is to sort through the chaos.[10]

We have seen how, with the development of patriarchy in the university, the phallic tends to become, or to merge with, the phrenic. And academia as a patriarchal institution is indeed prolific with its "seeds." I mean by this not only the tendency of some men to sow their carnal seeds in too many places but also the standards of "productivity" that face every academic person, woman or man—which often seem a confusing heap of duties, opportunities, and demands. We are likely to sit in front of these, as Psyche does, "in silent stupefaction, overwhelmed by the vastness of the task."[11]

Early in my work on this book, I corresponded with Rachel, a prolific writer and one of the top scholars in her field. She had just quit her job as a senior professor to develop some other interests related to her writing. "My decision to walk away from formal, institutionalized academia was very scary," she wrote me. "Sometimes I wonder if I did the right thing. I know I may never get a teaching job again, and on some days that's a wonderful thought, and on others it's frightening." Her e-mail message laments the difficulties that she and five other women she knew were having with the huge demands placed on them as academicians. All these women were immensely "productive"; anyone in their field would recognize their names. Rachel's message is a classic description of Psyche's pile of seeds:

> I was most intrigued by your comments about women in academia and how we're all feeling at mid-life, and how your goals seem to be changing. Jackie, Dana, and I have been having similar talks. How I wish we were close; it would be wonderful to talk with you about this. Our issues include these: We've always worked about 15 hours a day, often 7 days a week, on academic things. We've always said it was fun. And yes, we still like to write, but academia seems to be filling our days with "junk stuff" so that, if we want to write, it gets done after already incredibly long days. In addition, although we like to write, there are other things we like to do too, but we don't do them because we're

> spending all our time working. Our lives don't seem very balanced. Then we wondered why we couldn't work 8 hours a day on academic things and do other things the rest of the time. The thought of working only 8 hours a day made us all break out in laughter; it seemed so absurd. Then we thought about what we would do with those other hours every day, and the list of activities we came up with was very short—largely because we never have time to do them anyway.

Rachel told of how these demands had affected three other women that she knew:

> Add to all these items: Tanisha (who also works all the time) just had a stroke at age 37; they say it was caused by stress. Maureen has major back problems and often must walk with a cane; she's having to readjust her life in major ways. Krista took early retirement just to get out; in part it was because she had to do 400 tenure reviews and recommendations in one semester alone. (By the way, this is another issue we've talked about—how much of the work we do in academia is done for other institutions—for free!).

The ants who come to help Psyche are of the earth, showing that Psyche relies on her unconscious instincts to help her select and sift through the confusion of masculine demands placed upon her.[12] Unfortunately, the women Rachel knew were still in Aphrodite's realm of plenitude. They seemed to have lost touch with their helpful instincts, trying to deal with the outrageous piles of demands by *accomplishing* them rather than by *sorting* them. In the myth, the fact that the ants do the work for Psyche suggests that instinct is sorely needed here: *What is reasonable for me to do? What really must be done? What do I want to do?* Surely, the four hundred tenure reviews and recommendations is a twisted norm of "productivity"—masculine fertility completely out of control. Faced with such an absurdity, Krista was not able to sort out what had to be done from what didn't, and simply got out while she could. Neither were Tanisha and Maureen able to use their unconscious body-sense to sort through the pile of demands—and so the pile was ravaging their bodies.

Sorting this pile of demands is a constant task for academic men and women. But I believe it is especially a problem for women, whose relational orientation, like Psyche's at the beginning, often keeps them in the dark about who they are. Except for those who are more Amazonian, women are more likely to do what Rachel calls the "junk stuff" without adequate sorting, partly because their connectedness with others seems to require it, and partly because their inner sense of discrimination—which would be helped by a positive rather than critical *animus*—is not well developed. They do the tasks in front of them for friendship, duty, service, which others appreciate very much while they are ranking them low on their annual reviews or denying them tenure when their time has run out. Or these feminine-identified women accomplish the feat while also publishing prolifically, and end up sick or burned out—like Tanisha, Maureen, and Krista.

Sorting the seeds of academic productivity must be done daily but it can be done quickly, especially if a woman calls on her "ants" to cut through the crap and to say "I will do this and not *that!*" It also helps to practice until this response is almost automatic, or to say "Let me think about it," and use the delay for further sorting. There is another kind of discernment that takes longer, sometimes a lifetime, and that is sorting out who she *is* apart from the male influences in her life. Although Psyche has four distinct tasks to accomplish, they are all in the service of developing herself as a separate being from Eros, though she loves him deeply. Perhaps we could turn that around, too, and say that she cannot fully love him until she discovers herself. All of the women who shone the lamp on the men they loved were faced with this eventually; while gazing upon him they had to ask "Who am I?"

Because I married an older man who had been my professor, my sorting of this nature is ongoing. My task is complicated by the similarities, as happens in a marriage despite all our intentions otherwise, between my spouse and my father on a crucial dimension that affects my academic persona, and ultimately, the work of my Psyche. In this case, my dad did not speak with the voice of the Brainchild's "Almighty Father," who criticizes and denigrates by holding up a standard of perfection I cannot achieve. Instead, I idealized his voice into a heroic *animus* that I admired, but still disowned as a part of me. I was also afraid of this heroic dimension, for in my father it had cost me dearly as a child, and in Tom it continued to do so. The result was quite a medley of seeds to sort—and for a long time, I gave over what was in *me* to the stronger voices of *them*. Although this labor of distinguishing—which is also a labor of love—has several dimensions, here is a bit of it. I wrote this a couple of years ago in narrative form and presented it at a convention, because sometimes it helps me to shape a page from my life as a story. I can see what myth I was working on. And it seems to me now it was Psyche's.

~

Transgression is the only term I know of that stirs the blood of postmodernists as much as that of Christians. I didn't notice it much until I started speaking in tongues—of cultural studies, that is. This word is dangerously seductive, encompassing a wide array of behaviors, mostly within texts and cultural performances, which endow any critic who likes them with an aura of "radical alterity" that separates one from the herd. Among the cultural studies crowd with whom I often hang, transgression is definitely preferred to tradition.

But transgression is also an attitude bred in my bones, and so transgressive acts make me feel at home. Transgression both excites and scares me, and this affects a current turn in my academic writing. This all has something to do with my relationships with two men, the one I grew up with, and the one I live with now.

My husband Tom is currently on sabbatical, writing his ethnography in blissful tranquility while I, teaching too much and handling his advisees, but graciously *not* resenting it, am perpetually stressed out and cranky. He greets me as I walk in the door, lugging the bulging briefcase holding my evening's work and his mail.

"I got another episode of my cancer ethnography done," Tom gloats. "Wanna hear it?" I juggle the pride I feel for his disciplined productivity with the suspicion that I am not going to like what he's written. Tom looks like a boy holding a frog behind his back, which he intends to toss at his girlfriend just to hear her squeal. "Is this one going to be scatological too?" I ask. Sometimes I go to school this semester with the nagging sense that I've forgotten something important. Remembering the place in the movie when Kevin's mother realized she'd gotten on the airplane without him, I once shouted to my next-door office neighbor, who understands about Tom, *Oh no! Home alone!*

But I instantly regret my parental tone when I see the delight drain from Tom's face. He says nothing, almost always a sign of anger keeping the hurt at bay.

As I grope for the right words to amend my offense, I flash back to another time I tried to right a wrong with words, though the crime was not my own. I am in a sandy West Texas town, as flat as our ranch-style house, whose only saving grace is that its one air conditioner is in my room. I hate the cowboy wallpaper that we'll never get the chance to remove. But I bravely press on with what a girl's gotta do: I am writing a novel.

Having already mastered an Aristotelian sense of order, I write the preface first, clarifying that we just arrived in this red-dirt hellhole from Dallas, a greener metropolis much more fitting to my budding urbanity. My sister and brother and I bicker, I explain, because we have once again been ripped from our roots too young. Our backyard is a cotton field punctuated by a water tower. Our address is "Sand Road," which the Country Club set is trying to rename "Hillcrest Drive," a pretension not without some poignancy. You'd understand this if you could look out the picture window of our parsonage. The title of my first chapter, written in fat block letters on a Big Chief tablet, pretty much sums up my life so far: "Moving."

Even now, when I think about what I most want to be when I grow up, it's a *writer*. This calling has bested, in roughly chronological order, preacher's wife, fourth-grade teacher, track-and-field champion, and country-music star. Writing is the place I feel most *at home*, if home is where you feel the most grounded, the most located in one spot, the most together.

Academic writing, let's be clear, is not usually thought of as "creative." But since it doubles as vocation and avocation for me, it leaves traces of my "life's journey," even if I can't interpret them until I look back, like the flagman on the caboose as the train moves down the track. This journey includes my relationships with my father and my husband.

My father is a clergyman—a "preacher" to be exact—raised up in a small hill-country town dotted with bluebonnets, streams that run clear over limestone and muddy over sand, and groves of live oaks spreading the illusion of cool on a hot day. For landmarks you could use the Sinclair station with the faded green dinosaur or any one of the sturdy stone churches with stained-glass windows of Jesus feeding his sheep, pool-sized baptisteries behind the choir where you could be washed of your sins in real water, and holy billboards outside suggesting GOT TRUTH DECAY? BRUSH UP ON THE BIBLE.

My father likes to say his family placed the bathtub in the kitchen and filled it with hot water every Saturday night so that everybody got a bath once a week before church, "whether they needed it or not." His mother taught piano and was the church organist. For fifty-nine years, she never missed a Sunday, not even one, whether *she* needed it or not. She didn't cotton much to dancing on Sundays—actually to dancing any time at all, as long as boys were involved. Until my grandmother died, my mother reinterpreted our school dances as "banquets" so we could keep both the peace and the faith. My sister didn't even tell her about the really neat band from Lubbock that the student council hired for her junior-high prom, name of "Buddy Holly and the Starlighters."

My dad went to college in the city and, instead of getting religion, which he already had, he got philosophy, which he needed. He also got his Bachelor's of Divinity after narrowly missing admission to Yale, an injustice we all still blame on his rearing, not his brains. After a high-profile apprenticeship in the country's largest congregation of his denomination, he settled into preaching in the same kinds of towns and white-bread churches where he grew up. By the time I arrived, most of the lovely old sanctuaries had given way to modern colonial or pre-postmodern Gothic. But the church suppers still spawned fried-chicken contests among the ladies, and I got my fill of Jell-O salads and "Blessed Assurance, Jesus Is Mine."

The problem was, my Dad was kind of a head case. Philosophy had made him "liberal." Don't get me wrong, he was plenty straight-laced. He distrusted Elvis, beer, and the Twist. He believed one should save oneself for marriage. He told jokes that *Reader's Digest* would print on the spot. He was incapable of saying the F-word—if, indeed, he knew what it meant.

These latter qualities were fortunate, considering his profession. But eventually his college education caught up with him. When a black family accepted his invitation to walk up front during the last stanza of "Onward, Christian Soldiers," Dad welcomed them into the body of Christ and onto the official membership roster. He went door-to-door lobbying against capital punishment in Colorado. He slept on church basement floors in Washington while he helped form the Clergy Opposed to the War in Viet Nam. In time, he forgot to compliment Mrs. Boyd on her fried chicken and to use the word "Jesus" enough in his sermons, speaking instead of "situation ethics" and Martin Buber, who some suspected was not even a Christian.

In due time I came to understand that we moved on average every three years because that is how long it would take the church board to figure my father out and fire him. This in spite of my mother's tireless compensations for his inattentiveness to church politics, and her uncompensated, soothing accompaniment at every wedding, funeral, and hospital call. My father had principles and he stood up for them. He was not afraid of transgression, and I was proud.

Thus, of the many reasons I fell for Tom, his skill at transgression was surely one of them. I didn't know this about him at first. Tom had a slick, short haircut in the Beatles-into-BeeGees seventies and wore three-piece Bobby Kennedy suits while everybody else I knew was feelin' nearly faded as their jeans. He reveled in the arcane complexities of transformational grammar. "Billy raked the lawn with his sister," he would announce from the front of the classroom. "Who can give me the syntactical reason you're all laughing?" Tom went home early while the rest of us waited out the L.A. freeway crunch in the 901 Club. I didn't really get the big picture about Tom; I just thought he was smart.

Looking back, though, there were signs of Tom's penchant for transgression. Like when he entertained a group of us at a convention by mooning one of the great thinkers of our field to express his irritation at her long-windedness. Though thoroughly scandalized, I guess I felt somehow "at home." Perhaps from somewhere deep in the heart of Texas, I felt I could help.

Tom is a bona fide intellectual with passionately held principles. Some of his students even call him "brilliant"—which I regard as extravagant, especially since they're more likely to call me "nice." But few who know him well would call him a "head case." If both my father and my husband have transgressed with style, it is from opposite ends of their anatomies. Speaking mostly metaphorically, my excursion from one to the other has been from heads to tails. I recognized the depth of these two men's differences early in my marriage after spending a week camping with my parents, during which time Tom was very, very good. With no apparent provocation other than that we were finally alone, he spewed forth a string of expletives in Crested Butte's Wooden Nickel Saloon that turned the smoky air as blue as the Rocky Mountain high outside. "There!" he said, as if letting go a blown-up balloon, "now I feel better."

Tom and I soon formed a writing partnership that is still in progress. Although drawn to similar ideas, our alliance flourishes through opposites. I creep towards my main point like an inchworm, crawling over every intellectual building block within reach, prompting Tom to scream for a destination. Tom, on the other hand, has been known to outline a piece of film criticism before actually *seeing* the movie, which he does not regard as a problem. I put off writing by directing my urgent attention to a ruthless critique of my entire wardrobe, which has suddenly become outdated *today*, and have been known to bungee-cord myself to the desk chair to prevent an early escape. Tom thinks "writer's block" is a lame euphemism for lack of character. I am enamored with my infinitely nuanced words, whereas Tom relishes his ability to reduce them all down to bald black-and-white whenever a point is required.

All these binaries form a satisfying complementarity when our merger is working, when we are "in the flow." Tom and I get these moments occasionally despite, or perhaps because of, our battles to Near-Death Experience over the rightness of an idea or the turn of a phrase. And I am perversely gratified in my role as keeper of propriety. This is a *partnership*, and it affords a sort of control I never had at eight when my Dad was stirring up our next move. Or maybe it's that here *I* get to play parent. The tables are turned, for a change, and if Tom wants to dance at the feet of the church board dragon, I can at least lull it to sleep with my prose.

Lurking in our collaborative margins, though, is Tom's "other side"—his tendency toward transgression, a sort of dark Lacanian Imaginary always threatening to erupt into the Symbolic world of the Fathers. When Tom crosses the boundaries of my sense of decorum I get edgy, especially when he transgresses not just in his writing but in his actions. His indulgence, even when wrapped in a mantle of heroic victimage, has cost me dearly on occasion. Married life has not been the clean break from my early novel *Moving* that I craved, as Tom's transgressions against the system spilled over—much to his sorrow—into transgressions against me.

I want to say to Tom—*or is it to my father in a voice I wish my Mom had had?*—what Garrison Keillor has Pastor Ingqvist's wife say to her husband when he nobly gives up the trip to Orlando that she was so counting on as a respite from the Minnesota winter. "If you want to be a martyr, that's fine," Mrs. Ingqvist says. "But the great martyrs went off to their martyrdom alone. They didn't invite their wives along."

I alternate between Mrs. Ingqvist's well-earned indignation and the terror that fuels it. My vigilant parent crumbles into a scared child. For transgression also means "dislocation" to me—tearing apart what I've tried most of my life to build with words, where the center of bricks and parsonages would not hold. And I feel trapped in the bind that to be *home* means to be *homeless*.

But there is still this matter of Tom's injured face. I didn't support him when he wanted to amuse me with his ethnographic frog. He has not, as he often points out, dislodged my expanding rootedness in a long time. I don't really like playing parent that much, anyway, and my sentry act no longer feels right, like an old prom dress rescued from the closet to make me feel pretty, but instead just looking pretty *silly* as I model it in the mirror.

It's been a month or two since Tom finished his story. I am holding his head in my lap for a dark hour in which his fear has reappeared, as it does sometimes these days, that his cancer has returned. We are listening with two good friends to Tangerine Dream's "Tyranny of Beauty," an apt oxymoron for the sweet terror filling up our living room. As if carried atop the notes of the Dream, some words of Anne Lamott come to me. She was modeling a short dress at Macy's that she thought her boyfriend would like, and started worrying out loud about her big butt. Her friend Pammy, who was dying of cancer, was there in a wheelchair, a wig covering her baldness.

> [A]nd Pammy said, as clear and kind as a woman can be, "Annie? You really don't have that kind of time."[13]

The candles my friend Paula has placed in a star shape in front of us on the coffee table begin to glow with an inner light that is other-worldly, yet very much here. The ruby crystal plate at the center dissolves into fractals of multi-hued sight and sound, each distinct, yet all of a whole. Tom's features grow soft. This room in our house is alive, dancing with movement, yet it is going nowhere.

It is the morning after, and I am sitting at my computer. That familiar restlessness is gone for now; there is no place else I'd rather be. I'm trying to find a way to write what came to me last night when I was "in the flow": that if I stop chasing after Tom's transgressions like a one-woman posse, maybe I can round up a few of my own. I don't need to substitute a *presentable* professorial persona for who I am becoming. I really don't have that kind of time. Lately I feel as fenced in by the bloodless prose of academe as *Phaedrus*' unruly black horse of desire, constrained by the reins of reason—perfectly formed and perfectly still.

My gaze shifts from the still-bare trees of winter filtering the Ozarks outside to the twin posters above my desk. Startled, I realize, in that looking-back-at-the-tracks sort of way, that they are slightly surreal artists' renderings, in brilliant psychedelic colors, of a cowboy in full chaps-and-kerchief regalia, and of a girl standing tall atop her pony, twirling a rope around her waist, like a circle of containment within which she is protected and complete. I bought them on impulse last summer in Jackson, Wyoming. Maybe I was just choosing my own cowboy wallpaper this time. The grizzled cowboy has his lariat ready and, from this angle, it would encircle the girl if he threw it. The girl—who is blonde and looks to be about 8—is performing with complete joie de vivre, only the sagebrush and the Grand Tetons in attendance.

My eyes return to the computer screen, where I watch a personal narrative unfold. Given the academic career I've so carefully constructed over three decades, I suppose what I'm writing is "transgressive"—I cannot quite picture myself presenting something so personal, so "un-academic," to my peers—and yet I'm sure I want to do this. I'm writing *from* home now, not as an attempt to *save* it. I think I will call this "The Presentation of Tom in Everyday Life." But that's actually just for starters.

~

Psyche's hill of seeds is not something that can be dealt with once and for all. Unfortunately, it can reconstitute itself as yet another daunting pile of chaos, just when I think I have it all in order. I must go back to the task of sorting my self out from the men in my life, especially the important ones, whenever I become aware that my self is too closely intermingled with theirs. Like separating barley from oats from millet, I sift through my psyche, watching my own pyre expand as I discard what is not me.

GATHERING THE FLEECE

Having sorted the seeds of masculine fertility, Psyche takes some of its power for herself. In her second task, she must deal with horns, not seeds; phallic virility takes on greater intensity. The rams with the golden fleece are an elemental, natural force—like the burning bush, they glow with divinity.[14] We know from their significance in Egypt and from the legend of the Golden Fleece that they are the magical powers of solar masculinity.[15] The reeds tell Psyche, "'they borrow fierce heat from the blazing sun . . . '."[16] Solar masculinity is a wonderful thing—it is *logos*, bringing us the clarity of Apollo, the rationality of the Enlightenment, the clear eyes of science.

A dream I had, which I called "The Great Horned Ram," illustrates the numinosity, or glowing attraction, of this archetype to me.

> I am outside in a very open space, and Tom is with me. We come upon a corral with a horse in it. I go up to pet it, but the horse is so huge, and the fence so high, I can't reach him. The horse bends his head down over the fence to reach me, and I reach out to touch him. Then all of a sudden he jumps the fence, even though this seems like an impossible feat.
>
> He is running toward me with his head lowered, but I get the sense he is more playful than threatening. Then I see that this is not a horse at all, but a Great Horned Ram—of at least double the normal size. I get the feeling he is very special.
>
> I go inside somewhere and tell an authority that the Great Horned Ram has escaped, and I wonder if we should do something about it. But she says not to worry—we will just let him run free in the woods. I think this is right, and that she is wise.

Tom, my masculine helper, is with me here, and perhaps that is why I am open to these forces that so often are deadly to me. The horse is a common *animus* figure, especially for girls, who at ten or twelve often fall in love with a horse before they do with a man. The wounded young girl in *The Horse Whisperer* is a poignant example. But the horse in my dream is magical, as is evident from his great size and his shifting shape. By extension, I seem to transform from girl to woman here, as the horse turns into a ram, which wears its phallicism on its *head*, and this "special" ram runs straight toward me, horns lowered. I am more awed than threatened, and the Wise Woman corroborates my feeling that he should be left alone. Masculine ram energy, in and of itself, is an impressive thing.

But when I reach up to pet the horse at the outset, he jumps. Apparently, he should not be approached directly. The helpful reeds warn Psyche about this. As the hair of the earth connected with the waters of the depths, the reeds are the feminine counterpart to the rams' hair-rays of the sun. Psyche should not approach "those terrible sheep" during the day, they counsel. "For they borrow fierce heat from the blazing sun and wild frenzy maddens them, so that with sharp horns and foreheads hard as stone, and sometimes even with venomous bites, they vent their fury in the destruction of men."[17] The rams with the golden fleece are killing when they are inflated at high noon—that is, all puffed up with their own egotistical powers. This is masculine energy in its negative aspect that burns the feminine, Zeus who incinerates Semele when she sees him unprotected.[18]

Many women experience this lethal aspect of masculine *logos* within the academy—*animus* become *animosity*. It is present in women's guilt that they want to write or teach in more personal ways than the profession considers "academic," like Laura, who still felt inadequate even after a second PhD, or Abby, who didn't want to tell me she might leave academia for something more "creative." It can be found in the "Almighty Father" of the Brainchild, like the voice inside Claire's head that said she wasn't good enough, even with impeccable academic credentials and a recent book published by Oxford University Press. It is manifested in those Amazons who convert to the penetrative attacks of the patriarchy that co-opts them, turning their arrows upon their sisters. It is there, in one of the most frequently recurring dreams of women, that they must get another degree or retake the oral PhD exams—even though, like me, like the accomplished chairperson Ruth, and like the distinguished literary scholar Jane Tompkins, they already have a PhD. And it is certainly lurking in the bodies of women who, like Tanisha, Maureen, and Krista, get ill or depressed due to academia's relentless demands.

Women in academia sometimes adopt *animosity* in order to compensate for patriarchy's abuses. Annis Pratt, a professor of English and women's studies, expresses her concerns this way:

> Academic institutions are structured upon masculine ideas of domination and competition, tempting even women professors who devote all their time and energy to women's studies to atrophy their emotional and relational qualities in a wan mimicry of its aggressions and competitions. I consider this (often unconscious) masculinization of the self responsible for the fierce resistance of many women's studies professors to archetypal and theological scholarship, which often leads to their dogmatic restriction of their syllabi to patriarchal abuses and resistance against them.[19]

In terms of our myth, I think Pratt is saying that, grabbing the rams by the horns, trying to take the whole fleece, results in solar inflation among women. This kind of "wan mimicry" keeps the gifts of the feminine—including a valuing of emotion and relationship—from really counteracting negative masculine *logos* that is out of control.

In the story of Jason and the Golden Fleece, a ram with a glowing hide saved a girl and a boy from death at the hands of their father and stepmother. Gathering them up and flying off, the ram carried the boy safely to another kingdom, but dropped the girl into the sea, where she drowned (along with so many other feminine figures of myth). The boy sacrificed the ram, giving its fleece to his king. Eventually, Jason captured it with the help of Medea, whom he then rejected for a political marriage—a denial of the feminine that resulted in Medea's horrible vengeance of killing her own children to save them from exile.[20] When the compensating feminine aspect is dropped into the collective unconscious, both this myth of the Golden Fleece and Pratt seem to say, the feminine itself turns destructive.

But the reeds have a better way. Psyche should go after the sun sets and the sheep are asleep. "And, when once the sheep have abated their madness and allayed their anger, go shake the leaves of yonder grove, and thou shalt find the golden wool clinging here and there to crooked twigs."[21] Psyche need not expose herself to the destructive fullness of the ram's power; "if the feminine strove to take what it requires by confronting the ram directly, it would be doomed to destruction."[22] She should take just enough of the fleece, just what she needs. The reeds are the vegetative wisdom of nature: "'Wait, be patient. Things change. Time brings counsel. It is not always high noon, and the masculine is not always deadly. One must not attack with force.'"[23]

It may seem that Psyche is getting the raw end of the stick—that she is counseled to be passive, to wait endlessly like Penelope, or to be surreptitious and to get what she wants while the men are away, like Lucy Ricardo with the help of Ethel Mertz. But none of these are really Psyche's ways. Psyche does not wait forever, only long enough to figure out what to do. And although taking the sun's hair-rays is a symbolic castration similar to Delilah's shearing of the solar hero Samson, she does not disarm or enfeeble a man in order to kill him, as the Terrible Mother would, and she does not steal the fleece through violence, as does Medea. Rather, as is true throughout the story, she creates a fruitful contact between feminine and masculine—peacefully and without hurting anyone.[24]

Psyche's taking of just what she needs is a crucial feminine corrective to the Western notion of progress as a god-term that justifies dominating the world through knowledge and control. "Modern man needs to give up his godlike assumption of unnatural power over nature and the destiny of the entire world," says Robert Johnson.[25] The problem with ram energy at high noon, or *logos* not just running free in the woods but trampling things feminine, is an earth covered with pavement, goddesses buried underground, human flesh replaced by metal machines, industrial waste polluting the earth, and nuclear apocalypse hanging over our future. As I have heard it said, "You can't stop progress, but progress can stop you." But academicians can filter their choices concerning what to study and how to study it through a screen of human values, asking questions like: *What will this knowledge gain us? Am I just padding my vita or will this be helpful to someone? Who might it hurt? How will the knowledge be used?* Yielding just a bit of the gold to the goddess of Love seems, when we run with the alternative possibilities, to be a saner choice.

FILLING THE CHALICE

Each time Psyche's task just gets harder. This time, she is to fill a crystal jar with water from a spring that flows from the highest crag of a mountain and feeds the underground rivers, Styx and Cocytus. The stream is guarded by dragons who, unlike the rams, never sleep, and it emits forbidding voices that say ominous things to Psyche like "'Thou art doomed to die'!"[26] This third labor is a quest for the precious water of life, difficult to obtain. In fact, this stream really *can't* be contained; uniting the highest and lowest, it is uroboric, forming a never-ending circle—the snake eating its own tail. It is the river of life that flows without ceasing, and without beginning or end.[27]

A variation on the heap of seeds and the rams with the golden fleece, this river, symbolized in river gods all over the world, is male-generative energy. But this time the emphasis is not on its chaos, as with the seeds, or its aggression, as with the rams, but on its dynamism, or "animation." Water often symbolizes the unconscious, and so we could associate it with Psyche's *animus* energy. Aphrodite orders Psyche to contain this stream; her vessel is a feminine mandala-urn or grail-chalice, with which she is to "mark off a configured unity from the flowing energy of life, to give form to life."[28] She may take only one goblet—that is, she is to give shape to only one cupful of the *animus* energy running through and around her. As Johnson points out, "[t]he feminine way is to do one thing and do it well." Then, and only then, may she move on. "As the poet tells us, we may see the world in a grain of sand."[29]

We have delved into the lives of academic women enough to see that many of us are driven by our task-oriented *animus* within, the one with the ceaseless energy for what I call "getting life done." For most of my career, I have tried to do too much, deluding myself that, even though I know I *can't* scoop up the entire stream of academic life, I *should*. A kind of free-floating guilt pervades me; instead of immersing myself in whatever I'm doing, I think of whatever I am *not* doing, preventing my concentration on doing the one thing well. But, as the myth would have it, once the seeds are sorted and just enough fleece is gathered, Psyche can give feminine shape to that energy that is forever in motion.

Once I had this dream, which illuminates Psyche's third task for me. I call it "Gathering Joan Rivers' Jewelry":

> Tom and I are on a trip, and we stop at an exercise spa. We are about to go in when Joan Rivers comes out the door. She seems a little agitated because she needs to get to the airport and her driver isn't there. We volunteer to take her, even though it is out of our way. She thanks us, but says she'd prefer to find her driver. She's not paying a lot of attention to us—she seems mainly concerned about herself.
>
> All of a sudden, the jewelry she is wearing around her neck—lots of it—breaks and scatters all over the concrete floor. I start to pick it up—there are gold pieces and stones that could be diamonds or rhinestones. I give them to her, and she says none of these are important. There's only one jewel she's concerned about, and that is a faceted ruby in a casing. She's very distraught that it's lost; it seems of utmost importance. I vow to find it, and start looking all over the concrete. Then I realize there's a large red-carpeted area, and it's probably over there, but it will be almost impossible to find because the carpet is thick, the ruby is small, and they're the same color.
>
> Down on my hands and knees I look for it intently, and finally I see it. I'm elated—it shines and seems somehow very significant. I present it to her, and she seems happy to have it back.

This dream begins with almost frenetic movement: Tom (my masculine helper) and I are on a trip, we want to exercise, and Joan Rivers is eager to get to the airport. We seem to keep moving randomly, and are willing to waylay our trip to become her drivers, but she refuses our assistance. Suddenly our purpose changes when her necklaces—in continuous loops like Psyche's river of life—break. True to form, I am distracted by the glitter, and try to pick up *all* the scattered pieces, whether precious (gold and diamonds) or trivial (rhinestones). But Joan isn't interested in gathering it all back up; she just wants the one "pearl of great price," in this case a faceted ruby—like Dorothy's red slippers, a most feminine symbol.[30]

What is Joan Rivers doing in my dream? I don't even like her very much; in comedians I prefer the subtlety of a Lily Tomlin or a Steven Wright. I think her name is a pun suggesting I am dealing with Psyche's uncontainable river. Her surprise appearance also hints that my task must not always be so desperate as Psyche's. Maybe I need to lighten up, be irreverent, let my transgressive side out, say whatever comes to mind with no concern about offending, like Joan does each year in her impertinent fashion commentary at the Academy Awards. After all, as I revealed in "Sorting Seeds," I have been overly concerned with what C. G. Jung calls the *persona*, or the theatrical mask I wear to present myself to the world,[31] and must be less so if I am going to do my real work. Joan is also quite focused here, even selfish—as my dream says, "she seems mainly concerned about herself." Like so many women, I am often just the opposite—squandering my limited energy on others when the task requires a focus on my own work—at least for now.

Perhaps the red carpet references the one walked by the stars as Joan comments on their clothes, one of the most frequent dream symbols of the persona. Or maybe it alludes to the cheap red carpet I've had in my office for years, trying to warm up its cold interiors, just as Jane Tompkins did at Duke University. "'Come in under the shadow of this red rug,'" Jane would say to herself upon entering her office, playing on T. S. Eliot's line from *The Waste Land*.[32] Whatever the case, Joan seems to know what is important, despite her silliness. I must select the one ruby in a whole field of red—a feminine figure in a feminine ground. Not only is it important to contain the masculine stream of life, the dream seems to say, but also the stream of endless possibilities that women tend to generate.

Joan's faceted ruby is like Psyche's crystal chalice—fragile and precious. A human container for the vastness of life, it has to be carefully handled.[33] But I have at least had a crack at sorting the seeds of who I am and what I want to do, and have tried to dispense with my veil of overly rationalistic arguments—or with trying to take the entire golden fleece—of my early career. One of my colleagues says our job as faculty members is to "produce ink." Although this sounds funny, I think he's serious about it. It doesn't matter *what* you write, just write *something*, and preferably a lot. But this means dispersing your own energy, not shaping it. My dream thinks otherwise. *Be like Joan!* it seems to say. Try out a more impudent and self-centered stance, for a change. Maybe this will help me quiet the voice of my insistent *animus*' demands to be constantly in motion. I should give up my incessant attempt to pick up *all* the stones—to reassemble Joan's continuous river of jewels—and focus on just the one ruby.

~

As soon as Psyche climbs to the top of the mountain to have a look, she decides it would be easier to throw herself from its heights than to get the water. Many times, academic women are so busy that we stand perched looking down at the ever-flowing river, like Psyche, believing we cannot possibly hold even a cup. But help comes, this time in the form of Zeus' eagle, whose range of vision allows him the perspective to see all the stream's curves, twists, and changes, and who can fly above it to get exactly the right part.[34]

Perhaps such vision was what Rachel sought when she quit her professorship to pursue what she hoped would fulfill her. Shortly after she wrote me the e-mail lamenting her and her friends' impossibly busy lives in academe, she wrote me this:

> I did have a positive academic experience last Sunday. I'm teaching a class on theory at the Women's College of the university; the class meets Sunday mornings! This was absolutely wonderful. The women are largely in their mid-forties, smart, enthusiastic, and they just love it. One of them said to me after class, "What a trip!" After teaching that class, I remembered why I went into teaching in the first place, but I hadn't remembered that for quite a while!

For Rachel, getting above that never-ending stream of a full-time academic position by quitting seemed to enable her to "fill her cup" in ways that she hadn't for a long time. About a year later, she returned to academia as a chairperson, apparently better able to shape her own work than to be buffeted about by a river of no return. She was excited about leading a unique department that nurtured older adults in an urban environment. Her time away had been her "eagle's vision" that allowed her to dip into just the right place in the flowing stream.

~

You may remember Sophia, whom I introduced in the chapter on the "Veiled Woman." She was disturbed that academia was a "male space" that denied femininity to women who wished to be players. She was haunted by images of her exclusion from the Club, like the dream in which she held her tongue in her lap. She kept trying to wear the veil of respectability, in particular to publish a well-regarded university press book, and yet she was also angry that she could not express herself more metaphorically and passionately in her writing. Sophia's way of containing the ever-flowing stream was to try to shape her own life story more than academia shaped her. She felt a kindred spirit with Thelma and Louise from the movie, who she saw as trying to do that, too, but contending with forces of patriarchy that kept closing off space for them until they had nowhere else to go. She wanted to write a book that would reflect their struggle, as well as her own.

"I've become so much more aware that what I write is autobiographical," Sophia told me. "It's about a space to be heard—not to be silenced."

"You're one up on me," I replied. "I never realize what I'm working on when I'm doing it, only after the fact. I'd like to write more self-consciously."

"It's hard to work that way. Do you remember in *Thelma and Louise*, when they're going through the desert after she's robbed that store, and she looks around and says they've crossed the line, they won't be able to go back? You know that whole notion of the feminine spirit has got to grow! I mean for them it was either suicide or servitude." Then she exclaimed, in a passionate non sequitur, "That's our job!"

"As academics and writers?" I asked, somewhat startled.

"As people who are conscious of our own personal space as women. We have to begin to define our territory," she explained.

"So we don't have to drive off the cliff . . ."

"And keep that space open so it's not lost. It has to be rediscovered over and over and over again."

"Do you mean help other women so they can start from this level and not have to start all over again?" I wanted to know.

"Yes," Sophia answered. "I think the most interesting question you asked me to think about was 'Are you the author of your own career?' This one haunts me more than any of them. I mean in the sense that—to be an *author*—asks whether we can determine our own fate or destiny. If we could become conscious of that, look at what we could do! You know, a narrative has a structure to it, a comedy has a certain kind of structure. Can we structure our life?"

"Do you think you could really do that?" I said.

"Well, I think that life is so powerful and chaotic than you can never have that kind of control. But at the same time, with awareness, you could respond—in a free way."

"From your own self," I offered.

"I see that as a really hopeful point. It's a space out of any kind of depression or trap the institution puts you in," she said thoughtfully.

"Authoring is not the same thing as total control," I suggested. "Maybe it means a sense of not being knocked around, of being as conscious as you can be?"

"Thelma and Louise lose their authorship in the end. At some point they give it up," Sophia reflected.

"Their final act could be seen as an attempt to reclaim it, although it's tragic."

"Yeah," she said, "but why write that? I want us to have more choices than that."

Sophia understood that the river of her life could never be totally controlled, yet she did want to fashion some channels to her liking. Her way of gathering the water of life into a crystal chalice—to "mark off a configured unity from the flowing energy of life"—was to translate her own autobiographical struggles into a space to speak and write in order help other women to do the same. In fact, as I write she is hard at work, doing just that.

~

Earlier I quoted the first part of songwriter Iris DeMent's lyrics to "The Way I Should" to illustrate the voice of the Almighty Father, in her case a ghost that kept her up till dawn, telling her that everything she "thought was right was suddenly all wrong." He asked Iris what she had to show for herself, to which she felt obligated to present a long list. But the second half of the song reveals an epiphany in which she, like Sophia, realizes she cannot control the river of life. But she can concentrate on "the one thing" and let the rest drift by on its own.

> Then I realized I was playing into someone else's rules
> Tryin' to keep my score up in a game I did not choose
> Then I looked that ghost straight in the eye and said
> 'You'd better not be comin' back by again.'
> And it's true that I don't work near as hard
> As you tell me that I'm supposed to
> I don't run as fast as I could
> But I live just the way I want to
> And that's the way I should
>
> October's leaves were dancin' round
> Like angels dressed in robes of red and gold
> But November's come and gone now
> And they're lyin' in the gutter out along the road
> They're gonna make their way out to the ditch or someday
> to the sea
> But they'll get to where they're goin' without the help
> of you or me
> And if each life is just a grain of sand
> I'm tellin' you man, this grain of sand is mine.[35]

Like Psyche, like Joan Rivers, and like Sophia, Iris DeMent found her point of entry into the river that goes on and on, even without the help we too often think it needs.

DESCENDING INTO HADES

Up to now, Psyche has flirted with the land of death, repeatedly contemplating suicide each time she receives her orders. This time, she really has to go there. For her ordained marriage to death was never consummated, replaced instead by the blind paradise of Eros' palace. Eventually, she has to pay the piper, as the saying goes. She'll have to face it for real by meeting Persephone who, as Hades' abducted bride, rules the Dead. Aphrodite and Persephone are poles of the same goddess here—the one in the upper world and the other in the lower. Aspects of the collective feminine, they are hostile to Psyche's attempts to individuate. In the first three labors, Psyche wrestles with aspects of the masculine principle; here she deals with the feminine. Her work is to advance beyond the ancient Great Mother to a more conscious manifestation of femininity.[36] This will be her hardest task. Together, as the slighted beauty and Queen of the Shades, Aphrodite and Persephone are one formidable mistress.

As before, Psyche feels utterly defeated. But the tower that she climbs in order to throw herself from its heights becomes her unexpected counselor. Whereas all her other helpers came from the world of flora and fauna, the tower is a symbol of culture, crafted of human hands. Straight, tall, and made of stone, it is most obviously masculine, but as fortress or mountain, the equivalent of temple tower or pyramid, it is also feminine. Like the eagle, it is "far-seeing," but this time because it is of human consciousness.[37] Less of instinct than the ants, the reed, and the eagle, it is a set of rules, a tradition, or a system.[38] Psyche needs these rules now because her charge—to get Persephone's beauty ointment and bring it back to Aphrodite—is huge. The tower's rules are like the tribal elders' advice to an initiate who undergoes torments on a vision quest, or a shaman's regimen that prepares one for the journey. They are also like a priest's or a psychotherapist's watchful eye as a person delves into illness or personal history. The path is dangerous, these traditions attest, and one must have discipline to come out alive.

As is probably clear by now, I have a tendency toward Psyche's kind of descent—most often unplanned, but also unavoidable. I have found the tower's injunctions to Psyche, or at least the latter part of them, crucial, and I refer to them often, as when I realize I am on the downward path. The coin to the ferryman, the sops to Cerberus, and the rule against taking food into the underworld are motifs traditional to myth and not specific to Psyche.[39] But the rules against helping the people Psyche crosses on her way—the lame donkey driver, the dying man in the water, the old women weaving their webs—are a different story. These are all snares sent by Aphrodite to deter Psyche from her goal, the tower says. That is, they are the distractions of relatedness, which have such powerful appeal to many women, but which must be suspended when a woman is on descent.[40] The veil donned by the Handless Maiden when she wanders in the forest is another form of the tower's injunction: *Do not bother me now or even look at my face*, the veil implies. *I am on a mission. I am not available to the world.*

When the tower warns Psyche against the poor dying man who only wants her to pull him into her boat, it says: "But be thou not moved with pity for him, for it is not lawful."[41] This sounds harsh. It is "womanly" to be sympathetic to others' plights. But whereas men often stand their ground and achieve stability of self by enduring pain, hunger, and thirst, women often must do this by resisting their own pity and curbing their generosity, by "suspend[ing] the claim of what is close at hand for the sake of a distant abstract goal."[42] Johnson calls this temporary suspension "the creative no . . . not an indifferent one. . . . The myth tells us that a woman must not do good indiscriminately at this point in her life."[43]

Some scholars locate this attachment behavior that pulls at women, the prototype of which is the bond between mother and child, as the archetypal feminine itself—the foundation of all human community and culture.[44] It is the kernel of what Riane Eisler calls "partnership societies," which are goddess-based, as opposed to "dominator societies," which are god-based.[45] This kind of nurturing altruism is not only admirable but also fundamental to human survival and organization. But a woman must learn to discriminate—a lesson that underlies all four of Psyche's labors. When is it good to help others and when must she stick ruthlessly to the task at hand? Levy-Bruhl shows that "primitive" peoples are not "thankful" to their rescuers or helpers, such as doctors. Instead, they simply keep escalating their demands. Helping another person, like eating at their table or accepting gifts, establishes a communion. And sometimes the helper gets ambushed into more involvement than she intends.[46]

Here is a series of dreams that illustrates my emotional reaction to letting myself get more entangled with people than I wanted to while in the course of academic tasks. I have stuck with the titles I used in my journal:

Getting Derailed from Psyche's Tasks

I am riding my bicycle on campus. I am late for something, and I decide to go around to a different part of the building than I normally

> do, but I find this takes even longer. A very old woman stops me and asks me to hold her glasses while she walks down the hill and has her picture taken. I am annoyed, but she is an old woman, so I do it. It's obviously going to take her a very long time to get down that hill to the cameramen, and I'm not happy about it.

As dreams often do when the dreamer doesn't get the message, the next one in the series ups the ante on my commitment:

> **The Student with AIDS**
>
> I am passing back exams in a class. One guy has never been there except for the test, but I notice his wife is there. I start to tell her that he is going to fail if he doesn't attend, but she holds up a note that says he is HIV-positive, and that he isn't able to get to class very often.
>
> I then realize that he looked very sickly and had sores on his face. I feel very bad, and ask her if he wants to come see me in my office. She says yes, and then we start to choose a time to meet during my office hours. She says she will come too, and so will their children, and we can go out to lunch. Although I am sorry for them, I am very busy, and I start to feel taken over and resentful.

This is like the dying man reaching up for Psyche's help. How can she possibly resist him? But as if I were in one of Levy-Bruhl's tribes, this sick student's family now begins to take me over. The result is this third episode in the series:

> **Jewelry Repair**
>
> I am on my way to a jewelry store to get some piece of jewelry repaired that I have broken. When I get there, there is a massively long line of people at the customer service window, and I realize I will not have time to get mine fixed.

The problem with ignoring the tower's rules, these dreams seem to say, is that everybody else gets their needs met but me. I am not accessing my "inner Joan Rivers" here, and so my pearl of great price—my deep feminine self—remains broken.

Last night I was talking at a party with a colleague who had just accepted the chairpersonship of her department. As a productive scholar just finishing her third book, she was reluctant, knowing that the job would eat into her research time and whatever introverted peace she had crafted during the last few years at home, away from a diverse and politically charged department. She had taken the job in large part because she perceived no other viable candidate to deal with some problems of latent discrimination within her domain. I expressed my admiration for her commitment, especially since I knew that she had very much found her stride in her writing, and that she was passionate about her subject.

"Well, I'm not doing anything you wouldn't do if you were desperately needed," she said, knowing of my own zeal for writing and aversion to administration. "I'm sure if you were in the situation I'm facing, you would say yes . . . wouldn't you?" She was searching my face for an answer, I thought in part to corroborate her own decision.

"No," I replied, "I wouldn't."

"*Why not?*" she demanded. "You'd be so good at it!"

"Because I think it would kill me," I deadpanned, over-dramatizing a bit, but only a bit. After all, my insomnia has still not abated, and good days are hard to come by.

"But if all of us feminists decline to help when we're really needed, how is the university ever going to change?" she pleaded.

I was literally immersed in writing this section before turning off the computer to attend the party, and I was well aware of the pitiful man reaching up for Psyche's helping hand, as well as my own commitment not to extend mine too far while writing this book. The old familiar guilt immediately flooded over me, as I questioned the tower's injunctions anew. Yes, what if we all turned a blind eye to those in need, cutting off our pity and generosity at critical moments, when we really could put our missions aside—just for, say, three years—until the worst exigencies are removed? I must be a selfish bitch.

I have engaged in conversations like this one, either in my head or out of it, on countless occasions, "runnin' down a list of things," with Iris DeMent justifying "each breath that I'd been breathin' in this life." And many times I have said yes to things I didn't have to or want to do, forgetting the tower's rule, "pity . . . is not lawful." Too often for me and for many of my peers, it is the decision to go on a conscious descent, to keep the initiate's veil fastened firmly over our faces, that is not lawful.

Not too long ago, I felt pummeled by repeated requests to take on weighty editing and administrative jobs that I believe I could handle well, but that would delay this book even further, right when I wanted more than anything I could think of to complete it. The requests were persuasive, accompanied by appeals like "The field really needs you to do this," and "You are the best person for this job." Again, I faltered—seeing those old women on Psyche's path, the ones who are obviously weaving the fate of the world. Their task is important—don't they need my help? I dashed off an e-mail detailing my torments to my sister Joyce, who has understood me better than anyone since I was born, and who often is the Wise Woman in my life. She sent back this reply, which I have since forwarded to many women I know facing similar situations to mine. It has struck a chord, and so I will repeat it for you here:

> Hi Janice,
>
> Frederick Buechner said, "One's call is that place where the world's great need meets your own great Joy." I think you can take this in stages. A quick, definitive no to the editorships for now. You are enjoying your writing, and it would ruin your life to say yes. Other people's urgent/important plea is not your urgent/important yes.
>
> Administrative offices—not now, maybe later. You are in your early fifties, and are crafting a way to do the productive soul work you've always wanted. Not all people are alike. You could explain to anyone who cares that you give a great deal of personal mentoring, paper advice, keeping up with former students, etc., and that is valuable to you. Let them think what they think. It is your life, and YOU get to decide in what way you want to "give back" to the field, and on your own time. This is the time of fun, solitude, writing, and sanity.
>
> The "Central Female Gender Fallacy" comes in here: if they don't get it, you can't act. IF THEY DON'T GET IT, YOU CAN'T ACT. You can say to some people "I am at the peak of my creativity and I don't want to transfer that to others' creativity. I see myself doing that later." Or just say "No, my heart isn't in it and, while I would do a good job, because I'm duty bound I would be sad and lose what really fuels me." Be charming, polite, kind, clear, and firm,

then let it go. Remember, life does change, it's longer than you think, and you might want to do some of these things later. You have at least 12 to 13 more years, and the requests won't stop.

That's all the cheap advice I can think of before I go to work. Love you,

Joyce

Like a softly lit torch on Psyche's way into the underworld, Joyce's message kept me on track when I was once again contemplating abandoning it—or, more accurately, thinking maybe I could do my book and at least *one more Big Thing*. What I realized is that some people can juggle several demanding projects at once, sometimes happily. I have done this many times in my career, but it has always taken its toll. Maybe there is nothing wrong, when I have contained that one fragile crystal goblet of water, in "doing only one thing well" until it is time to move on.

Patricia, who I admired earlier as an Amazon forged in the sixties counter-culture and now fighting for many important causes as a vice chancellor, is one of those women who does handle many Big Things at once. I consider her an effective and altruistic Superwoman. I wanted to know if she ever said no, or if she really did have some kind of "Bewitched" nose she could wriggle, like the good witch Samantha, and get things done in a flash without breaking a sweat.

"Do you feel that you're good at juggling all the things in your life?" I asked Patricia toward the end of our conversation.

"Yes, I'm good at it," she replied without hesitation. "The good thing is, I'm never bored—have never been bored in my life. But it's true that I always have many more things I want to do than I have time for. I think I've finally realized that I can't do all of them. Maybe it's a function of growing older."

"Are you good at saying no?" I wanted to know.

"I've gotten better at it, I'm still not really good at it. One of the things that's really helped me is seeing women who have a lot fewer responsibilities than I do saying no—for things I consider really trivial—like, 'We're having company this weekend so I can't have the book club over at my house.' Then I think—I could do that!"

"What a concept!" I exclaimed.

"Yeah, what a concept! I also think it may be a kind of sickness to think you have to do everything, to think your whole self-worth is tied up in being able to do everything. But I still have that sickness pretty bad, it's just not as bad as it used to be when I was younger."

Even this strong but soft warrior, so accomplished at handling many more things than I ever could, admitted that wanting to do everything might be a sickness. I believe the reason is that such a juggling act keeps a woman from completing Psyche's descent, from entering Hades and securing Persephone's ointment.

With the tower's rules for her behavior in mind, the coins in her mouth for the ferryman, and the bread in her hands for the three-headed dog, Psyche heads for Hades—like a backpacker who has planned for contingencies, at least somewhat prepared. It is a fear-some journey, but Hades actually means not "bad," but "deep."[47] Something is waiting for Psyche in the depths of Hades. She has great courage, and she must get to the bottom of her quest.

Not all of us are as prepared as Psyche for the down going. Some-times our bodies force a descent, mandating our withdrawal from the upper world, as in the illnesses Rachel recounted among her friends. The cycles of creativity, as we have seen, are just that—ups and downs rather than straight lines—demanding periods of dryness alternating with moisture. My own mid-life descent, in which I could not accomplish the academic work I had done so faithfully for two decades, was one of these surprise attacks, in which I felt ambushed by my own listlessness and unprepared for my losses.

At the lowest point of my disorientation, I spent Christmas vacation wondering how I could possibly return to school in January, almost hoping for an illness that would save me with the sick leave I knew in my heart I would never take. At her urging, I accompanied my sister Joyce and twelve other women on a trip to Belize before the semester started for a week of meditation, geographic exploration, companionship, and fun. Joyce leads such retreats every year to some place in the tropics, partly to escape the cold Montana winters where she lives, and partly to help other women to do the reflective soul work they so often do not have time to do at home. Something about journeying below the equator, feeling the gentle rains of the deep forests and the soft breezes of the clear ocean, as well as getting to know peoples who aren't as infected with the chronic American sense of urgency, tends to bring about a welcome descent for many.

Joyce had titled this week "Dreaming from the Inside Out," with the intent of translating our dreams into guidance for living. Being an inveterate dream interpreter, I was up to the challenge. What I didn't count on was the failure of my carefully packed suitcase to navigate successfully the twists and turns of Third World travel. Somehow everyone else's luggage made it to the lush, overgrown jungles of Chaa Creek—everyone's, that is, except mine. In addition to my travel clothes (a blazer, skirt, pantyhose, and street shoes, all completely worthless in the rain forest) I had exactly one Razorback t-shirt, one pair of denim shorts, one pair of failing leather sandals, and one hair dryer (also not particularly useful in the electricity-less thatch huts in which we stayed). All week, I borrowed essentials from helpful people I'd just met. The Tevas one woman loaned me were half again as big as my feet, adding a new dimension to the term "flip-flops," and the swimsuits—well, we won't even go there. I felt out of control and beholden, and partly because I already felt naked from the loss of my familiar academic persona, I grieved for my clothes.

As a group, we role-played each other's dreams, trekked over Mayan ruins, and canoed the jungle river in a sudden downpour. We were invited into the home of Dr. Rosita Arvigo, an herbal practitioner from Chicago who had moved to Belize in search of Don Eligio Panti, a 100-year-old *curandero* from whom she was learning the medicinal uses of the rain forest's plants, trying to catalogue them before the forests were destroyed by industry.[48] The world's strongest link between the art of herbal healing and the test tubes of the National Cancer Institute, Rosita was also a profoundly spiritual woman. She included us in traditional ceremonies to honor the nine Mayan spirits—all very present in her life—and read to us from her journal of experiences and dreams regarding her long apprenticeship to her shaman. During the days spent with Rosita and the other women, I slowly felt the weight of my former school life evaporate into the mists of the Maya Mountains, although the depression was still heavy on my shoulders.

Toward the middle of the week, I had this dream:

> Rosita invites our group into her home. She tells us that last night the spirits visited and left a gift. She leads us into a large kitchen, and there is something hanging from a hook on the ceiling. It has a very mysterious presence, and I feel I am somehow connected with it. She indicates that it is some kind of meat—like chicken—but we can't eat it today. We must let it hang there for an indefinite time. As I get closer, I can smell that it is rotten.

I immediately recognized the motif in my dream as that of Inanna-Ishtar, the Sumerian goddess of heaven and earth, whose story we know from third millennium B.C. clay tablets discovered in the 1920s. Inanna's story is similar to Psyche's and Persephone's descents into Hades. Inanna journeys into the underworld for the funeral of her brother-in-law, her dark sister Ereshkigal requiring that guards strip her of her regalia and clothes at each of the seven gates, until she appears "naked and bowed low" before her. At this point, Ereshkigal kills Inanna and hangs her corpse on a peg, where it turns into rotting meat. Eventually, Ereshkigal hands over Inanna's corpse to mourners who come to secure her release, and she is restored to life. But upon her return to the upperworld, she must send down a substitute, and she chooses her beloved consort Dumuzi as a sacrifice.[49]

Just like Inanna, I had gone down below what is familiar and been stripped of my "regalia and clothes." With my vocation having lost its luster, I felt like that rotting piece of meat that Ereshkigal, or the Mayan spirits, had hung on the hook. As I said before, in my descents I often feel like I'm composting, although while in the process I don't expect any results. But Rosita, with her deep communion with the plant and spirit world, had become my Wise Woman for that time and space, and she referred to the meat as a gift. No one could touch it yet, in fact we could not determine when, but its time would come. The next day our group moved out of the jungle to the ocean, and for the rest of the week I learned that I could indeed depend on the kindness of strangers, and that it was a sort of weightless freedom to have so few accoutrements to keep up with. I danced to the music of the Garifuna tribespeople, snorkeled with borrowed gear, let the oceans' waves calm my perpetually hyped-up body. In the wet sand between my toes as I lay at the border of land and sea, or out where the colorful fishes swam among the seaweed floating like loosened hair ribbons, could I hear the voice of the long exiled goddess? *Let it go, my child,* she was whispering, *all of it. You will survive.*

Joyce read us a poem each morning to contemplate during the day. On the last morning it was "In Blackwater Woods," by Mary Oliver. The last part of it goes like this:

> . . .
> Every year
> everything
> I have ever learned
>
> in my lifetime
> leads back to this: the fires
> and the black river of loss
> whose other side
>
> is salvation,
> whose meaning
> none of us will ever know.
> To live in this world
>
> you must be able
> to do three things:
> to love what is mortal;
> to hold it
>
> against your bones knowing
> your own life depends on it;
> and, when the time comes to let it go,
> to let it go.[50]

I had indeed held my love for the rarefied heights of academic intellectualism against my bones now for a long time, as if my life depended on it. But the veil of respectability, which had worked so well for me as a loyal Brainchild, had hardened into something like armor; it had lost its ephemeral suppleness, and perhaps the time was coming to let it go. Upon my return to the Ozarks I would still owe a sacrifice to the dark sister below, and it would have to be dear. But I still had a little more time before it would come due.

PSYCHE'S FAILURE

Psyche does find her way to Persephone, obtains her treasured beauty ointment, and makes it back to the upper world. How frustrating, then, that just as she is almost home free, she falters and opens the cask. This seems on the surface like Pandora's fateful curiosity or Eve's greediness—both patriarchal overlays on older myths that blame the woman for vanity or, worse, the ills of the world. Indeed, the beauty potion may be seen as a woman's preoccupation with physical desirability, a superficial mask that prevents serious relationship.[51] But again we need to look deeper than that. Psyche's act is more like the last gasp of her maidenhood, trying desperately to keep its hold on her before she gives it up for good.

When Persephone's beauty ointment escapes the jar, Psyche falls into a death-like sleep, similarly to what happens to Sleeping Beauty and Snow White, who are also bewitched by the Bad Mother. Aphrodite/Persephone would prefer that Psyche "die," to regress back to her self-contained maiden stage before she met Eros. In all these stories, it is the seduction of carefree narcissism that threatens to overcome the heroine. "This beauty of existence in the unconscious gives the feminine a natural maidenly perfection. But preserved forever, it becomes a beauty of death, a beauty of Persephone, who is inhuman since her existence is one of divine perfection, without fate, suffering, or knowledge."[52]

The enchantment does not ultimately succeed, however, because Psyche is pregnant by Eros—that is, imbued with love and consciousness. In fact, it may well be love that motivates Psyche's "failure." Psyche's desire for beauty brings the story full circle, for it all started with this same concern of Aphrodite's. Eros will not be able to resist her, she must be thinking, if she is besprinkled with divine beauty. But, by preferring beauty to duty, Psyche re-evokes the feminine in her nature—not her earlier maidenly narcissism, and not the promiscuity of a goddess concerned only with fertility, but the beauty of a woman who loves a specific man. Knowing in some part of herself that she may die as a result, Psyche sacrifices her whole being for love; this repairs the injury that drove Eros away. More than that, it "transforms the burned fugitive into a savior" because he encounters the human and feminine mystery of rebirth through love.[53] Taken as *animus*, Eros can now arouse Psyche to life on a new plane, for the two now are in proper relationship, whole and complete. "She is his queen."[54]

Psyche's failure reminds her of her humanity, and us of the necessity of failure in all human growth.[55] It also seems finally to melt Aphrodite's icy heart. "A Psyche who fails, who for the sake of love renounces all principles, throws all warnings to the winds, and forsakes all reason, such a Psyche must ultimately find favor with Aphrodite who assuredly recognizes a good part of herself in the new Aphrodite." The ancient goddess does at length ordain Psyche's deification. And the two goddesses, divided by the patriarchate into Good and Bad in countless manifestations, are now one.[56]

When an academic woman risks everything for love, it may be for a specific man, but often it is for *what she loves*. When Juliana burned her dissertation, she gave up a promising academic career—with much less assurance of success—for her love of writing fiction. When Laura left her professorship and got a second PhD, it was because another profession met her one great joy. When Abby contemplated resigning as director of her research clinic, she was pursuing her love of "something creative," however incompletely defined. But I would like to relate the stories of two women who sacrificed all for love, yet stayed in academia. Both of them describe their experiences in the terms of descent. One of them, Amelia, shared her story with me. The other, Jane Tompkins, tells hers in her book, *A Life in School*.

When I met with Amelia, she had just gotten tenure, but it had not been easy, and she had left a major university for an urban college that was on nobody's map of prestige points. This was surprising, given that she had achieved acclaim for her publications while still a graduate student, and was even better known as an assistant professor. She qualified as a "rising star," and her name routinely appeared in "three best women in the area" lists (which always annoy me because there is never a "three best men" list in any area). Her articles blended faultless scholarship with an entertaining, edgy writing style that drew me to her; after all, she was enacting the transgressive tendencies I wanted to exhibit myself. She seemed to nod toward patriarchal standards of argumentation while simultaneously flipping them off; many could not quite put their finger on just how she managed to be both *de rigueur* and insubordinate, and it made them vaguely uneasy. At any rate, everyone thought she was going to be BIG.

Amelia's demeanor, however, was warm and personal. I asked her why her tenure case had been so hard.

"Well, being at that university was like a descent and a re-emergence," she began, unexpectedly writing Psyche for me. "When you go to an Ivy League graduate school, you always are indoctrinated that you're supposed to go back into the Ivy League."

"Do they say it's OK to go out to a non-Ivy League school first—the minor leagues—and then go back?" I asked.

"Yeah. You just know that's the trajectory that you're supposed to follow. And so I went to a state school first, and then I went to the university, and then I thought, well, after that I'll get back in the Ivy League. Of course, nobody ever talks about the economic situation—the fact that you can fit the jobs there on the head of a pin."

Amelia told me of her husband's serious illness and difficult recovery. "When I was single I thought about wanting to publish as much as possible. After his illness, I started thinking about what would make us both happy, and what we would have to sacrifice together. We thought about maybe commuting in a major way. But there were so many petty things going on at school. I called it a major time-suck kind of a place. I mean, it's always like, what's the next thing?"

"When Tom and I finished our book," I volunteered, "somebody on the personnel committee said they were disappointed there wasn't another one. And that one wasn't even out yet!"

"I truly loathe the constant pressure," she continued. "I can't tell you how unhappy it makes me. I hate the sense of threat all the time, and the feeling that I can't stop to celebrate any achievements. I think academia is destructively set up for someone like me. I need the chance to think more deeply and develop ways of teaching and a coherent scholarly niche, and I resent the fact that's not possible in your pre-tenure years."

Amelia said that the difficulties in her tenure case—the committee didn't like it that she was interdisciplinary—along with her husband's illness, put her into an emotional tailspin, which made her question the "success track" she was on. She thought seriously about becoming a yoga instructor.

"That would be so different!" I exclaimed, very surprised she would consider giving up the reputation she had gained. She laughed uproariously.

"Oh, I see, that's the point!"

Amelia decided to "give academia one more try," with the thought that if another job didn't work out, she would leave for good. "I gave up the white phallus of the Ivy League as a goal. I didn't want to keep moving around, and I didn't want the time pressure." She chose an inner-city college where she could become rooted in the community, especially in humanitarian causes. Currently, she is the director of an interdisciplinary program, but spends much of her time linking its activities in research and service to the needs of poor families in the area.

"I'm really happy," she reported. "I don't miss the Ivy League at all. I will never go back." Amelia had given up her burgeoning reputation as a "player" in the big leagues—what some would call "everything"—for what she loved to do, what made her feel whole.

~

Jane Tompkins is a famous feminist literary critic who was professor of English at Duke University. I met her once at an American Studies convention and invited her to Tom's and my room. Having read her works and knowing of her fame, we were both honored and nervous when she said yes. We had planned to ask a lot of questions about her criticism, and maybe even what it was like to work with her husband, the also-famous critic, Stanley Fish. Tom even threatened to ask for her autograph. Imagine our surprise when she immediately kicked off her shoes, put her feet up on the bed, took out a tablet and pen and started asking questions about *our* work! "Now," she said, "I want to know more about this 'perennial philosophy' thing you have written about." Somehow, I am always amazed when eminent scholars turn out to be so human. Little did I know.

Jane's book, *A Life in School: What the Teacher Learned*, is a revelation. She begins with this rather shocking statement:

> At the age of forty-nine, having spent most of my conscious years inside the walls of academic institutions, I realized I no longer had much use for the things I'd learned in school.[57]

Her book set off a firestorm of reaction, as other teachers and her former students attacked and defended what she had done, which amounted, in my mind, to a very Psyche- or Inanna-like descent, in which she threw off almost everything she had learned about college, and particularly about teaching. "By this I don't mean that what I had learned was worthless," she clarified, "but that the subjects I had studied and taught, and the way I had studied and taught them, were secondary to the real concerns of my life."[58]

What followed upon her initial disaffection was a period of internal change in which she lost her familiar anchors. Her life goal had always been achievement, and she had lived in perpetual fear that whatever she did was not enough. Now it became clear that her primary goal was not to make a career for herself but to give something back to others. Like so many who felt the ground shifting beneath their feet, however, she did not know what that would be. She could only tell that school was no longer the place for her. She came to believe that our entire educational system fails to nourish the inner lives of students or to provide the safe and nurturing environment that people need in order to grow.[59]

In descents such as those of Psyche and Inanna, as the song goes, "What goes up must come down." So, too, Jane sought out experiences that were totally antithetical to what we normally consider "academic." Her new teachers, she said, were no longer celebrated literary critics, but "a dog, a course of massages, Alzheimer's patients, homeless people, Buddhist meditation, a nondenominational charismatic African American church." Whereas she had always resisted these nonintellectual ways of knowing, they became her central focus of learning.[60] Like Psyche (and like me), Jane did not set out intentionally to change herself; it was more like she was dragged under by an inability to go on in the old way.

In her book, she goes back over the founding experiences of her life in school, from kindergarten on, to see how they had shaped her.[61] Whereas college at Bryn Mawr was an ideal cloister for her, the PhD at Yale was another story. Jane remembers the "desperate striving to achieve barely obtainable goals."[62] She describes her graduation ceremony at Yale: driving home afterward to Middletown, Connecticut, with her family in another car, she arrived home first, went straight to the bedroom of their second-floor apartment, lay down on the bed without removing her gown, and burst into tears. When I read this I thought of my own bodily eruption, and wondered if they are not all that rare. But whereas I was mystified by mine, Jane was not by hers. "I knew why I cried," she writes. "No one, not one person in the world, knew what that PhD had cost me."[63] She also tells how she became a professor, how she grew dissatisfied with teaching her students what was in her head, and how she progressively took apart and gave up everything about the way she taught, as "all the moorings [came] loose."[64]

Jane started teaching classes with no syllabi but only with some readings for starters, letting the structure emerge from the group. She stopped preparing or working through a body of material in an organized manner. "It was not about the mastery of knowledge or the acquisition of a skill. It was about letting chaos in, about not knowing, not being in control."[65] She had conducted these "trials by liberation" for the benefit of her students, seeing how "straitjacketed" they were in the need to please their teachers. But she eventually realized that she was also trying to free *herself* from the authoritarian training that had kept her in the chains of "mind-numbing and spirit-breaking discipline." She needed to get back to "a time and space before school began."[66] She describes the stripping away of her preparedness and her teaching principles as "an avalanche, a hemorrhage" that she couldn't stop. "Everything became a throw of the dice. I called it teaching nothing."[67]

Jane's loss of her traditions, rules, principles, and ultimately her familiar self is what spiritual teachers call *kenosis*—an emptying out or becoming nothing that makes a person receptive to new insights. It is the kind of descent she recognized in T. S. Eliot's *Ash Wednesday*, a spiritual death, or the day of ashes that precedes resurrection. Although she had read this work in college, she saw for the first time, up close and personal, Eliot's suffering. It was "unappetizing. . . . His innards are half rotted; they send up a kind of stink that curls between the lines but is denied." "I feel him swing between a complete undoing of himself," she writes, "his bones scattered in the desert, himself forgotten—and the first starting up of hope."[68] Again, we sense Inanna's corpse—as well as Jane's, and my own. When Psyche journeys to Hades, she cannot be sure whether she will return.

Jane's courage reminds me of Psyche's "failure"; for the sake of love, she renounced all principles, threw all warnings to the winds, and forsook all reason. What she loved, I think, was her own emerging vision of a different kind of education, a more holistic approach to learning that echoed her own desire to be whole. "I wish that the college I bound my identity over to had introduced me to my heart. I wish it had set mercy and compassion before me as idols, instead of Athena's cold brow. I wish I had been encouraged to look inward, been guided on a quest for understanding my own turmoil, self-doubts, fears."[69]

Seemingly reiterating the moment when the eagle gets the water of life for Psyche, Jane observed that "if your cup can become empty momentarily, it can be filled."[70] The latter part of her book outlines what she thinks a university can and should be. It is a vision that is radical in its simplicity. She wants a form of higher education "that would take responsibility for the emergence of an integrated person."[71] No more, and no less.

I returned from Belize not exactly rotten and stinking, but tenderized. As I alluded to earlier, I did not write anything academic for two years. I continued to teach pretty much as I had been because I didn't know what else to do, but I was excited about my screenplay, which I kept hidden from all but my co-author and Tom. I read only those academic journal articles I absolutely had to for the sake of my classes or my editing duties. Like Jane Tompkins, Sophia, and many other women I spoke with, I was drawn to the garden. Without a particularly green thumb, mine never looked that great, but what mattered was just to have my hands in the earth rather than my head in the clouds.

I didn't make it in Hollywood, but that was OK, too. Writing a film script taught me the importance of stories, which I had known since I was a child and had over-zealously defended since I was a graduate student. Though I had long left my honors professor behind, I came to see, through writing this book, that I have tried much of my career to live up to an imagined collective Pygmalion/Zeus, who I believed wanted me to be the Brainchild he would reward. But I began—slowly, tentatively—to break Pygmalion's mold. Or was it breaking me? I started to speak without Athena's rational armor, and it felt like the last part of my week in Belize, unencumbered by the weight of props I could do without.

But Athena's armor is close to the skin, if not to the bone and, taking it off, I feel naked again. Suddenly, I am back in college, and my honors professor is turning on *me*, not my friend Margo. *You don't have what it takes*, he is sneering. *You're not as smart as I thought.* I seem to be still standing. *You are not desirable*, he scoffs, but I am dry-eyed. Yet I still owe a sacrifice to the dark sister below, something precious I must give to her in exchange for my liberation. Could it be Psyche's maidenhood? In my case, this was more like the beauty of unstained rational perfection than her innocent bliss of a marriage. If I relinquished that, which I had held so dear, I would also have to see that the Father's critical voice, like Eros to Psyche, was not apart from me, but *in* me.

As a loyal Brainchild I've been imitating Pygmalion's, and especially Zeus', suppression of the Goddess' origins: swallow the mother source whole and deliver through the head a maiden who emerges fully armored, with a mighty shout. But I have loved myth, that soft and fully rounded underbelly of the harder, more chiseled logic, since I was disguised as a girl. And it is *mythos* from which the Brainchild's *logos* was born. Perhaps now, at the tender age of 54, I can begin yet again to claim my birthright, and to speak with a voice that is more Virgin than made.

CHAPTER 11

DIVINE CHILD

"It's a girl!"

We have seen Eros and Psyche endure a great ordeal; now it is time to celebrate. Here is the last line of Apuleius' tale:

> Thus did Psyche with all solemnity become Eros' bride, and soon a daughter was born to them: in the language of mortals she is called Pleasure.[1]

Eros and Psyche consecrate their union in the presence of all Olympus, in the light rather than in the dark. It is a *hieros gamos*, or sacred marriage of god and goddess, such as those celebrated in the temples of Aphrodite by the priest and the sacred prostitute; it is a coming together of the masculine and feminine as one. But Psyche has also been pregnant during all her tasks. There has always been promise of a reward for her labor, even when she seemed to forget she was carrying a child and thought to end her life, and there is definitely something new afoot. My favorite Christmas card this year came from a graduate student who just finished a class I was teaching in mythology. The Three Wise Men are looking at the manger in the stable and one of them says "It's a girl!" Contrary to Eros' presumptions, their child, too, is a girl.

Although this is a myth of love and relationship, it is most centrally Psyche's story. If the child had been a boy, he would have stood for the renewal and deification of her *animus*. But a divine daughter! This is an unexpected mystery; it is the rebirth of her very *self*, Psyche's discovery of her own goddesshood. Apuleius calls the child "Pleasure," but this event far surpasses the pleasure of the senses. The daughter is the bliss that is described in many traditions as the fruit of the highest mystical union, and thus could more fittingly be called "Joy" or "Ecstasy."[2]

Masculine mysteries, or the myth of the solar hero, are concerned with the heroic struggle of the ego to separate from the Great Mother, capped with the disclosure of "atonement" (at-one-ment), or "I and the father are one."[3] Matriarchal mysteries, such as those of Eleusis and Isis, have to do with death and rebirth. Masculine mysteries generally end in *gnosis* or knowledge, whereas feminine ones end in love. Masculine mysteries view matter as the creation of the spirit—as in the Genesis story when God creates the heavens and the earth; matriarchal mysteries view spirit as created from matter—as in Psyche's work that transforms Eros from monster-husband to sleeper to redeeming god.[4] These themes of rebirth, love, and grounding in the phenomenal world of matter weave throughout the stories that academic women tell about finding their joyful selves.

THE DIVINE MENAGERIE

It is clear to me now that my inner Psyche has been laboring for some time to deliver a Divine Child. In fact, as I go through my journals, I find evidence of this process spanning back over two decades. But this very long gestation is intertwined with dreams of Critical Fathers, of not being good enough, of mental and bodily exhaustion, of being crowded out of my self by others' demands, and of the neglect of my instinctual and spiritual selves. No wonder this is a difficult birth! It is also multiple, occurring over and over again—sometimes aborted, sometimes stillborn, sometimes premature and too small to live, occasionally whole and vibrant. Apparently, this nativity cannot be accomplished once and for all.

Neither are my offspring always human. I have, in fact, an entire menagerie of animals that come to visit me at night. I think this is due, in part, to my very mental waking life as a professor—and a

Brainchild at that. Like the ants who arrive to help Psyche sort the seeds, my instincts show up when I am not on guard against them. They also need help themselves. Earlier I referred to my ongoing series, consisting of hundreds of episodes at least, of "starving puppies" dreams. I call them that because they are most often puppies, but almost any baby animal can stand in, and has.

The motif is always the same: I wake up or remember, with a start, that I have a puppy in my back yard or garage that I have forgotten to feed. It's been a week or ten days and I am frantic. I rush out to find it, and it is weak and sick, almost dead. Sometimes it has black spots where it has started to "spoil," or it can barely lift its head to eat. I desperately feed it whatever I can find, hoping against hope it is not too late. By going unconscious and forgetting to feed my instincts, these dreams seem to say, I have endangered them almost to the point of death. I always revive the animal, but the dreams always return. Mary Oliver's poem, "Wild Geese," begins this way:

> You do not have to be good.
> You do not have to walk on your knees
> for a hundred miles through the desert, repenting.
> You only have to let the soft animal of your body
>   love what it loves.[5]

But I have not yet "gotten it," these starving puppies dreams imply, and I continually slip back into overwork and starvation of the soft animal of my body. Many of these series occur in escalating episodes. Once the sequence began with kittens, went to puppies, then to hippos, elephants, and whales. I am not a quick study in this department.

One series, in fact, featured hippopotami. It started in the same old way:

> I am having trouble walking through the house because the floor is absolutely covered with baby hippopotami. They are all sick or injured.

Granted, hippos are a bit extreme, but at least this one is familiar. I am appalled, as usual, and want to do something about it. Actually, my dream life does this for me in the next installment:

> With someone else, I come upon a pen in a forest, in which there is a mother hippo and her baby. The mother breaks out of the pen and,

> abandoning her baby, she tumbles and rolls down a steep mountain, landing in a pool of water with a big splash.
>
> The baby looks very forlorn and helpless without its mother, as if it doesn't know what to do. So my companion and I help it out of its pen. Once unconfined, the baby hippo seems to know what to do, and he runs and tumbles, somersaulting playfully, and lands in the pool beside his mother.

Something about hippopotami here? This one comes from deeper in my unconscious, as it is not in my own back yard or house, but in the forest—symbol of the Great Mother. The hippopotamus goddess Ta-urt, who is benevolent and protective, in time came to be identified with almost every goddess in the Egyptian pantheon.[6] In my dream, this mother seems to abandon her child, but I pick up the slack, and mother the little one myself. I think, though, that this animal mother is simply modeling for her progeny what to do, like a mother bird kicking its young out of the nest—in this case, how to "break out" and play. Once we free the baby, she or he figures out what to do.

This dream then picks up again with an abrupt scene shift that intensifies the motif to the level of a feminine mystery:

> A woman is giving birth, and several people are standing around watching. She talks about what is happening, and shows the "child" that is half-born. We are all astonished to see that she is giving birth to a hippopotamus! We wonder how this could be. Somehow, we get the impression that she has *swallowed* it, and is now giving birth. The event seems to be imbued with religious importance.

This is now a collective ritual, for the birth is communal; the mother explains for the group what is happening, as if it is not just for her but for them. The dream taps into another Egyptian motif, for swallowing before giving birth is also typical of that culture's mythology. It refers to the goddess religions' seasonal rite, in which the mother gives birth to herself as a maiden.[7] And it is a feminine reversal of the patriarchal co-optation theme of swallowing a goddess in order to give birth through the head, like Zeus' consumption of Metis and cranial delivery of Athena. This dream may seem a bizarre "magical mystery tour," but it has religious importance for me; it is about the birth of the creative feminine.

My birthing babies dreams do not all come from *Animal Kingdom*. When they evolve to the human domain, they dramatize more of my self than the animal parts I have continued to disown. In the second season of television's *Ally MacBeal*, Ally was visited by several visions of a computerized, be-diapered dancing baby. He appeared because her biological clock was ticking, and her infamously chaotic love life was not promising relief from her anxiety. My version is the "talking baby"—appearing to remind me, not of my biological clock, but that I cannot wait forever to deliver my innermost creative self. These infants talk to me, I am guessing, to give me important messages I can't hear when I'm awake. My talking babies come in many varieties. One I held in the palm of my hand; he looked like Willie Nelson—braids, beard, and all. His words escape me, but maybe he was trying to tell me my music—or creativity—was both full-grown (ready to be delivered) and undersized (malnourished). "Quit messin' around," he might have lyricized, and "get downtown." When I completed an especially difficult theoretical article once, another tiny "palm-pilot" appeared in my hand and said with a Christ-like flair, "It is finished." I did have to wonder whether he meant the essay or *me*.

As in the hippo series, these human baby dreams escalated into one containing a numinous mystery. This baby didn't talk, but its symbolism did. I called it "Divine Child in a Barrel":

> I am walking in the back yard at someone's house, and this person shows me that there are flowers in bloom, even though it's winter. After showing me around, he asks it I want to see something secret, and guides me to a barrel with a top on it. It is at the left edge of the yard. I have an eerie feeling about the barrel. I don't really want to see what's inside. But I follow him to it, he takes off the lid, and I see that the barrel is filled with grass clippings and leaves that are rotting and mildewing. He digs into the mulch with his hands, pulls out an ugly creature and asks if I want to touch it. I am repulsed, but also morbidly drawn to it.
>
> He asks if I know what it is. My first thought is that it looks like a stick-bug—a large insect so perfectly camouflaged that it's almost indistinguishable from a twig. But when I touch it, I realize it's softer than a stick, and has tufts of brown fur on it. He puts the creature, which seems to be alive but slowed down, perhaps hibernating, back in the organic mess in the barrel. I have an uneasy intuition that the

> thing is more alive than it looks, and that we really should not put the lid back on and leave it there; I'm not sure it will survive.
>
> We start to put the lid back on and leave, and my uneasiness grows as it dawns on me that this creature may be a human child. As I look closer, I realize it probably is. I am horrified, but also transfixed—the baby has a numinous feel about it—not like a halo, but like a deep connection with me. I feel strongly that it needs a real home, and to be nurtured. I also know that if I take the baby, it will need total devotion, for its "formative months" have probably been irreparably damaged by its solitary life in the grass. It will probably never be a normal human being. I stand there staring, totally conflicted between taking the child with me and leaving it there.

As in my starving-animal dreams, there is a forgotten creature in the back yard who may be sick or malformed. There is more hope here than before, though, because there are flowers blooming in winter, a sign of unexpected fertility. My *animus* is more helpful here than in most of my dreams; he leads me toward the "secret," which hints not just at my disregarded instincts, but a mystery. The secret is in *his* back yard, not mine, indicating he still retains the key to it. However, this is a feminine mystery, as evident from its location on the left side, which has been associated with the feminine at least as long as women have been considered the "second sex." The creature in the barrel is also nesting in rotting matter, the *prima materia* that gives birth to the spirit in feminine mysteries. Like Inanna's corpse—and mine hanging on the hook back in Belize—it is composting, but this time it evolves into something more advanced.

It would be easy to ignore or kill an insect. But when I connect to it with my senses (touch), it has fur, making it the kind of mammal that has already tugged at my emotions in many dreams. Then when my intuition kicks in, I become deeply connected as it dawns on me it is human. It is calling to me now on all levels of *my* humanity. My anxiety grows, as I am torn between nurturing this abandoned child and sacrificing everything to give it the total devotion it needs in order to thrive.

The divine child in mythology represents the potential of wholeness, creativity, and joy—that which is nascent in all of us but so often covered up or ignored. It is typically abandoned and in danger, like Moses in the bull rushes, the Christ child hunted by King Herod, and E. T. when he is left behind in the back yard of Elliott's house.[8] The child has to be detached from its parents, or given a fresh start, in order to evolve. But its condition is hazardous because there are huge difficulties to face. As C. G. Jung puts it, "Nothing in all the world welcomes this new birth, although it is the most precious fruit of Mother Nature herself . . . ."[9] The divine child symbolizes "the powerlessness and helplessness of the life-urge, which subjects every growing thing to the law of maximum self-fulfillment, while at the same time the environmental influences place all sorts of insuperable obstacles in the way of individuation."[10] The stories of academic women, including my own, reference many of those "insuperable obstacles"; certainly, if our divine children need challenges to test themselves, they get them.

Should I remove the child from the barrel and take care of it, or should I leave it? I seem to feel both love and dread, and I am undecided as the dream ends. Perhaps the composting is not quite yet what gardeners call "black gold," or maybe I am not quite ready.

PLACES IN THE HEART

Some women seemed to come through difficult times in academia to give birth to a Divine Child of new possibilities. Juliana, for example, who burned her dissertation in an initiatory departure from academia, has written three novels of surpassing elegance and excitement. I read all three, sometimes guiltily because I consumed them while I was supposed to be editing journal articles or reading student papers. I was hooked by the first page of the trilogy and simply could not put them down. She has been through all of Psyche's labors to produce them and now she must go through them again to get them published. Like Psyche, however, she was "pregnant" from the beginning, and the promise of Eros is obvious in the result.

Although she burned nothing but (symbolically) her lesson plans, Jane Tompkins also made plans to leave academia. She made up her mind to retire, the paths of the university and of her professional and personal lives being too divergent to tolerate. But she had a sense of unfinished business, something within her "that didn't want to just fade away." She decided to return to Duke for one last year. Team-teaching a course called "Writing Spiritual Autobiography" with a friend, and another on advanced composition, she writes, "I am experiencing a certain amount of happiness and peace in the classroom. This is ironic, and also, perhaps, inevitable, after so much tumult and trauma." She felt a greater kinship with students than she used to, and most significant for her, a diminution of her fear. "You might say that my fear has been replaced in a general way by faith, faith that things will work out and that if I pay attention to the moment, without too much pressure to make it come out a certain way, I'll be all right."[11] She owes this newfound pleasure to several things, not all of which are known to her: workshops in personal growth; learning to make the classroom a safer place for students and for herself; and, of course, the classroom experiments that she had conducted before her hiatus. By the end of her book, she was going ahead with her retirement plans and reaching out in new directions, including teaching a beginning course in meditation. But, she says, "I realize I need the classroom as a base. I'm still learning what it is to teach, and the students feed me."[12] Jane seems to know that the birth of this divine child is far from a one-time thing.

I think Patricia knows that, too. She is the busy 57-year-old vice chancellor I have typed an Amazon, although she is also much more than that. Patricia has had her battles, from raising two children mostly by herself while progressing from undergraduate school through her doctorate, to being the lone woman in upper administration at her university for many years, to fighting for women's issues on a campus that was mostly unaware that there were any. In talking with her, I got the sense that she is now living the life and career she wants. She is comfortable in her own skin as a force on campus and in her community. Still, she is open to new potentials, to the birth of another "child."

When I asked Patricia if she had any dreams about academia, she related a recurring one:

> I am in a building with a lot of rooms in it. It's not quite a house or a public building—it's somehow neither and both, sort of ambiguous.

> There are lots of parts of it to explore, and usually there are other people I'm going through it with. It seems they are academics.

"In a way I've always lived in an academic community—even my homes were either in college towns or right across the street from a college," Patricia elaborated. "I love the academic world. I love learning and talking about ideas. I miss that a lot, because I don't think it happens as much as it did when I was young."

"Is that because you're in administration, or because of the era?" I asked.

"I don't think it happens as much now as it did in the sixties and seventies. These days I don't really experience the kinds of intellectual discussions I had at one time."

"What are you doing in the dream in terms of the rooms?" I probed.

"There's a sense in which it's my house and I'm exploring it and creating it at the same time," Patricia said. "I think the whole building is my self. The rooms are places where I have the potential for doing practical things, but I'm also exploring. It's wide-ranging curiosity, balancing a lot of things—maybe I could create that environment where I could talk more with others about ideas."

Patricia's dream is actually a recurring one for many people. I have variations on it too. What a delight it is to find a room in our own house or school we didn't know was there. It is a room to explore the unknown, a space to be opened, a place in the heart. Like the child in the barrel I didn't know was there, it calls to us.

A VOICE OF HER OWN

Several of the women in our stories have lamented their loss of voice in academia. When the Handless Maiden gives birth to her child, if you recall, the Devil sends a message that it is an abomination, and that the old queen must kill it and cut out its tongue and eyes as proof it is dead. Sophia's dream in which her tongue was cut out and in her lap symbolizes the feeling she and so many others expressed—that they could not speak when in the company of academic men.

For years after leaving the university, Laura has been concerned with strengthening her own voice and the voices of other women. She had many dreams in which she tried to say something but people turned their backs on her, or she was talking but couldn't be heard. She owed her trouble with voice not only to the difficulty academia has listening to women in general but also to her romantic involvement with academic mentors early in her career. Recently, however, she told part of her story to a group of women who were also trying to reclaim their voices so as to be heard within a variety of professions.

"I told that story," Laura said, "and my voice broke—literally. This is twenty-six years later." Her voice broke again as she told it to me.

"Do you feel as if you have your voice now?" I wanted to know.

"Yes. I have a good sense of myself. I was eager to have my own life and job that didn't depend on anybody else to evaluate me. I knew I would work hard at this. I don't feel second-rate."

"Do you have any regrets about your relationships with the men?" I asked, remembering that several of the Maiden Lovers had no regrets at all, whereas others did.

"I regret all of them," Laura replied.

Laura had worked extremely hard to reclaim her self and to develop her voice apart from the men with whom she had been in relationship. And yet, she did not feel bitterness toward any of them. I asked her if she held the men responsible for what she perceived as her loss of voice.

"No, the era of the seventies was different," Laura reflected. "Do I blame the men? I can't blame them as individuals. I feel the cultural responsibility of the privileged group not understanding and seeing their privilege—not understanding the impact of their actions. I have a lot of anger about the culture—about what men learned they could get away with, their sense of entitlement, the feeling that they had the right to young women's attention all of the time. They used our brightness to shine their own mirrors. I have rage about that—and sorrow. Sorrow that I didn't get a chance to really fly in that field. But I don't have rage about any of the individual men. I would now, because the cultural dialogue has progressed to the point that ignorance is no excuse."

Instead of blaming others for her struggles, Laura had done

Psyche's labors—many times. She had sorted the seeds to distinguish herself from her romantic mentors. She had decided she did not have to take the entire golden fleece, which for her meant to produce a long list of refereed journal articles. She had filled her crystal chalice with the water of life by shaping a specialty, highly valued in her community, within a profession she loves. She had descended to a Hades of depression over the injuries to her voice many times, and sacrificed herself to the beauty ointment of love, not for a man or a manly institution, but for her own gifts. Now she was feeling a profound sense of calm with herself, much like what comes through at the end of Jane Tompkins' book. Like many others, she wanted to help other women to understand the trials they had faced or were facing, and to speak with a voice of their own.

WATERING THE WASTELAND

Laura did not blame the men who had badly botched her initiation into academia. She rightly pointed out that something is very wrong with a culture that could grant one of the sexes such entitlement while tainting the voices of the other. What happened to Laura, as it did to many of the other Maiden Lovers, Muses, Mistresses, and Brainchildren, is a radical reversal and profanation of the sexual initiation, or *hieros gamos*, of the Great Goddess traditions. As we have seen, this sacred rite, occurring in the temple of Aphrodite or another goddess of love, united body and spirit in a religious offering that produced *gnosis*—that is, the man and the woman became god and goddess. In the religion of the Great Mother, a king or a priest could only become divine through sexual union with a high priestess. It was she who was in control. As Lynn Picknett and Clive Prince put it, "Without her he was nothing."[13] This sacred marriage had significance not just for the individuals but for their culture. "Their union was believed to infuse both themselves and the world around them with a regenerative balm, and actually echo the creative impulse of the birth of the planet."[14]

But we saw what happened to Galatea. She was demoted from the Great Goddess to an inert statue, while her male consort stole her powers for his own (understandably so, since his fate was to die) as the patriarchate slowly replaced the goddess religions. Men became sexually dominant, and women's sexual status was reduced to that of wife, servant, or whore, and demarcated by the presence or absence of the veil. Furthermore, as the seat of masculine power rose in general from the phallus to the brain, and nowhere more thoroughly than in academia, sexual domination went underground. In the university, this has resulted in the unacknowledged license of men to women's sexuality, where it is still interspersed with *gnosis*, defined as *logos* rather than divine transformation. Although many women have initiated themselves into the university, the road for others has been rocky.

I am certainly not suggesting that we should return to ancient traditions. The world has changed too much, and we are still too firmly rooted in what Riane Eisler calls a "dominator society" for anything resembling a rite of sacred marriage to be sanctioned within a mass institution such as academia. If you want a picture of a *hieros gamos* gone bad—that is, infused with the domination of men—watch the ending of Stanley Kubrick's last film, *Eyes Wide Shut*, in which the sacred rites of a secret society are inflected with violence. It is the more general subordination and burial of the Goddess by the patriarchy that needs to be changed. Ever since aspects of the feminine began to be violated, interred, and co-opted, images of the Wasteland and the Grail have become pervasive in Western cultures. The lost Goddess takes the form of the princess submerged under the lake, the Lady of the Night, the undersea Amazons, the cave-dwelling Furies, the deep-sea monster, the oceanic Siren, the Alien mother, and on and on. In Plato's cave there are many mistresses.

The myth of the Holy Grail embodies this condition as hauntingly as any. The Fisher King's wound festers because without the Grail the world has turned arid—dry, brittle, and devoid of new life. Originally the Grail was probably pagan, although medieval myth translates it into the chalice containing Christ's blood and symbolizing the divine spirit.[15] But, more generally, the cup is the sacred emblem of feminine containment, as in the womb of the mother goddess, Psyche's urn, the cup suit of the Tarot cards (which becomes hearts in the modern deck), or the inverted pyramid of esoteric societies that honor the feminine. Wild female power is symbolized in many religions by blood and the color red, which stand for vitality and fertility.[16] The quest for the Grail, which is also the quest for the blood of life, is, then, a search for the lost feminine.

Helen Luke vividly depicts the condition of the earth when it has become a wasteland:

> And as the Goddess withdrew, so the earth dried up and withered, the sap and growth departed, and the land lay dying. The wasteland around the Fisher King in the Grail legend carries the same meaning—when it is time for a transformation of the whole personality, the birth of a totally new attitude, everything dries up inwardly and outwardly and life becomes more and more sterile until the conscious mind is forced to recognize the gravity of the situation, is compelled to accept the validity of the unconscious.[17]

But wait. Is there a ray of hope here, an absence before a presence, in what Luke says? In her words, when the world becomes a wasteland, something new is on the horizon. Apparently, everything must dry up until the land is parched and crying out for a drop from a merciless sky before we are forced into digging down deep, as Emmylou Harris sings, "Lookin' for the water from a deeper well . . . Reachin' out a hand for a holier Grail."[18] The land dries up into a desert before Zeus finally has pity on the grieving Demeter and strikes a bargain for her daughter Persephone; Psyche almost dies several times before Eros resurrects her and their child is born.

Images of aridity abound in the stories women tell about academia. Sophia, consistently in touch with the rhythms of creativity, articulately translated her feelings about university life into metaphors. She spoke of her sadness that academia allowed no time for getting stuck when you're involved in a creative project, and no downtime to experience the inevitable losses in life.

"I mean, what if somebody very, very close to you died when you were working on tenure?" she lamented. "You cannot allow yourself the liberty to mourn that. You have to set that aside and go on because the structure is so rigid. But you know it's going to come back—you're going to have to deal with it at some point. And it comes back as rage. There's no time to celebrate the joy or suffer the sadness."

Sophia suggested that we need rituals to mark the passages that we go through in academia, instead of "'OK, what are you going to do next?' There's this image before you go into academia that there'll be time for reflection, but there isn't, really."

"It kind of violates the creative process," I lamented. "You can't experience those hills and valleys. How do you get a seed growing when you haven't had time to water it and let it grow?"

"It's like the Dust Bowl, where you take the land and keep plowing it and plowing it and plowing it. And all you get is locusts and dust."

This kind of academic dryness scorches the feminine in men as well as in women. One of my brightest and most creative graduate students went to a prestigious PhD school, excited about pursuing his unorthodox ideas with advanced studies. But his teachers tried to fit him into a mold, just as, assuredly, Pygmalion did to his statuary bride. After two years this student left in order to avoid having his creative soul drilled out of him. "You have to learn to say things like 'X is the very condition of the possibility of Y,'" I remember him saying. Eventually he found a program to nurture his talents, but not in a conventional academic setting.

Another extremely talented student graduated from an MA program to enter an equally distinguished PhD program. After a year, he was sprouting a mirthfully sardonic attitude toward school that replaced the innocent enthusiasm he had as a younger student.

"I learned a lot this year, in general, but remarkably little about my area of study," he wrote me in an e-mail. "If anything, my understanding of the field has been confounded by the sometimes cavalier and unnecessary complication of what are essentially graspable concepts. Reading the position papers of some of my colleagues tonight for the upcoming conference convinces me that we students are groping to make sense of amorphous and tangential—yet chic—issues, and I think we all sound like we don't know what the hell we're talking about." He was managing to make stellar grades and had determined to stick it out until graduation, but I detected a new tone of dehydration in his words.

If our culture is producing more and more images of the wasteland, perhaps a Divine Child is being gestated. No wonder Dan Brown's *The Da Vinci Code*, which casts the search for the feminine Grail in the context of a fictional thriller, is still number 1 on the bestseller list as I write. But, whereas academics sometimes study "objective historical facts," we are probably the last to acknowledge that these drought conditions affect us. We adulate the myth of the solar hero, who brings light from heaven into the world, but not that of the goddess, who draws water up from under the earth. Thus, whereas individual women are rediscovering the submerged feminine in themselves, their under-recognized gifts, for the most part, are not put to use.

~

Toward the end of our time together, Laura reflected on the entire story that she had been courageous enough to tell me. I sensed that, like the Handless Maiden, she had her own Divine Child bound firmly to her breast, but that this was not quite enough, that there was something else she needed to say or do.

"You don't need to get anything 'right' any more, do you?" I asked, searching for what still chafed at her. "Do you still feel you need to get 'untainted'?"

"No, I don't. I feel that I've come through a very difficult time and have made it just fine, and I used to say, 'Well, it's not that hard to make it in this small town,' but I don't say that any more. I don't think about fame or being known. I care about doing good work."

At that moment her black cat brushed against her leg and then jumped into her lap. Stroking her sleek fur, Laura seemed at ease thinking out loud. "In a way, I feel as if I've come, not to the end, but to the present."

"You have a fascinating story," I said.

"I'm very interested in women's stories being heard with an intelligent ear," Laura said. "I don't have a sense of ownership on the personal level about my story. But I do believe in the power of stories to educate, inform, enlighten."

"I think stories are what get to people."

"One of the things I don't have any idea how to do is, I'd like to make a difference to men and not just women," Laura said earnestly. "I have a burning desire for men to understand how it is with women. I have so many intelligent feminist friends that I feel as if that battle, for me, in my life, is won."

"We know a lot," I bragged.

"We know the content of our fields, and we know about the

culture and sexism. Men only have to know their fields—and enough about relationships to build their intimate lives and get along, but they don't have to be bi-cultural in the ways we have to be. I'd like to change that. The thing that's difficult is that most men don't want to be in a group for personal growth, at least for themselves. And the men who would sign up are mostly already there!"

We laughed as her cat bounded from her lap to her desk to the top of her bookcase. Cats have a rule that they can't touch the floor when navigating a room.

"I'm a little concerned that I'll be writing for women who already know these things," I said uneasily. "Men won't read these stories. And most women don't have the power to change things radically."

"Well, women who know that they can push back and hold on to their sense of self. . . "

"You're right," I interjected, "they do make a difference."

"I don't believe it's just women 'in power' that matter," Laura continued. "Understanding your own story is important, and so is telling it. Any woman with a voice makes a difference."

As we reflected on what Laura's academic story meant to her and to others, I realized that we were imitating Zeus' eagle, come to provide the heightened vision for getting just the right drops for Psyche's cup. Shaping and containing it inside that fragile crystal just might water the wasteland, if only a little bit at a time.

THE DANCING GODDESS

Surviving trials that could deter the most ardent lovers, Eros and Psyche finally make a sacred marriage. Each helps the other; Eros helps Psyche to find the divinity within and Psyche helps Eros to ground his tendency towards flight in the love of one woman. But it is Psyche who first questions their ecstasy of darkness, who lights the lamp of awareness, and who leads Eros into maturity. While I am not suggesting that all of academia is a wasteland—it is, after all, the scene of my own calling, as well as that of many others—I do believe it is ailing from the Fisher King's wound, in need of being brought to life by what women, and the feminine in men, have to offer.

John Welwood writes that we often portray male-female relations in our society in terms of men as active or dynamic and women as passive or receptive. Whereas this one-dimensional perspective is limited, often wrong, it does have some legitimacy on the physical plane. A man's body, for example, is typically more muscular and better able to sustain forceful exertion. Many sacred traditions, however, claim that the polarities reverse when we move from the outer to the inner plane. "If a man is often a woman's teacher, protector, and guide in the visionary, intellectual, and worldly spheres, a woman often leads and inspires a man by teaching him to come into his body, rouse his vitality, listen to his heart-consciousness, dance with life's energies."[19] Many spiritual traditions, although not in the West, see the woman in this way. The Hindu's dark goddess-mother Kali dances with a necklace of skulls, symbolizing the great ocean of blood at the beginning and end of life. The Tibetan Buddhist wild woman is the wrathful/playful "dakini" or "sky-dancer," often depicted drinking blood or dripping menstrual blood on a mirror.[20] And the Indian Tantric tradition has for a thousand years considered women to be the supreme fire of transformation.[21]

Welwood echoes many other psychologists in describing men's psychological development in three stages. In the first, men are tied psychically to their mothers; in the second, or heroic stage, they escape the mother and find their own individuality; and, in the third, they become receptive at a new level to what women can teach them.[22] These stages are similar to what Joseph Campbell describes in the heroic monomyth, in which the hero first separates from the tribe to which he has been attached as a child, is initiated into personhood on a road of trials, and then joins with the goddess of the world in a sacred marriage.[23] But a problem in our contemporary male-dominated society is that men often get stuck in one of the first two stages, either tied to the maternal, or else reacting to their fear of engulfment by the feminine by adopting a hardened, macho stance. If a man is stuck in the first phase, he will remain a child; if in the second, an adolescent.[24]

It is certainly not my purpose to type individual men within the universities at any one of these stages. In fact, I believe many academic men are far more advanced than the institutions they serve. As men have told me repeatedly while I was writing this book, they feel many of the same things that women feel—oppressed by "publish or perish" ("publish *and* perish," it is often called) and by the lack of time to be creative. They too are tired of the relentless demands to be ruthlessly "up," never "down," and are often sad at the toll academic life takes on their bodies and their emotions.

Yet I believe that academia, considered as an institution—as one of the "men" to which many women are married—is stuck, in large part, in the second stage of the hero's journey. Moreover, I believe it is reactive in the sense that Welwood depicts—that is, afraid of feminine engulfment— as we have seen in the way Siren and mother symbols are treated, and in the many ways in which things associated with the feminine are trivialized, dismissed, ridiculed, dominated, banished, veiled, and buried. "Our modern heroes," Welwood observes, "are those who endlessly ascend—to the top of the Hit Parade or bestseller charts, to the top floors of skyscrapers where the corporate headquarters reside, into the heavens in rocket ships, or into the disembodied mental realm via computers or virtual reality."[25] Notice how similar Welwood's portrait is to the academic who amasses an intimidating *curriculum vita* or million-dollar corporate grant, whose intellectual constructions attain the detached aura of flight, or whose brilliant calculations enable the whole world to disembody itself toward a *Matrix*-approaching computerized reality?

"The heroism of stage three, by contrast," Welwood says, "involves facing and overcoming some of our deepest fears—about coming down to earth, coming into our body, relating with our feelings, and committing ourselves to a path of passionate engagement with the world."[26] I believe that women who take the time to pour their experiences within the university into the "crystal chalice" of their own stories have a crucial role to play in leading the patriarchal institution to confront these fears that have been assigned a feminine face. As Robert Johnson says of the "Eros and Psyche" myth, "Joy is a gift from the heart of woman."[27]

A BEGINNING

I wrote earlier of Linda Leonard's "man with heart," her inner *animus* who loves and guides her within her dreams—a hard-won gift as a result of her labors to extricate herself from the grip of a bevy of

Critical Fathers.[28] Others have told me, too, of their helpful and beloved man inside. Elizabeth, for example, may have left behind her romantic "Abelard" partner Michael, but she now has a "gray man" who loves and helps her in her dreams. So far, mine has not shown up. I am beginning to wonder if he will. This may have something to do with the insomnia that still haunts me, despite my best efforts to banish it with calmer days and a less frantic pursuit of academic perfection. Perhaps he needs more sleep time to make his entrance. I have, however, been visited with some divine gifts as a result of my psyche's labors.

As a critic of popular culture for several decades now, I have had visitors from movies, television, and music in my dreams. It has been a continuing mystery for me that the women I met for this book have also had their nighttime appearances, as my story blends with theirs to form a rich tapestry in my mind. Here is one I call "Sophia's Wedding Veil":

> I am at a convention. Too many of the important events are scheduled at once. I am hiding out in my room because I have met a man who seems to be interested in me, but I am not interested in him.
>
> There is a panel on women or feminism that I am supposed to attend, although I don't really want to. When I get there, I see that Sophia is performing. She is all dressed up, in her wedding dress. She is dancing and singing with great gusto as a wind machine blows against her so that her hair billows wildly, straight up through a hoop that holds her veil. It is a schlocky romantic song, and although she sings it with great enthusiasm, I get the impression it is camp, and for the purpose of being deconstructed by the feminists.

Sophia was one of my main teachers about the Veiled Woman. Painfully aware that she wore the veil of patriarchy, she wanted desperately to shed it, to be her unorthodox playful and creative self. Here she appears in the garb of the Maiden with the veil of matrimony, hardly a liberating symbol in our culture that still asymmetrically pronounces many couples "man and wife." But there is no actual wedding here; she is more like a Wild Woman—gleefully dismantling the veil of patriarchy with cosmic humor. And I am much more interested in her performance than I am in the academic scene, with its typically overstuffed program and a man I don't need.

Lately, I have been laughing more at the foibles of academic structure than I did when I was younger. Like Sophia's campy song and the hunt for Joan Rivers' nocturnal appearance, irreverence is an effective tool for deconstructing institutional pomposity. I really like it better than the deconstructive theories bequeathed us from literary criticism (although these have their uses). I think the Goddess enjoys this full-blooded laughter more than she does the dangerously dry Derridean analytical knife.

Even in the midst of an overcrowded schedule at school recently, this dream occurred to me:

> I go into my office at school, and find that it is overgrown with large trees and plants. It is a lush, forested green jungle. There is hardly anywhere for me to sit or work.

I think I have mentioned how sterile our building is; it is an architectural aberration from the seventies, a descendant of the modernist "box" without the stark aestheticism of that era, as if it inherited only its bleak genes and not its soaring loftiness or chrome-plated kitsch. But here it is, sprouting greenery I didn't place there. Or, maybe I did, in a moment unguarded by academic propriety—as when I added the misguided throw pillows to plump up a bare-bones skeleton with feminine padding. I don't mind it that I can't find a place to work; in fact, I am entranced with all these trees. It feels magical.

As if to complete my floral dream landscape with fauna, this dream occurred to me two days after "finishing" this book:

> I am in some kind of showroom where a crowd of people is looking at a beautiful painting. It has incorporated various animals, including a donkey and a buffalo and dogs, into a semi-abstract collage design with a rich gold background. It is all perfectly balanced and beautiful, like a tapestry, and it glows. Everyone is admiring it. Then I realize I painted it. I am surprised, because I don't even know how to draw, much less paint! But I have to admit it is gorgeous.
>
> One man and his wife want to buy it. I have no idea what to charge. I think maybe it's worth $1,000, but Tom says at least $1,800. I think this man would pay just about anything for it. The dream ends without my knowing what the price is.

Although there are two old themes here—I am unconscious about my own work and I tend to undervalue it—I eventually acknowledge that I can do more than I thought. This dream seems to incorporate my entire "divine menagerie" into a design that makes sense, that tells a story. In fact, it "glows"!

~

Maybe Helen Luke is right—a dry spell is the precursor to a lushness that is overdue. Not too long ago, I dreamed this:

> I enter a big building—it's either a convention hotel or a college building. I am walking toward a large banquet hall to hear a speech some important person is giving. There is a crowd in the lobby. Ahead of me, I see my high school boyfriend, then another man I have dated, and then an important scholar in my field. I don't have my makeup on, so I don't want to see any of them. I stop, turn a corner, and put on some lipstick.

This one begins, like so many of my dreams, in a large indeterminate building. The only thing definite is that it is academic. I am not at all lost here, as in my earlier "Lost in the Halls of Science" dream; I know right where I'm going. But I get deterred by three men who have been romantically and intellectually important to me. I feel I am not good enough as is, and must touch up my face.

> When I get to the banquet room, it is full of several hundred people eating, talking, and milling around, even though the speaker has already begun. I find Tom and some friends to sit with. The speaker is some important person in the field; I listen to him for awhile, but he's bombastic and isn't saying anything. He reminds me of an arrogant chairperson I once worked for. So I leave.

But this time I know an egotistical puff-bag when I see him. I am not a starry-eyed maiden any more, and I have no trouble exiting this place.

> I run outside, then glide above the ground, then fly way up high, barely brushing the treetops. It feels fantastic; I feel that I can fly anywhere. I become aware that a little blonde girl (she feels as if she is mine) is running along the ground underneath me. There seems to be

> some danger following us. I swoop down and pick her up. It is harder to fly while carrying her because I can't move my arms, but I manage to stay aloft by moving my legs. I tell her that I can manage it, assuring her that I won't leave her behind. I am determined to take her with me, and I feel very strong, confident, and free.

Unlike the situation in the "Divine Child in the Barrel," I leave my *animus* figures—romantic and academic—behind at the end. I'm even going to do this thing without my beloved Tom. I soar above the empty academic ritual—fittingly, for my profession, it's *rhetorical!*—in a crescendo of freedom. Now the endangered child beneath me is not only clearly human but she's also a *girl*. She looks like the quiet little one who used to read inside my chest of drawers. I do not intend to drop her into the sea, as the Great Ram with the golden fleece did. There is simply no question, as there was with the child in the barrel, of my leaving her behind.

~

In my family, all the girls' names begin with a "J." My mother is Jean, my sister is Joyce, and I am Janice. My mother and father thought these J-names sounded strong. The one in my arms now will fit right in. I don't know exactly where I will go next, but I am definitely taking her with me. I think I will name her Joy.

NOTES

PART ONE THE MAN-MADE MAIDEN

Chapter One—Alma Mater

The epigraph to this chapter is drawn from *The Oxford English Dictionary*, 61.

1. de Beauvoir, *The Second Sex*, 146.
2. Markale, *Women of the Celts*, 57.
3. hooks, *Teaching to Transgress*; Ellis, *Final Negotiations*; Tompkins, *A Life in School;* Bochner, "It's About Time."
4. Lamott, *Bird by Bird*, 181.
5. Bochner, "It's About Time."
6. Bochner and Ellis, *Ethnographically Speaking*; Ellis and Bochner, *Composing Ethnography*; Goodall, *Writing the New Ethnography*.
7. Goodall, *Writing the New Ethnography*, 9.
8. Ibid., 13.
9. Ellis, "What Counts as Scholarship."
10. Goodall, *Writing the New Ethnography*, 12.
11. Ellis, "What Counts as Scholarship."
12. Lopez, *Crow and Weasel*, 48.
13. Estes, *Women Who Run with the Wolves*.
14. Powers, *The Heroine in Western Literature;* Brown, *The Da Vinci Code*.
15. Daly, *Gyn/Ecology*.
16. Markale, *Women of the Celts*; Weinbaum, *Islands of Women and Amazons*, 130–31.
17. Eisler, *The Chalice and the Blade*, 59–77.

18. Fletcher, *Disappearing Acts*; Jordan et al., *Writings from the Stone Center*; Tannen, *You Just Don't Understand*.
19. Fletcher, *Disappearing Acts*, 3.
20. Eisler, *The Chalice and the Blade*; Lerner, *The Creation of Patriarchy*; Powers, *The Heroine in Western Literature*.
21. Cited in Hiles and Hiles, *The Daybook*, 1999, 12.
22. Ibid., 2000, 2.
23. Campbell, *Myths to Live By*, 11.

Chapter Two—Maiden Lover

The epigraph for this chapter is spoken in the opening voiceover by the main character in the film *Guinevere*.

1. This rendering of the myth is based on Hamilton, *Mythology*, 112–15.
2. Graves, *The Greek Myths,* 498, 657–58; Harding, *Womens' Mysteries,* 127–43; Walker, *The Woman's Encyclopedia of Myths and Secrets,* 332–33.
3. Campbell, *Oriental Mythology*, 4–6, *Primitive Mythology*, 151–69; Lerner, *The Creation of Patriarchy*, 125, 141–60; Powers, *The Heroine in Western Literature*, 51–52.
4. Gimbutas, *Goddesses and Gods*; Harding, *Women's Mysteries*, 144–54; Lerner, *The Creation of Patriarchy*, 125–31; Qualls-Corbett, *The Sacred Prostitute*, 39–40.
5. Graves, *The Greek Myths*, 211.
6. Ibid.; Walker, *The Woman's Encyclopedia*, 332–33.
7. Graves, *The Greek Myths*, 211–12.
8. Lerner, *The Creation of Patriarchy*, 145.
9. Bolen, *Goddesses in Everywoman*, 241.
10. hooks, "In Praise of Student/Teacher Romances," 37.
11. Young–Eisendrath, *You're Not What I Expected*, 88.
12. Ulanov, *The Feminine in Jungian Psychology*, 159, cited in Qualls-Corbett, *The Sacred Prostitute*.
13. Tannen, *You're Not What I Expected*, 95.
14. Ibid., 96.
15. hooks, "In Praise of Student/Teacher Romances," 38.
16. Qualls-Corbett, *The Sacred Prostitute*, 39.
17. Tannen, *You're Not What I Expected*, 89.

Chapter Three—Muse

The epigraph for this chapter is taken from Douglas, *Translate This Darkness*, 151.

1. Young-Eisendrath, *You're Not What I Expected*, 96–97.
2. Hamilton, *Mythology*, 38.
3. Young-Eisendrath, *You're Not What I Expected*, 96–97.
4. Walker, *The Woman's Encyclopedia*, 701.
5. Graves, *The Greek Myths*, 55.
6. Lindemans, *Encyclopedia Mythica*.
7. Walker, *The Woman's Encyclopedia*, 956.
8. Douglas, *Translate This Darkness*, 12, 279.
9. Ibid., 15.
10. Ibid., 15–16.
11. Ibid., 20–21.
12. Ibid., 12–13.
13. Ibid., 15.
14. Ibid., 12.
15. Ibid., 299.
16. Ibid., 132–51.
17. Ibid., 125–31.
18. Ibid., 131–32; 302–18.
19. Ibid., 151.
20. Ibid., 152.
21. Ibid.
22. Ibid.
23. Ibid., 304–06.
24. Hynes, *The Lecturer's Tale*, 230–31.
25. Douglas, *Translate This Darkness*, 133.

Chapter Four—Mistress

The epigraph for this chapter is from *Hamlet, Prince of Denmark,* lines 129–30.

1. Lerner, *The Creation of Patriarchy*, 131.
2. Ibid., 131–33.
3. Young-Eisendrath, *You're Not What I Expected*, 87–88.
4. Douglas, *Translate This Darkness*, 305–06.
5. Ibid., 264–65.
6. Ibid., 312–13.
7. Ibid., 314.

Chapter Five—Brainchild

The epigraph for this chapter is from Aeschylus, *Oresteia*, 161.

1. Bolen, *Goddesses in Older Women*, 6–8; Walker, *The Woman's Encyclopedia*, 74.
2. Hamilton, *Mythology*, 30.
3. Bolen, *Goddesses in Everywoman*, 75–76.
4. Ibid.; Graves, *The Greek Myths*, 96–97.
5. Bolen, *Goddesses in Everywoman*, 35.
6. Ibid., 78; see also Harding, *Women's Mysteries*.
7. Graves, *The Greek Myths*, 96.
8. Bolen, *Goddesses in Everywoman*, 39.
9. Bolen, *Goddesses in Older Women*, 11–13.
10. Bolen, *Goddesses in Everywoman*, 81–92.
11. Murdock, *The Heroine's Journey*, 30–35.
12. Ibid., 12.
13. Lamott, *Bird by Bird*, 116–17.
14. DeMent, "The Way I Should."
15. Kornfield, *A Path with Heart*, 14.
16. Young-Eisendrath, *You're Not What I Expected*, 92–93.
17. Ellis, *Final Negotiations*, 18–19.
18. Ibid., 19.
19. Ibid.
20. Ibid., 333.
21. von Franz, *Interpretation of Fairy Tales*, 33–82.
22. On April 11, 2002, the University of Arkansas received $300,000,000 from the philanthropic arm of the Wal–Mart dynasty, the Walton Family Charitable Support Foundation, to further the economic development of the state of Arkansas.
23. Shelley, *Frankenstein*; Rushing and Frentz, *Projecting the Shadow*, 71–72.
24. Estes, *Women Who Run with the Wolves*, 387–455.
25. Ibid., 395; see also Leonard, *The Wounded Woman*, 25–36.
26. Estes, *Women Who Run with the Wolves*, 395.
27. Ibid., 403.
28. Ibid., 419.
29. Ibid., 427.
30. Leonard, *The Wounded Woman*, 113–14.
31. Murdock, *The Heroine's Journey*, 156.
32. Leonard, *The Wounded Woman*, 87.
33. Rushing, "*Alien and Aliens.*"
34. Ibid.
35. Murdock, *The Heroine's Journey*, 17–18.
36. Woodman, *Addiction to Perfection*, 19.

37. Bolen, *Goddesses in Everywoman*, 35.
38. LaMott, *Bird by Bird*, 28–29.
39. Graves, *The Greek Myths*, 98.
40. Bordo, "Reading the Slender Body."
41. Caputi, "*Jaws* as Patriarchal Myth"; Rushing and Frentz, *Projecting the Shadow*, 85–86.
42. Bordo, "Reading the Slender Body."
43. Woodward, *Identity and Difference*, 140–41.
44. Woodman, *Addiction to Perfection*, 23.
45. Ibid., 9–10, 23.
46. Walker, *The Woman's Encyclopedia*, 65.
47. Woodman, *Addiction to Perfection*, 32.

PART TWO FATAL ATTRACTIONS

Chapter Six—Sirens

The epigraph for this chapter is taken from James Hynes, *The Lecturer's Tale*, 165.

1. Walker, *The Woman's Encyclopedia*, 940; Graves, *The Greek Myths*, 716–27.
2. Walker, *The Woman's Encyclopedia*, 162.
3. Graves, *The Greek Myths*, 721.
4. Markale, *Women of the Celts*, 49, 53.
5. Ibid., 100.
6. Deida, *Intimate Communion*, 150.
7. Walker, *The Woman's Encyclopedia*, 168.
8. Graves, *The Greek Myths*, 723.
9. Weinbaum, *Islands of Women*, 142.
10. Markale, *Women of the Celts*, 43–44, 51.
11. de Beauvoir, *The Second Sex*, 166; quoted in Markale, *Women of the Celts*, 50.
12. Markale, *Women of the Celts*, 48, 99.
13. Walker, *The Woman's Encyclopedia*, 168.
14. Hynes, *The Lecturer's Tale*, 164–66.
15. Young-Eisendrath, *Gender and Desire*, 76.
16. Young-Eisendrath, *Gender and Desire*.
17. Graves, *The Greek Myths*, 148.
18. Walker, *The Woman's Encyclopedia*, 768–69.
19. Graves, *The Greek Myths*, 723.

Chapter Seven—Veiled Woman

The epigraph for this chapter is cited in Lerner, *The Creation of Patriarchy*, 134.

1. Lerner, *The Creation of Patriarchy*, 128–30; 134.
2. Ibid., 134–36.
3. *BBC News* Home page, June 27, 2001.
4. Havelock, *Preface to Plato*, 197–214.
5. Plato, *Gorgias*; *Phaedrus*.
6. Aristotle, *Aristotle's Rhetoric and Poetics*.
7. Sutton, "The Taming of *Polos/Polis*."
8. *Publication Manual of the American Psychological Association*, 61.
9. Rushing, "*E.T.* as Rhetorical Transcendence."
10. Lerner, *The Creation of Patriarchy*, 139.
11. Estes, *Women Who Run with the Wolves*, 392–93.
12. Ibid., 437.
13. Ibid., 440.
14. Sutton, "Women in the House of Speech," 5–6.
15. Ibid., 14–15.
16. Ibid., 15.
17. Estes, *Women Who Run with the Wolves*, 441, 443.
18. Ibid., 441.
19. Leonard, *On the Way to the Wedding*, 217.
20. Estes, *Women Who Run with the Wolves*, 442–43.
21. Lewis, *Till We Have Faces*.
22. Estes, *Women Who Run with the Wolves*, 442.
23. Ibid.
24. Sutton, "Women in the House of Speech," 11.

Chapter Eight—Amazon

The epigraph for this chapter is taken from "Xena Quotes."

1. Salmonson, *The Encyclopedia of Amazons*, xi.
2. Weinbaum, *Islands of Women*, 21; Salmonson, *The Encyclopedia of Amazons*, 20.
3. Engle, "The Amazons in ancient Greece," 512–44; cited in Weinbaum, *Islands of Women*, 30.
4. Weinbaum, *Islands of Women*, 125–27.
5. Ibid., 67; see also Pratt, *Archetypal Patterns*.

6. Kleinbaum, *The War Against the Amazons*, 223–24.
7. Leonard, *The Wounded Woman*, 60.
8. Salmonson, *The Encyclopedia of Amazons*, xi.
9. Weinbaum, *Islands of Women*, 63.
10. Kleinbaum, *The War Against the Amazons*, 1.
11. Weinbaum, *Islands of Women*, 81.
12. Ibid., xix, 77–79, 147; Weinbaum is relying partly on the work of Anderson, *Religious Cults*.
13. Weinbaum, *Islands of Women*, 67–127; see also Harding, *The Way of All Women*.
14. Harding, *Women's Mysteries*, 103, 105, 125.
15. Powers, *The Heroine in Western Literature*, 38.
16. Kleinbaum, *The War Against the Amazons*, 1.
17. Weinbaum, *Islands of Women*, 127.
18. duBois, *Centaurs and Amazons*, 35.
19. Salmonson, *The Encyclopedia of Amazons*, 9.
20. duBois, *Centaurs and Amazons*, 33; Salmonson, *The Encyclopedia of Amazons*, 118; Hamilton, *Mythology*, 172.
21. Kleinbaum, *The War Against the Amazons*, 24–25; Salmonson, *The Encyclopedia of Amazons*, 210–12.
22. Weinbaum, *Islands of Women*, 125, 127.
23. Ibid., 19.
24. Ibid., 128–51.
25. Ibid., 68.
26. Powers, *The Heroine in Western Literature*, 39.
27. Doyle, *The Male Experience*, 150.
28. Pratt, *Archetypal Patterns*, 288–89.
29. Salmonson, *The Encyclopedia of Amazons*, 20.
30. Powers, *The Heroine in Western Literature*, 24.
31. Ibid., 26–28; Weinbaum, *Islands of Women*, 72.
32. Powers, *The Heroine in Western Literature*, 24.
33. Ibid., 28.
34. Ibid., 56; Markale, *Women of the Celts*, 15.
35. Hamilton, *Mythology*, 30.
36. Nussbaum, *The Fragility of Goodness*, 118.
37. For a fuller explication of this position, see Rushing, "Putting Away Childish Things."
38. Nussbaum, *The Fragility of Goodness*, 216.
39. Vogt, *Return to Father*, 103.
40. Markale, *Women of the Celts*, 64, 74.

41. Kolodny, *The Lay of the Land.*
42. Slotkin, *The Regeneration of Violence*; Rushing and Frentz, *Projecting the Shadow.*
43. Campbell, *The Hero with a Thousand Faces*, 109–120.
44. Woolger and Woolger, *The Goddess Within*, 34–39.
45. MacKinnon, "Desire and Power," 105.
46. Mulvey, *Visual and Other Pleasures*, 14.
47. Ibid., 16.

PART THREE ONE-IN-HERSELF

1. Harding, *Women's Mysteries,* 103.

Chapter Nine—Psyche's Marriage

The epigraph for this chapter comes from Lucius Apuleius, 1910, *Amor and Psyche,* 25.

1. Fletcher, *Disappearing Acts*, 9.
2. Powers, *The Heroine in Western Literature*, 4.
3. Ibid., 130.
4. Ibid., 11.
5. Neumann, *Amor and Psyche*, 157.
6. Murdock, *The Heroine's Journey*.
7. Neumann, *Amor and Psyche*, 156–61.
8. The abstract of the myth in this chapter as well as the next is condensed from versions by Apuleius (1910), which is reproduced in full in Neumann, *Amor and Psyche*, 3–53, and from Robert Johnson, *She*. Following both Neumann and Johnson, I use "Aphrodite" rather than "Venus," and "Eros" rather than "Amor" or "Cupid," which has become sentimentalized as a cherubic boy through Valentine's Day traditions and contemporary popular songs.
9. Powers, *The Heroine in Western Literature*, 77–78.
10. Walker, *The Woman's Encyclopedia*, 44.
11. Neumann, *Amor and Psyche*, 58–59.
12. Ibid., 59–60.
13. Johnson, *She*, 10.
14. Neumann, *Amor and Psyche*, 90; Johnson, *She,* 6.
15. Neumann, *Amor and Psyche*, 61–62.
16. Johnson, *She*, 23.
17. Apuleius, *Amor and Psyche*, 8.
18. Neumann, *Amor and Psyche*, 127.

19. Ibid., 143.
20. Walker, *The Woman's Encyclopedia*, 826.
21. Keirsey and Bates, *Please Understand Me*, 47–57.
22. Kerényi, *Prometheus*, 46.
23. See Frentz, "Stayin' Alive."
24. Kerényi, *Prometheus*, 47.
25. Ibid., 46.
26. Apuleius, *Amor and Psyche*, 9.
27. Walker, *The Woman's Encyclopedia*, 826; Neumann, *Amor and Psyche*, 158.
28. Apuleius, *Amor and Psyche*, 13.
29. Neumann, *Amor and Psyche*, 70–71.
30. Estes, *Women Who Run with the Wolves*, 39–73.
31. Brown, *The Da Vinci Code*, 125.
32. Rushing and Frentz, "The Gods Must Be Crazy."
33. Harris, *Jubilee Time*, 35; Kerényi, *Dionysos*, 206–33; Walker, *The Woman's Encyclopedia*; Rushing and Frentz, "The Gods Must Be Crazy," 241–42.
34. Apuleius, *Amor and Psyche*, 10.
35. Powers, *The Heroine in Western Literature*, 83.
36. Ibid., 104.
37. For the last metaphor, see Blair, Baxter, and Brown, "Disciplining the Feminine."
38. Neumann, *Amor and Psyche*, 72–74, 128; Johnson, *She*, 22; Downing, *Psyche's Sisters*, 41–52.
39. Apuleius, *Amor and Psyche*, 24.
40. Neumann, *Amor and Psyche*, 72.
41. Apuleius, *Amor and Psyche*, 25.
42. Neumann, *Amor and Psyche*, 77–78.
43. Ibid., 79–80.
44. Johnson, *She*, 42.
45. Neumann, *Amor and Psyche*, 82.
46. Apuleius, *Amor and Psyche*, 26.
47. Johnson, *She*, 42.
48. Neumann, *Amor and Psyche*, 80.
49. Campbell, *The Hero with a Thousand Faces*, 90–95.
50. Neumann, *Amor and Psyche*, 74–75.
51. Ibid., 84; Johnson, *She*, 30.
52. Neumann, *Amor and Psyche*, 107.
53. Apuleius, *Amor and Psyche*, 28.
54. Ibid., 5.

55. Johnson, *She*, 18; von Franz, *Puer Aeternus*.
56. Apuleius, *Amor and Psyche*, 5.
57. Neumann, *Amor and Psyche*, 84; Hillman, *The Puer Papers*, 102; Bly, *Iron John*, 207–17.
58. Neumann, *Amor and Psyche*, 84–85; Johnson, *She*, 41.
59. Apuleius, *Amor and Psyche*, 28.

Chapter Ten—Psyche's Labors

The epigraph for this chapter is taken from Jane Tompkins, *A Life in School*, xviii.

1. Apuleius, *Amor and Psyche*, 29.
2. Estes, *Women Who Run with the Wolves*, 404.
3. Ibid.
4. Ibid., 402.
5. Pirsig, *Zen and the Art of Motorcycle Maintenance*, i.
6. Neumann, *Amor and Psyche*, 76, 108–10; Johnson, *She*, 74.
7. Neumann, *Amor and Psyche*, 107.
8. Johnson, *She*, 68.
9. Ibid., 49.
10. Neumann, *Amor and Psyche*, 95.
11. Apuleius, *Amor and Psyche*, 42.
12. Neumann, *Amor and Psyche*, 95–96.
13. Lamott, *Traveling Mercies*, 235.
14. Johnson, *She*, 55.
15. Neumann, *Amor and Psyche*, 98.
16. Apuleius, *Amor and Psyche*, 43.
17. Ibid.
18. Neumann, *Amor and Psyche*, 99; Johnson, *She*, 55.
19. Pratt, "Demeter," 153.
20. Johnson, *She*, 54–55.
21. Apuleius, *Amor and Psyche*, 44.
22. Neumann, *Amor and Psyche*, 191.
23. Ibid., 100.
24. Ibid., 99–102.
25. Johnson, *She*, 56.
26. Apuleius, *Amor and Psyche*, 45.
27. Neumann, *Amor and Psyche*, 102–03; Johnson, *She*, 61.
28. Neumann, *Amor and Psyche*, 108.
29. Johnson, *She*, 61–62.
30. Payne, "The Wizard of Oz," 30.

31. For a discussion of the *persona*, see Storr, *The Essential Jung*, 94–101.
32. Tompkins, *A Life in School*, 130.
33. Johnson, *She*, 62.
34. Ibid., 63.
35. DeMent, "The Way I Should."
36. Neumann, *Amor and Psyche,* 112–16.
37. Ibid., 111.
38. Johnson, *She*, 65.
39. Neumann, *Amor and Psyche*, 112.
40. Ibid.
41. Apuleius, *Amor and Psyche*, 48.
42. Neumann, *Amor and Psyche*, 113.
43. Johnson, *She*, 67.
44. See, for example, Briffault, *The Mothers*, 151ff; Powers, *The Heroine in Western Literature*, 12–22.
45. Eisler, *The Chalice and the Blade*.
46. Lévy–Bruhl, *Primitive Mentality*, cited in Neumann, *Amor and Psyche*, 114.
47. Downing, "Persephone in Hades," 227.
48. See Arvigo, *Sastun*.
49. Perera, *Descent to the Goddess*.
50. Oliver, *American Primitive*, 82–83.
51. Johnson, *She*, 71.
52. Neumann, *Amor and Psyche*, 118, 119.
53. Ibid., 119–25.
54. Johnson, *She*, 73.
55. Ibid., 74.
56. Neumann, *Amor and Psyche*, 124, 128–29; see also Rushing, "*Alien* and *Aliens*."
57. Tompkins, *A Life in School*, xi.
58. Ibid.
59. Ibid., xii.
60. Ibid.
61. Ibid., xvi.
62. Ibid., 74.
63. Ibid.
64. Ibid., xviii.
65. Ibid., 132.
66. Ibid., xviii.
67. Ibid., 122.
68. Ibid., 130–31.

69. Ibid., 220.
70. Ibid., 124.
71. Ibid., 218.

Chapter Eleven—Divine Child

1. Apuleius, *Amor and Psyche*, 53.
2. Neumann, *Amor and Psyche*, 140; Jung, *Secret*; "Psychology of the Child Archetype"; *Psychology and Alchemy*; Johnson, *She*, 75.
3. Campbell, *The Hero with a Thousand Faces,* 126–49; Neumann, *Origins*, 265ff; *Amor and Psyche*, 148.
4. Neumann, *Amor and Psyche*, 139, 149–50.
5. Oliver, *Dream Work*, 14.
6. Spence, *Ancient Egyptian Myths*, 294.
7. Powers, *The Heroine in Western Literature*, 51.
8. Rushing, "*E.T.* as Rhetorical Transcendence."
9. Jung, "Psychology of the Child Archetype," 87.
10. Ibid., 85.
11. Tompkins, *A Life in School*, 227–28.
12. Ibid., 226–27.
13. Picknett and Prince, *The Templar Revelation*, 257.
14. Ibid.
15. Markale, *Women of the Celts*, 173, 174.
16. Welwood, *Journey of the Heart*, 153.
17. Luke, "Mother and Daughter Mysteries," 194.
18. Olney, Lanois, and Harris, "Deeper Well."
19. Welwood, *Love and Awakening*, 186–87.
20. Welwood, *Journey of the Heart*, 153.
21. Welwood, *Love and Awakening*, 189.
22. Ibid., 182–83.
23. Campbell, *Hero with a Thousand Faces.*
24. Welwood, *Love and Awakening*, 182–83.
25. Ibid., 183.
26. Ibid.
27. Johnson, *She*, 75.
28. Leonard, *The Wounded Woman.*

BIBLIOGRAPHY

Anderson, Florence Bennett. *Religious Cults Associated with the Amazons*. New York: AMS Press, 1967. Originally published in 1912.

Apuleius, Lucius. "Amor and Psyche." In *The Metamorphoses* or *Golden Ass of Lucius Apuleius*, 1910. Translated by H. E. Butler. In *Amor and Psyche: The Psychic Development of the Feminine: A Commentary on the Tale by Apuleius*, by Erich Neumann. Translated by Ralph Manheim (3–53). Princeton University Press: Bollingen. Series 54, 1971. First published in 1956 by Bollingen Foundation.

Aristotle's Rhetoric and Poetics. Translated by W. Rhys Roberts (*Rhetoric*) and Ingram Bywater (*Poetics*). New York: The Modern Library, 1954.

Arvigo, Rosita. *Sastun: My Apprenticeship with a Maya Healer.* New York: Harper San Francisco, 1994.

Aeschylus, *Oresteia*. Translated by Richard Alexander Lattimore. Chicago: University of Chicago Press, 1953.

BBC News Home page, June 27, 2001. http://news.bbc.co.uk.

Blair, Carole, Leslie A. Baxter, and Julie R. Brown. "Disciplining the Feminine." *Quarterly Journal of Speech* 80 (1994): 383–409.

Bly, Robert. *Iron John: A Book About Men*. Reading, MA: Addison–Wesley, 1990.

Bochner, Arthur P. "It's About Time: Narrative and the Divided Self." *Qualitative Inquiry* 3 (1997): 418–38.

Bochner, Arthur P., and Carolyn Ellis, eds. *Ethnographically Speaking: Autoethnography, Literature, and Aesthetics.* Walnut Creek, CA: AltaMira Press, 2002.

Bolen, Jean Shinoda. *Goddesses in Everywoman: A New Psychology of Women.* New York: Harper Colophon, 1985.

______. *Goddesses in Older Women: Archetypes in Women over Fifty.* New York: HarperCollins, 2001.

Bordo, Susan. "Reading the Slender Body." In *Identity and Difference*, edited by Kathryn Woodward, 167–81. London: Sage, 1997.

Briffault, Robert. *The Mothers: A Study of the Origins of Sentiments and Institutions.* 3 vols. New York: Macmillan, 1927.

Brown, Dan. *The Da Vinci Code.* New York: Doubleday, 2003.

Burke, Kenneth. *The Philosophy of Literary Form: Studies in Symbolic Action*, 3rd ed. Berkeley and Los Angeles: University of California Press, 1973. First published in 1941 by Louisiana State University Press.

Campbell, Joseph. *The Hero with a Thousand Faces.* Bollingen Series 17. Princeton: Princeton University Press, 1968. First published in 1949 by Bollingen Foundation.

______. *The Masks of God: Oriental Mythology.* New York: Penguin Books, 1976. First published in 1962 by Viking Press.

______. *The Masks of God: Primitive Mythology.* New York: Penguin Books, 1976. First published in 1959 by Viking Press.

______. *Myths to Live By.* New York: Bantam Books, 1972.

Caputi, Jane. "*Jaws* as Patriarchal Myth." *Journal of Popular Film* 6 (1978): 305–26.

Daly, Mary. *Gyn/Ecology: The Metaethics of Radical Feminism.* Boston: Beacon Press, 1990.

Deida, David. *Intimate Communion: Awakening Your Sexual Essence.* Deerfield Beach, FL: Health Communications, Inc., 1995.

DeMent, Iris. "The Way I Should." From *The Way I Should.* Warner Bros. Records, 1996, compact disc.

Douglas, Claire. *Translate This Darkness: The Life of Christiana Morgan, the Veiled Woman in Jung's Circle.* Princeton: Princeton University Press, 1993.

Downing, Christine, ed. *The Long Journey Home: Re–visioning the Myth of Demeter and Persephone for Our Time*. Shambhala: Boston, 1994.

______. "Persephone in Hades." In *The Long Journey Home: Re–visioning the Myth of Demeter and Persephone for Our Time*, edited by Christine Downing, 149–54. Princeton: Princeton University Press, 1993.

______. *Psyche's Sisters: Re–Imagining the Meaning of Sisterhood*. San Francisco: Harper & Row, 1988.

Doyle, John Andrew. *The Male Experience*, 3rd ed. Dubuque, IA: William C. Brown, 1997.

duBois, Page. *Centaurs and Amazons: Women and the Pre–History of the Great Chain of Being*. Ann Arbor: University of Michigan Press, 1982.

Eisler, Riane. *The Chalice and the Blade: Our History, Our Future*. San Francisco: Harper & Row/Perennial, 1987.

Ellis, Carolyn. *Final Negotiations: A Story of Love, Loss and Chronic Illness*. Philadelphia: Temple University Press, 1995.

Ellis, Carolyn. "What Counts as Scholarship in Communication? An Autoethnographic Response." *American Communication Journal* 1 (2001): http://acjournal.org/holdings/vol 1/iss2/special/elis.html.

Ellis, Carolyn, and Arthur P. Bochner, eds. *Composing Ethnography: Alternative Forms of Qualitative Writing*. Walnut Creek, CA: AltaMira Press, 1996.

Engle, Bernice Shultz. "The Amazons in Ancient Greece." *Psychoanalytic Quarterly* 11, (1942): 512–44.

Estés, Clarissa Pinkola. *Myths and Stories of the Wild Woman Archetype*. New York: Ballantine Books, 1992.

Fletcher, Joyce K. *Disappearing Acts: Gender, Power, and Relational Practice at Work*. Cambridge: MIT Press, 1999.

Frazer, James. *The Golden Bough: A Study in Magic and Religion*. Vol. I, Abridged Edition. New York: Touchstone, 1996. First published in 1922 by Macmillan.

Frentz, Thomas S. "Stayin' Alive: Surviving Cancer and the Academy." Unpublished Manuscript. Fayetteville, AR: University of Arkansas, 2005.

Gimbutas, Marija Alseikaite. *Goddesses and Gods of Old Europe.* Berkeley: University of California Press, 1982.

Goodall, H. L. Jr. *Writing the New Ethnography*. Walnut Creek, CA: AltaMira Press, 2000.

Graves, Robert. *The Greek Myths*. Complete Edition. New York: Penguin Books, 1992. First published in 1955 by Pelican Books.

Guinevere. Film directed by Audrey Wells, Miramax, 1999.

Hamilton, Edith. *Mythology: Timeless Tales of Gods and Heroes*. New York: Warner Books, 1999. First published in 1942 by Edith Hamilton.

Harding, M. Esther. *The Way of All Women: A Psychological Interpretation*. London: Longman, 1934.

______. *Woman's Mysteries: Ancient and Modern*. New York: Harper, Colophon Books, 1976. First published 1971 by C. G. Jung Foundation for Analytical Psychology.

Harris, Maria. *Jubilee Time: Celebrating Women, Spirit, and the Advent of Age*. New York: Bantam, 1995.

Havelock, Eric A. *Preface to Plato*. New York: Grosset & Dunlap/ The Universal Library, 1967.

Hiles, Marv, and Nancy Hiles, eds. *The Daybook: A Contemplative Journal* 34 (Fall 1999). Healdsburg, CA: Iona Center.

______. *The Daybook: A Contemplative Journal* 37 (Summer 2000): Healdsburg, CA: Iona Center.

Hillman, James. *The Puer Papers*. Irving, TX: Spring Publications, 1979.

Hynes, James. *The Lecturer's Tale*. New York: Picador USA, 2001.

hooks, bell. "In Praise of Student/Teacher Romances: Notes on the Subversive Power of Passion," *Utne Reader*, March–April, 1995, 36–37.

______. *Teaching to Transgress: Education as the Practice of Freedom*. London: Routledge, 1994.

Johnson, Robert A. *She: Understanding Feminine Psychology*. New York: Harper & Row/Perennial, 1977.

Jordan, Judith V., Alexandra G. Kaplan, Jean Baker Miller, Irene P. Stiver, Janet L. Surrey, eds. *Women's Growth in Connection: Writings from the Stone Center*. New York: Guilford, 1991.

Jung, C. G. *Psychology and Alchemy*. Vol. 12, Collected Works. Herbert Read, Michael Fordham, and Gerhard Adler, eds.

Translated by R. F. C. Hull. Bollingen Series 20. Princeton: Princeton University Press, 1953.

______. "The Psychology of the Child Archetype." In *Essays on a Science of Mythology*, 70–100. By C. G. Jung and Carl Kerényi. Translated by R. F. C. Hull. Bollingen Series 22. Princeton: Princeton University Press, 1973. First published in 1949 by Bollingen Foundation.

Keirsey, David, and Marilyn Bates. *Please Understand Me: Character and Temperament Types*. 4th edition. Del Mar, CA: Prometheus Nemesis Book Co., 1984.

Kerényi, Carl. *Dionysos: Archetypal Image of Indestructible Life*. Translated by Ralph Manheim. Bollingen Series 65–2. Princeton: Princeton University Press, 1976.

______. *Prometheus: Archetypal Image of Human Existence*. Translated by Ralph Manheim. Bollingen Series 65–1. Princeton: Princeton University Press, 1991. First published in 1963 by Bollingen Foundation.

Kleinbaum, Abby Wettan. *The War Against the Amazons*. New York: New Press, 1983.

Kolodny, Annette. *The Lay of the Land: Metaphor as Experience and History in American Life and Letters*. Chapel Hill: University of North Carolina Press, 1975.

Kornfield, Jack. *A Path With Heart: A Guide Through the Perils and Promises of Spiritual Life*. New York: Bantam Books, 1993.

Lamott, Anne. *Bird by Bird: Some Instructions on Writing and Life*. New York: Anchor Books, 1995.

______. *Traveling Mercies: Some Thoughts on Faith*. New York: Anchor Books, 2000.

Leonard, Linda Schierse. *On the Way to the Wedding: Transforming the Love Relationship*. Boston: Shambhala, 1997.

______. *The Wounded Woman: Healing the Father–Daughter Relationship*. Boston: Shambhala, 1985.

Lerner, Gerda. *The Creation of Patriarchy*. Oxford: Oxford University Press, 1986.

Lévy-Bruhl, Lucien. *Primitive Mentality*. Translated by Lillian A. Clare. London: George Allen & Unwin, 1923.

Lewis, C. S. *Till We Have Faces: A Myth Retold*. New York: Harvest/HBJ, 1956.

Lindemans, M. F. "Muses." In *Encyclopedia Mythica*. http://www.pantheon.org/articles/m/muses.html, 1995–2003.

Lopez, Barry. *Crow and Weasel*. Illustrations by Tom Pohrt. San Francisco: North Point Press, 1990.

Lu, Donbgin, Richard Wilhelm, and C. G. Jung. *The Secret of the Golden Flower: A Chinese Book of Life*. Translated by Cary F. Baynes. New York: Causeway Books, 1931.

Luke, Helen, "Mother and Daughter Mysteries." In *The Long Journey Home: Re-visioning the Myth of Demeter and Persephone for Our Time*, edited by Christine Downing, 190–96. Shambhala: Boston, 1994.

MacKinnon, Catherine. "Desire and Power: A Feminist Perspective." In *Marxism and the Interpretation of Culture*, edited by Cary Nelson and Lawrence Grossberg, 105–16. Urbana: University of Illinois Press, 1988.

Mulvey, Laura. *Visual and Other Pleasures*. Bloomington: Indiana University Press, 1989.

Murdock, Maureen. *The Heroine's Journey: Woman's Quest for Wholeness*. Boston: Shambhala, 1990.

Neumann, Erich. *Amor and Psyche: The Psychic Development of the Feminine, A Commentary on the Tale by Apuleius*. Translated by Ralph Manheim (3–53). Bollingen Series 54. Princeton: Princeton University Press, 1971. First published in 1956 by Bollingen Foundation.

———. *The Origins and History of Consciousness*. Translated by R. F. C. Hull, with a Foreword by C. G. Jung. Bollingen Series 42. Princeton: Princeton University Press, 1970. First published in 1954 by Bollingen Foundation.

Nothstine, William L., Carole Blair, and Gary. A. Copeland, eds. *Critical Questions: Invention, Creativity, and the Criticism of Discourse and Media*. New York: St. Martin's, 1994.

Nussbaum, Martha. *The Fragility of Goodness: Luck and Ethics in Greek Tragedy and Philosophy*. Cambridge: Cambridge University Press, 1986.

Oliver, Mary. *American Primitive*. Boston: Little, Brown and Company, 1978.

———. *Dream Work*. New York: Atlantic Monthly Press, 1986.

Olney, Dave, Daniel Lanois, and Emmylou Harris. "Deeper Well." *Wrecking Ball*. Hayes Court Music, Irving Music, Inc., 1995, compact disc.

Payne, David. "*The Wizard of Oz*: Therapeutic Rhetoric in a Contemporary Media Ritual." *Quarterly Journal of Speech* 75 (1989): 25–39.

Perera, Sylvia Brinton. *Descent to the Goddess: A Way of Initiation for Women*. Toronto: Inner City Books, 1981.

Picknett, Lynn, and Clive Prince. *The Templar Revelation: Secret Guardians of the True Identity of Christ*. New York: Touchstone, 1998.

Pirsig, Robert. *Zen and the Art of Motorcycle Maintenance: An Inquiry into Values*. New York: William Morrow & Co., 1974.

Plato. *Gorgias*. Translated by W. C. Helmbold. Indianapolis: Bobbs–Merrill Co., The Library of Liberal Arts, 1952.

______. *Phaedrus*. Translated by W. C. Helmbold and W. G. Rabinowitz. Indianapolis: Bobbs–Merrill Co., The Library of Liberal Arts, 1956.

Powers, Meredith A. *The Heroine in Western Literature: The Archetype and Her Reemergence in Modern Prose*. Jefferson, NC and London: McFarland & Co., 1991.

Pratt, Annis. *Archetypal Patterns in Women's Fiction*. Bloomington: Indiana University Press, 1994.

______. "Demeter, Persephone, and the Pedagogy of Archetypal Empowerment." In *The Long Journey Home: Re-visioning the Myth of Demeter and Persephone for Our Time*, edited by Christine Downing, 149–54. Boston: Shambhala, 1994.

Publication Manual of the American Psychological Association, 5th edition. Washington, DC: American Psychological Association, 2001.

Qualls-Corbett, Nancy. *The Sacred Prostitute: Eternal Aspect of the Feminine*. Toronto: Inner City Books, 1988.

Rushing, Janice Hocker. "*E.T.* as Rhetorical Transcendence." *Quarterly Journal of Speech* 71 (1985): 188–203.

______. "Evolution of 'The New Frontier' in *Alien* and *Aliens*: Patriarchal Co–Optation of the Feminine Archetype." *Quarterly Journal of Speech* 75 (1989): 1–24.

Rushing, Janice Hocker, and Thomas S. Frentz. "The Gods Must Be Crazy: The Denial of Descent in Academic Scholarship." *Quarterly Journal of Speech*, 95, (1999): 229–46.

______. "The Frankenstein Myth in Contemporary Cinema." *Critical Studies in Mass Communication* 6 (1989): 61–80.

______. *Projecting the Shadow: The Cyborg Hero in American Film*. Chicago: University of Chicago Press, 1995.

______. "Singing Over the Bones: James Cameron's *Titanic*." *Critical Studies in Media Communication* 17 (2000): 1–27.

Salmonson, Jessica Amanda. *The Encyclopedia of Amazons: Women Warriors from Antiquity to the Modern Era*. New York: Anchor Books, 1992.

Shakespeare, William. *The Tragedy of Hamlet, Prince of Denmark*, 880–934. In *Shakespeare: The Complete Works*. Edited by G. B. Harrison, New York: Harcourt, Brace & World, Inc., 1968.

Shelley, Mary, *Frankenstein*. New York: Bantam, 1981. First published in 1818.

Slotkin, Richard. *Regeneration Through Violence: The Mythology of the American Frontier, 1600–1960*. Middletown, CT: Wesleyan University Press, 1973.

Spence, Lewis. *Ancient Egyptian Myths and Legends*. New York: Dover Publications, 1990. First published in 1915 by George G. Harrap & Company.

Storr, Anthony, ed. *The Essential Jung*. Princeton: Princeton University Press, 1983.

Sutton, Jane. "The Taming of *Polos/Polis*: Rhetoric as an Achievement Without Woman." *The Southern Communication Journal* 57 (1992): 97–119.

Sutton, Jane. "Women in the House of Speech." Unpublished Manuscript. York, PA: Pennsylvania State University, 2005.

The Compact Edition of the Oxford English Dictionary. New York: Oxford University Press, 1971.

Tompkins, Jane. *A Life in School: What the Teacher Learned*. Reading, MA: Addison–Wesley, 1996.

Ulanov, A. *The Feminine in Jungian Psychology and in Christian Theology*. Evanston: Northwestern University Press, 1971.

Vogt, Gregory Max. *Return to Father: Archetypal Dimensions of the Patriarch*. Dallas: Spring Publications, 1991.

von Franz, Marie–Louise. *Interpretation of Fairy Tales*. Dallas: Spring Publications, 1982. First published in 1970 by the Analytical Psychology Club of New York, Inc.

______. *Puer aeternus: A Psychological Study of the Adult Struggle with the Paradise of Childhood*. Second Edition. Santa Monica, CA: Sigo Press, 1981.

Walker, Barbara G. *The Woman's Encyclopedia of Myths and Secrets*. San Francisco: Harper & Row, 1983.

Welwood, John. *Love and Awakening: Discovering the Sacred Path of Intimate Relationship*. New York: HarperCollins, 1996.

______. *Journey of the Heart: Intimate Relationship and the Path of Love*. New York: HarperPerennial, 1991.

Weinbaum, Batya. *Islands of Women and Amazons: Representations and Realities*. Austin, TX: University of Texas Press, 1999.

Wood, Julia. *Gendered Lives: Communication, Gender, and Culture*, 4th ed. Belmont, CA: Wadsworth, 2003.

Woodman, Marion. *Addiction to Perfection: The Still Unravished Bride*. Toronto: Inner City Books, 1982.

Woolger, Jennifer Barker, and Roger J. Woolger. *The Goddess Within: A Guide to the Eternal Myths that Shape Women's Lives*. New York: Fawcett Columbine, 1989.

"Xena Quotes," http://www.geocities.com/ skachild29/xenaquotes.html. Accessed September 21, 2003.

Young-Eisendrath, Polly. *Gender and Desire: Uncursing Pandora*. College Station: Texas A & M University Press, 1997.

______. *You're Not What I Expected: Learning to Love the Opposite Sex*. New York: William Morrow, 1993.

INDEX

ABOUT THE AUTHOR

Janice Hocker Rushing was professor of Communication at the University of Arkansas, Fayetteville. She has published three books, six book chapters, and twenty-four scholarly articles, and presented over thirty papers at academic conferences. She taught courses in myth, gender studies, rhetorical theory and criticism, film, and popular culture. Throughout her career, she won numerous awards for teaching and scholarship, including the prestigious Michael M. Osborn Teacher-Scholar Award in 2001 and, posthumously, the Douglas W. Ehninger Distinguished Rhetorical Scholar Award in 2005. Dr. Rushing succumbed to cancer in 2004.